Books are to be returned on or before
the last date below.

URBAN TRANSPORTATION: THE NEW TOWN SOLUTION

'The starting point for any new town project must be human needs'.

Arthur Ling

'Transportation is civilisation'.

Rudyard Kipling

Urban Transportation: The New Town Solution

HARRY DUPREE

Gower

Published by
Gower Publishing Company Limited,
Gower House,
Croft Road,
Aldershot,
Hants GU11 3HR,
England

Gower Publishing Company,
Old Post Road,
Brookfield,
Vermont 05036,
USA

ISBN 0 566 00839-4

Printed and Bound in Great Britain by
Redwood Burn Limited, Trowbridge, Wiltshire

Contents

Colour plates

The author gratefully acknowledges the sources of the photographs as indicated and the permission to reproduce. Photographs not acknowledged here were taken by the author.

Between pp. 74 and 75

1. *Primary and secondary distributor roads*
   (a) Pattern of roads at East Kilbride. *East Kilbride Development Corporation.*
   (b) Basildon: a primary road.
   (c) Approaching the town centre at Glenrothes. *Glenrothes Development Corporation.*
   (d) Skelmersdale: a primary distributor. *Skelmersdale Development Corporation.*
   (e) Peterborough: one of the parkways. *Peterborough Development Corporation.*
   (f) Washington: grid roads. *Washington Development Corporation.*

2. *Primary roads and junctions*
   (a) Hemel Hempstead: a surface roundabout junction.
   (b) Hemel Hempstead: 'The Plough' roundabout.
   (c) Telford: the expressway. *Telford Development Corporation.*
   (d) Telford: Hollinswood interchange. *Telford Development*

Corporation.
- (e) Grade separation at Cumbernauld. *Cumbernauld Development Corporation.*
- (f) Cloverleaf intersection at Livingston. *Livingston Development Corporation.*
- (g) Northampton: grade-separated junction. *Northampton Development Corporation.*

Between pp. 106 and 107

3. *Residential areas*
   - (a) Traditional street pattern at Harlow. . . .
   - (b) . . . Stevenage and . . .
   - (c) . . . Hemel Hempstead.
   - (d) Pedestrian/vehicle segregation: footpath access at Bracknell. *C.S Minchell A.R.I.B.A., A.R.P.S.*
   - (e) Basildon: pedestrian access at Laindon East and
   - (f) . . . vehicular access and parking from cul-de-sac. *Basildon Development Corporation.*

4. *Residential areas*
   - (a) Cumbernauld: footpath access at Kildrum 3. *Cumbernauld Development Corporation.*
   - (b) A more recent housing development at Cumbernauld. *Cumbernauld Development Corporation.*
   - (c), (d) and (e) The birth of the "shared access" concept was at Runcorn's The Brow estate. *Warrington and Runcorn Development Corporation.*
   - (f) Shared access at Cwmbran. *Cwmbran Development Corporation.*
   - (g) A development at Irvine. *Irvine Development Corporation.*

5. *Housing layouts of the 1970s*
   - (a) Washington: shared access. *Washington Development Corporation.*
   - (b) Glenrothes: a development of the 1970s. *Glenrothes Development Corporation.*
   - (c) and (d) Washington villages. *Washington Development Corporation.*
   - (e) and (f) Basildon: Noak Bridge village: return to the traditional street pattern?

6. *Residential: access to houses in the Mark III towns*
   - (a) Milton Keynes: courtyard access. *Milton Keynes*

Development Corporation.
- (b) Formal arrangement at Peterborough. *Ronald Adams and Associates.*
- (c) Looking out on Milton Keynes. *Milton Keynes Development Corporation.*
- (d) Looking down at Central Lancashire's culs-de-sac and footpaths. *Central Lancashire Development Corporation.*
- (e) Traditional layout at Warrington. *Warrington and Runcorn Development Corporation.*
- (f) A Northampton square. *Northampton Development Corporation.*

Between pp. 138 and 139

7. *New town shopping*
- (a) General view of town centre at Glenrothes. *Glenrothes Development Corporation.*
- (b) Hemel Hempstead: a traditional High Street.
- (c) Stevenage: the first all-pedestrian centre. *Stevenage Museum.*
- (d) Central Milton Keynes: the open market.
- (e) Irvine new town's shopping mall spans the River Irvine. *Irvine Development Corporation.*
- (f) Inside Queensgate shopping centre at Peterborough. *Peterborough Development Corporation.*

8. *Access to industry*
- (a) Central Lancashire – the M6 motorway runs alongside this employment area. *Central Lancashire Development Corporation.*
- (b) Road layout for a Northampton factory area. *Northampton Development Corporation.*
- (c) The Genesis Building at Warrington's Birchwood Science Park. *Warrington and Runcorn Development Corporation.*
- (d) Milton Keynes – the Volkswagen headquarters in its lakeside setting. *Milton Keynes Development Corporation.*
- (e) Unit factories at Washington. *Washington Development Corporation.*
- (f) An industrial estate at Glenrothes. *Glenrothes Development Corporation.*

Between pp. 170 and 171

9. *Public transport*
- (a) Stevenage Superbus. *Stevenage Museum.*

(b) and (c) Runcorn: the Busway in residential areas. *Warrington and Runcorn Development Corporation.*
(d) and (e) Runcorn: the Busway at Shopping City. *Warrington and Runcorn Development Corporation.*
(f) The bus station at Livingston. *Livingston Development Corporation.*
(g) Northampton's bus and coach station. *Northampton Development Corporation.*

10. *Footpaths and cycleways*
(a) Journey home from school at Milton Keynes. *Milton Keynes Development Corporation.*
(b) . . . and from the day's work at Stevenage.
(c) Cycleway and footpath at Stevenage.
(d) Skelmersdale footpaths. *Skelmersdale Development Corporation.*
(e) Cycling on the Redways at Milton Keynes. *Milton Keynes Development Corporation.*
(f) Pedestrian/cycle underpass at Bracknell. *Bracknell Reference Library.*
(g) Stevenage: pedestrian shopping in the town centre. *Stevenage Museum.*
(h) Warrington: an elegant new footbridge (photographed prior to landscaping works). *Warrington and Runcorn Development Corporation.*

11. *Parking the car in the residential areas*
(a) Kerbside parking: an early housing development at Harlow and . . .
(b) . . . the same at Hemel Hempstead.
(c) Residential parking provision at Bracknell. *Bracknell Reference Library.*
(d) A Radburn layout at Basildon: back access and car park.
(e) Washington: parking provision in one of the villages. *Washington Development Corporation.*
(f) Bracknell: car park at an early neighbourhood centre. *Bracknell Reference Library.*
(g) A village centre car park at Washington. *Washington Development Corporation.*

12. *Parking the car at work and at the town centre*
(a) A factory car park at Basildon.
(b) Surface car park: Stevenage town centre. *Stevenage Museum.*

(c) A car park in Central Milton Keynes. *Milton Keynes Development Corporation.*

(d) Stevenage: a multi-storey car park. *Stevenage Museum.*

(e) Multi-storey at Bracknell town centre. *C.S. Minchell, A.R.I.B.A., A.R.P.S.*

(f) Well landscaped car park access at Redditch. *Redditch Development Corporation.*

(g) Redditch: exit from another of the multi-storey car parks. *Redditch Development Corporation.*

Between pp. 202 and 203

13. *Townscape*

(a) Tree and shrub planting on a primary distributor at Washington. *Washington Development Corporation.*

(b) A well landscaped road at Skelmersdale. *Skelmersdale Development Corporation.*

(c) Beautifying the Busway at Runcorn. *Warrington and Runcorn Development Corporation.*

(d) Skelmersdale: road bridge and footbridge across the River Tawd. *Skelmersdale Development Corporation.*

(e) Shrubs and hard landscaping in a Washington residential area. *Washington Development Corporation.*

(f) Established planting at Runcorn. *Warrington and Runcorn Development Corporation.*

(g) Washington: man-made lake alongside the River Wear. *Washington Development Corporation.*

14. *Townscape: road bridges*

(a) Runcorn: a district road passing over the Expressway. *Warrington and Runcorn Development Corporation.*

(b) Road bridge over British Rail main line at Warrington. *Warrington and Runcorn Development Corporation.*

(c) Skelmersdale: bridge carrying primary road over district road. *Skelmersdale Development Corporation.*

(d) Northampton: viaduct carrying primary road over British Rail main line. *Northampton Development Corporation.*

15. *Townscape: footbridges and underpasses*

(a) A footbridge at Warrington. *Warrington and Runcorn Development Corporation.*

(b) A Skelmersdale design. *Skelmersdale Development Corporation.*

Black and white illustrations

The author gratefully acknowledges the source of each photograph as indicated, and permission to reproduce.

Figures

Tables

Foreword by the Trustees of the Rees Jeffreys Road Fund

From the beginning of the present century, William Rees Jeffreys, the founder of the Road Fund that bears his name, was an ardent advocate of the belief that the building and maintenance of safe, adequate and pleasant roads was one of the surest ways to raise the standard of living, to advance civilisation and to promote the social and economic well-being of the people they serve. Recognition of the validity of this belief by the general public and by their national and local elected bodies has been slow to come, notwithstanding a continuous growth in the dependence on road transport of all communities and all members of the community which has already exceeded by far even the visionary perceptions of Rees Jeffreys himself. Indeed, it would be true to say that, although even today that dependence is virtually total, the so-called man in the street shows little interest in the quality of the place where he finds himself. He adopts an ambivalent attitude towards any suggestions for the improvement of his environment which would lessen the damaging effects of the growing number and size of road vehicles and to make it safer and more pleasant to be there.

It is not perhaps surprising, therefore, that at no time has any government in Britain addressed itself to a long-term comprehensive policy directed towards the achievement of the greatest benefits of road transport, whilst containing as far as possible its harmful effects. Nevertheless, the past forty years have seen two major programmes involving the investment of considerable public monies, namely the building of the inter-urban network of motorways and the creation of the twenty-eight New Towns. The Trustees of the Road Fund believe that the separate story of the achievement of each of these projects should be told, and so earlier this year they agreed to sponsor the publication of *A History of British Motorways* by George Charlesworth, and to commission this story of British New Towns in their transportation context.

Unlike the motorway programme, where the requirements were comparatively straightforward, and for which considerable experience had been gained in other countries, the New Towns programme had to deal with a complex range of factors and needs far less clearly defined, and it was, moreover, innovatory. As with so many of life's problems, there is no simple and universal answer to the question: what is the best way to deal with the movement of people and their needs in towns? It is therefore of the greatest interest and importance that each New Town was given the political, professional and financial freedom to develop its own preferred answer to this question. The book which follows is an impartial though sympathetic attempt to record and analyse the thinking and planning that went into these answers, to highlight some of the difficulties that were met and to assess the degree to which the desired objectives were achieved in each of the New Towns built.

The Trustees were fortunate in finding in Harry Dupree an author in every way suitably qualified and experienced and they commend the book to all who believe that there are lessons to be learned in the building of towns that are agreeable, convenient and safe places to live in.

Preface and acknowledgements

This book examines the ways in which present and future transportation needs have been catered for in the new towns of Great Britain. Just what do we mean by 'transportation'? The seventeenth-century meaning was the removal of convicted criminals to a penal colony. In the second half of the twentieth century the word is much used in studying the problems caused by movement of the motor vehicle in its present-day, large and ever increasing, numbers. But suppose we decide not to get the car out but to walk to the shops instead. Is that transportation?

I really prefer the simple word movement because it so clearly covers all the trips we are likely to make, whether in the car, going by bus, sending goods by lorry or van, cycling, or just walking. It covers the child at play in the cul-de-sac or playground and, if we pause in the shopping centre to chat to a friend, or sit down and rest awhile, I like to think that this too is part of the movement pattern.

The book traces the history of the towns through the planning and construction stages in the context of transportation. History does not change over time but it does extend, and I regret that, partly due to publication delays the story is in some respects not quite up to date.

My researches in 1982 and 1983 were greatly helped by the technical officers of the New Town Development Corporations and (in those towns where development corporations had already been wound up) by the technical officers of the Commission for the New Towns. I am grateful for the information they so generously provided and for their comments and encouragement along the way. I hope I have presented the information they gave me accurately and fairly but, if mistakes have crept in, the fault is mine alone. I am indebted also to those who so patiently read the whole or part of the manuscript and gave me the benefit of their views. Amongst these I would particularly mention John Jefferson, Maurice Milne and a gentleman in the Department of the Environment's New Towns Directorate (who by tradition must remain anonymous); they waded through the whole manuscript. I must also mention Anthony Beetham and Simon Coventry, who advised in particular areas of the work, and Jack Pincombe and Brian Roberts who helped in various ways.

Here and there I have quoted shamelessly from the writings of other and more distinguished authors. I have obtained their permission and hope they will accept my acknowledgements as a token of my gratitude. Most of the illustrations are from photographs provided by the development corporations and all are acknowledged individually in the lists of illustrations.

The idea of writing this history was not mine. It emanated from the Trustees of the Rees Jeffreys Road Fund. I feel honoured to have been appointed to carry it out and grateful to the Trustees for their interest and encouragement throughout.

Lastly I must add a word of thanks to Anne Murphy who prepared the artwork for most of the figures and to Rosalind Kingdon-Saxby who somehow succeeded in educing an orderly manuscript from my frenzied scribbles.

Amersham 1986   H.W.D

1 The making of towns

It is sometimes suggested that all towns were originally 'new towns'. This is not strictly true because a great many towns developed from villages – which, in their turn, grew out of small settlements. Those settlements that did not progress in this way simply withered and died. There were several requirements if a settlement was to survive and succeed. It needed to be well sited in relation to climate and topography, in order to retain the families who had settled there and to attract others. A plentiful supply of water was another essential, and also good dry soil. To live and prosper the inhabitants had to work – growing food and making things for themselves and each other. The next stage was trade with neighbouring communities and this pinpoints a fourth requirement of the successful settlement – good communications with other nearby communities. This evolution took a very long time.

> The village is the completed expression of centuries of colonisation and change, the end product of man's adaptation to natural conditions in a given place. There is clear evidence in many places that the process began in the Iron Age, even before the Romans came.
>
> (Hoskins, 1973)

The Romans were in Britain for 400 years and many of our towns, Bath and Chester, Colchester and London, were founded and built during their occupation of the country.

This book is about the new towns which have been planned and built in Britain since the end of the Second World War, under very special conditions of induced growth. The project was a bold sociological experiment and, more than this, it was a practical contribution to the post-war need to relieve over-crowded cities, clear the slums and provide homes and employment opportunities in a clean and healthy environment.

Yet perhaps the concept was not as novel or as unique as many people believe, for a fairly close analogy to this twentieth century establishment of towns occurred in the Middle Ages, when English kings decreed that a number of new towns should be 'planted', where no previous settlement had existed, on sites in England and Wales, and also in south-west France. When Edward I convened Parliament at Bury St Edmunds in 1296 it was in order:

> to elect men from among your wisest and ablest who know best how to devise, order and array a new town to the greatest profit of Ourselves and of merchants.

> (Beresford, 1967)

Among these mediaeval 'plantings' were the towns of Chelmsford, Baldock, Dunstable, Wokingham, Maidenhead and Reigate – a ring of towns centred on London at a radius of about 35 to 40 miles (56 to 64 km).

The idea of designing and building a new town from scratch continued to be mooted from time to time by visionaries over the centuries, but seldom if ever was it carried through. Sir Thomas More, for example, wrote in 1516 of *Utopia*, wherein he described his vision of 'a number of medium-sized towns of generous layout and fine quality, designed to be spaced about twenty miles apart in open countryside'. Nothing came of the proposal.

With the coming of the industrial revolution in Britain in the eighteenth century, life in many towns was transformed from the peaceful rural ways to the industrialised rigours of the factory, the mill and the mine. The remarkable programme of canal construction by Thomas Telford and other engineers of the eighteenth century ensured industrial prosperity to many an inland town – until the railways took over these transport functions a century later. Attracted by the lure of the bigger wages of industry, workers flocked from the land to the cities. Innumerable terraces of workers' cottages rapidly sprang up to meet the demand for shelter; they were huddled together as closely as possible, to be within walking distance of the factory. The towns grew bigger and bigger, and so the foundations were laid for inner city slums – overcrowded and insanitary. By the end of the nineteenth century, this insupportable situation seems nevertheless to have been accepted by most people as part of the natural order of things.

Yet not quite everyone was so ready to accept these conditions. At least one reformer had a clear idea of how the situation could be improved. Sickened by the ever-increasing size of London and other large cities, by the dirt and insanitary, overcrowded conditions in which people lived and worked, in 1898 Ebenezer Howard unfolded a bold and imaginative plan to reduce the swollen populations of cities, transferring both people and employment to 'garden cities of limited size to be built in a healthy country environment' (Howard 1898). It can be said that British new towns emerged largely from these radical ideas and his pioneering work.

Two wealthy, philanthropic industrialists had meanwhile sponsored two imaginative housing projects at the end of the nineteenth century – at the new villages of Bourneville and Port Sunlight; but these projects, specifically to provide good housing for their workpeople, were rather special cases.

Howard was not a man of wealth. He was a man of remarkable vision and conviction and in addition he was a man of action. His idea was to establish a number of medium-sized industrial towns on selected rural sites to provide homes with gardens for families from the over-crowded cities, with workplaces close at hand and easy access to the countryside. He visualised towns of about 30,000 inhabitants, conforming to a predetermined circular pattern with a number of wide tree-lined ring roads and radial roads. These would divide up the town to form the residential areas, with shops towards the centre of the circle and factories on the outside. Other essential features would be a town park in the centre, and a broad belt of unspoilt farmland encircling the town and preventing future enlargement. With this arrangement the journey to work, to the shops or to school would be no more than a few minutes' walk, indeed the whole town would be only about 2 km (1.2 miles) across.

The road plan was remarkable, seeing that there were so few motor vehicles to be catered for in 1898. Those 'magnificent boulevards' were luxurious even by late Victorian standards – a reflection of the grand design rather than a prediction of the future traffic such roads might be expected to carry. Public transport was not forgotten: a tramway was proposed alongside the radial roads and continuing on to the open country beyond; and there was to be a main-line railway connection with sidings to serve the factories (Figure 1.1).

The town was referred to as 'Garden City', a rather grand name for an industrial town of no more than 30,000 inhabitants. However, Howard was not thinking of one town. To make appreciable inroads into the congested inner areas of London, the *raison d'être* of his proposal, would require far more than that. Like Sir Thomas More he

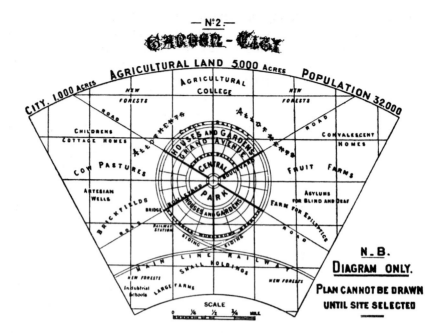

Figure 1.1 Ebenezer Howard's Garden City concept from the 1902 edition of Tomorrow: a Peaceful Path to Real Reform.

was proposing a cluster of towns – perhaps ten 'Garden Cities' encircling a rather larger 'Central City', all linked together with good road and rail connections, so that the entire population of about 240,000 inhabitants of Howard's 'Social City', 'though in one sense living in a town of small size, would be in reality living in, and would enjoy the advantages of, a great and most beautiful city.'

Although Howard was primarily a social reformer, it is remarkable to find so much planning insight, innovation and wisdom compressed into only eight pages of this little book; what, it may be pondered, would the feasibility study for a comparable project amount to in the 1980s, in terms of verbiage, charts, printout and all the rest of the present-day paraphernalia? It is also remarkable that the size and layout of roads in each Garden City were so suited to traffic in the motor age. 'In reading this book', wrote Frederic Osborn, 'we are studying a blueprint nearly fifty years old' (now, it is over eighty years old). 'What is astonishing is not that it has faded on the edges, but that its centre remains so clear and bright.' (Osborn in preface to Howard 1898, 1945 edn).

It was not long before Howard's theory was tried out. He founded the Garden Cities Association to promote the ideas laid down in his book and set about finding backers to support a specific project. In 1903 a company, First Garden City Limited, was formed to develop an estate of nearly 4,000 acres at Letchworth, Hertfordshire. The company was fortunate to secure the services of Raymond Unwin and Barry Parker to undertake the planning and architectural design of the project; they so well understood the need to plan for increasing traffic levels. The project got under way but was hampered from the start by lack of funds, and many of Howard's ideas had to be scaled down or laid aside. Grand avenues, for example, were transformed into narrow carriageways of minimum specification, but with ample grass verges to allow for future road widening.

At the end of the First World War, prime minister Lloyd George was calling for 'A fit country for heroes to live in' and a prodigious house-building programme was embarked upon in villages and towns – many already inflated beyond reasonable limits. The Garden Cities Association was continuously trying to sell the new town idea to the government, but with no tangible result. Then in 1919, with the cries of post-war reconstruction and rehabilitation all around him, the remarkable Ebenezer Howard could wait no longer. He scraped up the money to pay a deposit on about 1,500 acres of land at Welwyn, Hertfordshire, and launched another company, Second Garden City Limited. Frederic Osborn was appointed manager and Louis de

1. *Letchworth: a photograph taken early in the twentieth century.*

Soissons architect and planner. Once again there were serious financial difficulties leading to departures from the ideals of the original concept. The main road pattern bore little resemblance to the ring and radial form of the original thesis but, sixteen years later than Letchworth, the planning was far more car-orientated; roads were wide enough to allow kerbside parking and there were individual garages for many of the houses.

The residential roads in both towns were laid out, initially to minimum standards to save money, with all houses fronting onto the roads. Many culs-de-sac were included in the layouts, often with short-cut footpath connections between adjacent dead ends. Howard's ideas for public transport did not materialise. Neither company had the financial resources to provide tramways, and anyway it seems doubtful if this size of town could have supported the system; and, if regional bus services were slow to materialise, the towns both had the benefit of a railway station, centrally located.

In a transportation context these towns demonstrated in their day the best in planning for urban movement; but their main significance was the social achievement of bringing many families from the slums of early twentieth century London to good new homes and gardens in a country town environment. Both towns attracted wide interest and acclaim at home and abroad, and the government, which had done

2. *A Welwyn Garden City housing estate; photographed in 1927.*

little or nothing to aid the developments, was later to benefit greatly from the examples and experience of the Garden Cities. For they were the prototypes of at least the first batch of the British new towns, providing a depth of practical experience and setting an enviable standard. Yet the term Garden City cannot be included amongst the benefits. It clung to the new towns in their early years and, together with the other misnomer of satellite towns, came to be used by their critics (of whom there were many) in the pejorative sense; it took a lot of living down.

A further advance in planning for twentieth century living took place in America, where the level of car ownership was far higher than in Britain. It was the work of architects Clarence Stein and Henry Wright, and the foremost example was the design and construction of a new town for a population of 25,000 at Radburn, New Jersey. Stein and Wright were self-confessed disciples of Parker and Unwin, but they had some additional, novel ideas. Their principal theme was safety through the segregation of pedestrians from moving traffic. The main features of the Radburn plan (Figure 1.2) were:

- main roads to be for the sole purpose of traffic circulation; no frontage development whatsoever;
- the development areas enclosed by these main roads would be 'neighbourhoods', based on a population of about 7,000 per neighbourhood – the right size to support a primary school;
- within the neighbourhoods would be a grid of secondary traffic roads, again with no frontage development dividing the neighbourhood into 'superblocks';
- within the superblocks the houses would face each other across a wide landscaped reserve through which, instead of a road, as in traditional layouts, there would be a footpath;
- this landscaped footpath system would be an important feature of the project connecting with a park and playground in the centre of the superblock. Where the footpaths crossed a road, it would be through a subway; and
- access by car would be at the back of the house from a cul-de-sac off the secondary road system.

Thus, there was, theoretically at any rate, no direct interfacing between people on foot, in particular children at play, and moving vehicles. It is important to note that Radburn was built to a low density of seven houses to the acre (seventeen per hectare). The system gives less happy results as we shall see, when the density is doubled or trebled. Radburn and other developments by these architects were described in a book, *Toward New Towns For America* by Clarence Stein which was published in 1950. Yet surprisingly the Radburn

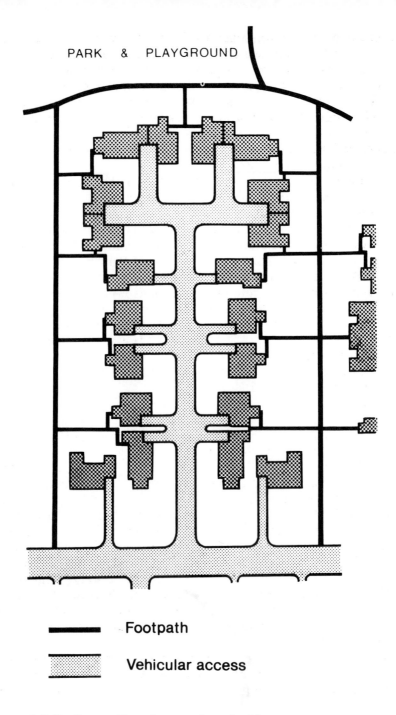

PARK & PLAYGROUND

———— Footpath

▨▨▨ Vehicular access

Figure 1.2 Radburn, New Jersey: A typical layout

8

example appears to have generated little interest in America; it seems to have disappeared from sight for twenty years, only reappearing with the ideas incorporated in modified form in British New Towns.

During the inter-war years, another stepping stone towards a New Towns programme was the influence of several government committees. The Chamberlain Committee on Unhealthy Areas recommended restrictions on factories in the London area and removal of some industry and workers to garden cities; the Marley committee recommended a programme of new town building. Neither had any tangible result. Meanwhile, the Town and Country Planning Association, which was the Garden Cities Association under its new name, was lobbying on its central theme of establishing a government-sponsored programme of New Town building, and giving evidence before all the government committees of the day. The Barlow Royal Commission was set up in 1938 by prime minister Neville Chamberlain, with Sir Patrick Abercrombie as one of the members. The members of the Commission appear to have had great difficulty in agreeing on the formulation of a national policy. The Commission's Report and an accompanying minority report appeared in 1940 and were promptly filed away until the end of the Second World War. Sir Frederick Osborn concluded: 'The Barlow Report did in the event prove the historical turning point in the governmental concern with urban development'. (Osborn, 1977).

In order to boost morale for the forces and on the Home Front, quite early on in the war the Government embarked upon some fairly specific planning for post-war reconstruction. Lord Reith, the Minister of Works and Planning, was made responsible and he accepted the Barlow Report as the basis of his study. He also set up two further committees, resulting in the Uthwatt Report on land values, compensation and betterment and the Scott Report on the protection of agricultural interests and the countryside. The Minister also commissioned Sir Patrick Abercrombie to prepare a plan for the whole Greater London area; this plan defined, probably for the first time, the nature of the problem of 'overspill' population and put forward a viable solution for dealing with it. This included proposals for the creation of a number of new towns, sited about 28 miles (45 km) from the centre of London. All the Reports and proposals were well publicised to a war-weary population at home and in radio broadcasts to the forces overseas.

Thus the outline of a comprehensive plan for providing new homes and rebuilding the bombed cities was ready to hand. Yet there was still no decision as to whether new towns would feature as part of this strategy.

9

2   The transport scene

The story of the foundations of Britain's transport system will only be touched upon here in so far as it leads up to the situation in the mid 1940s, the start of new town development. Britain's road pattern was haphazard, having emerged over many hundreds of years. Indeed some of the ridgeway routes of the Iron Age could still be traced. They had survived mainly as footpaths and bridleways and were seldom incorporated into the road system. Many of the Roman roads, on the other hand, had survived to become the backbone of the country's highway system (although changed of course in constructional detail). Where these roads have gone out of use, for example at Hadrian's Wall, the original construction can still be traced. The remainder of the road system must have evolved partly from the routes of footpaths and bridleways, often tortuous in alignment for reasons no doubt important once, but long since forgotten.

With the departure of the Romans, roadmaking skills, like so many others, were lost. Roads gradually fell into disrepair, and this neglect continued through the centuries. Responsibility for the roads shifted from the lords of the manors to the parishes, to the Turnpike Trusts; then, by the Highway Act 1862, the duties of road construction and maintenance were vested in local highway authorities; and, by the Public Health Act 1872, the Local Government Board was made the central body administering all the highway authorities. Another major change was made in 1910, when the Road Board was set up. This independent body, with William Rees Jeffreys as Secretary, was funded by motor taxation revenue and was empowered to make grants to the country's 2,000 or more road authorities. However, it did not last very long, perhaps partly due to the effects of the First World War, and it was replaced in 1920 by the Ministry of Transport.

The technique of roadbuilding improved dramatically in the early nineteenth century when John Loudoun Macadam, a Scottish engineer, introduced the method of grading the stone used in road construction, filling the interstices, and watering and rolling the surface to the correct camber to produce a sound, reasonably impervious, running surface. Meanwhile his famous contemporary, Thomas Telford, who had a flair for route planning, was building a prodigious number of roads, bridges, canals and docks. His name is honoured both in the civil engineering profession and in the new towns sphere.

Sadly, the advances attributable to Telford and Macadam were not followed through, almost certainly because Britain was entering the age of the train. The Stockton and Darlington Railway had opened in 1825 and a remarkable band of gifted engineers, including George Stephenson and Isambard Kingdom Brunel, were devoting their skills to steam locomotion and to the building of the railroads for the numerous railway companies which were competing with each other to build and open their particular railway line. Later on these railroads were all connected together to form the fine railway system that served Britain so well for many years.

Therefore, when Howard's book *Tomorrow, a peaceful path to real reform* (Howard, 1898) was published towards the turn of the century, industry was booming, labour was abundant and cheap, there was a magnificent railway system, and the cities had expanded beyond recognition – stately squares of Victorian elegance for the minority and slum dwellings in the industrial cities for the majority. With so much engineering talent, labour strength and capital investment devoted to the railways, not much advance was made in improving the road network or the technique of roadbuilding. An exception was in the metropolis, where some fine new thoroughfares were planned and constructed as well as the Blackwall Tunnel and many of the bridges over the Thames. But as regards road transport the all-powerful railway companies were going to tolerate no competition. They had seen off the stage coaches and, when steam driven vehicles on the roads appeared as another possible rival, an Act of Parliament was passed limiting their speed to four miles an hour and requiring them to be preceded by a man on foot with a red flag. Yet, the petrol-driven vehicle had arrived and it soon became apparent that, rival or not, it was there to stay.

At this time it is doubtful whether many people foresaw the

enormous upsurge in the numbers and speeds of motor vehicles or realised how quickly Britain's roads would be proved inadequate. One thing that could not fail to be noticed, however, was the dust menace on the roads – an old problem in dry weather but a worsening one. William Rees Jeffreys therefore initiated experiments leading to the process of tar-spraying, which was quickly adopted as standard practice in many parts of the country.

The number of motor vehicles continued to increase during the inter-war years, but little was done about roadbuilding or road improvement. 'The motor vehicle', wrote Rees Jeffreys,

> became a practical means of transport early in the twentieth century and the numbers put on the road increased rapidly. Road design however had not progressed beyond the stage it had reached at the peak of the coaching period and was consequently about eighty years behind the times.
>
> (Jeffreys, 1949)

Once the Ministry of Transport had been set up several important schemes, which had been planned for a long time, were put in hand and completed; for instance, Western Avenue and the North Circular Road in London, and the London-Southend Arterial Road. Some of these roads demonstrated the considerable advance in road planning. Southend Arterial Road, for example (destined later to serve as the chief access route to Basildon New Town), had a consistent layout comprising dual carriageways, separated by adequate grass verges, footways; and in some sections there were separate cycle tracks. The principal junctions were well spaced out, taking the form of surface crossings with good-sized roundabouts. Gradients and bends were easy. Here at last was a road for the motor age catering for fast-moving motor vehicles with satisfactory segregation for pedestrian and cyclist.

Few roads built in the 1920s and 1930s reached the standard of the Southend Road, and a generally approved road for heavy traffic had a single 30 feet (9.1 m) wide carriageway, with its inherent danger of, in those days, few road markings and indifferent driving standards. Sir Colin Buchanan commented:

> We always seem to have been a lap behind the motor car: by the time we had thought of 30 foot carriageways, it was duals that were really needed, by the time we had thought of duals it was motor roads that were wanted, by the time we had thought of roundabouts it was flyovers that were needed.
>
> (Buchanan, 1958)

In the few instances where cycle tracks were provided, these had a mixed reception. Many cyclists and some cycling clubs were jealous of their right to use the carriageway, preferring its better maintained surface to that of the cycle track. Equestrians meanwhile found the grass verges ideal for the morning canter.

A serious defect of the inter-war roadbuilding was in the lack of planning legislation. The roads encouraged the indiscriminate opening up of adjoining land for building development and, worse still, sometimes the establishment of ribbon developments of houses, factories, shops and public houses alongside the roads themselves. It was a planning disaster.

Within the towns not much new road construction had yet taken place, the road patterns remaining substantially as they had been for many years – although some towns, Crawley for example, already had a bypass to syphon off the main traffic flow. It was easier before the days of urban motorways, expressways and ring roads, to identify types of road pattern; in many towns they could be classified under three main headings:

- *radial* The commonest form in Britain, with the town centred on the intersection point of the main traffic routes, as at York, Tunbridge Wells and Crawley;
- *gridiron* A form on which Roman towns had often been based and which was widely adopted in the United States; British examples were Hove and Southend; and
- *linear* With the developed area mainly strung out along the dominant traffic route, perhaps through a valley, as High Wycombe, or where there was only a single river crossing, as at Tonbridge.

The main town roads mostly had single carriageways, with here and there the occasional duals (at Birmingham, for instance), and mostly continuous frontage development with unlimited access. Geometry, gradients and road surfaces left much to be desired. Most roads had street lighting although the standard was indifferent whether electric or gas. Maintenance of the roads was comparable with today's standard and that of street cleansing probably higher.

Public transport started to be motorised early in the twentieth century, the first vehicles literally being converted horse buses. Those were days when anyone could start a bus service and in the early 1920s competition became so intense that the established companies felt threatened by poaching on their routes and timetables and by cut-price fares. An act of Parliament was passed, enabling the Ministry of Transport to control the situation. There then developed an efficient service of local buses in towns, regional buses and long-distance coaches; this service continued to improve right up to the start of the Second World War. Combined with the pre-war train service, and

13

trams or trolley buses in many cities and larger towns, this allowed townsmen and countrymen alike to enjoy an enviable degree of mobility by public transport that has never since been equalled.

If the rise in vehicle numbers in the inter-war years was remarkable, the figures for accidents on the roads were truly appalling. Between 1929 and 1939 nearly 70,000 people were killed on the roads of Britain and over 2 million were injured. The newspapers headlined this depressing message each bank holiday. Yet little improvement was achieved. The motor car appeared to have outpaced man's ability to control it; perhaps he had not attained the required level of discipline or of civilisation. The techniques of road design and road maintenance were imperfect, the condition of tyres and maintenance of vehicles were not good enough, the standard of driving was low, and the discipline of pedestrian and cyclist was lax.

An exposé of the situation came in 1942 from a former Assistant Commissioner of Police at Scotland Yard, Sir Alker Tripp (Tripp, 1942). Analysing the accident statistics for the metropolitan area in great detail, and primarily in relation to road standards and layouts, he noted that, while only about 2 per cent of accidents had been attributed to road defects as the principal cause, some 50 per cent were said to be due to pedestrians or pedal cyclists; he drew the logical conclusion that if the walkers and cyclists had not been there these accidents would not have happened. Tripp recognised the time-honoured arrangement whereby everybody – pedestrian, cyclist, equestrian, motor vehicle, driven cattle – were all equally entitled to use the 'King's highway', but, with the sudden introduction of large numbers of motor vehicles moving at considerable speed on the old tracks, this arrangement was no longer valid. Tripp pointed to the railway tracks on which casualties over the years had been negligible by comparison, for they had been specifically designed for fast-moving mechanical transport – everything else was excluded. He demanded similar treatment for the primary roads.

> Despite legislation to restrict ribbon development, modern homes still spring up beside main traffic roads . . . Pedestrians must be guided away from the fast traffic, just as they are excluded from the railway lines. And at the same time the fast through traffic must be debarred from the places where people live and work, where they do their shopping and have their recreation. This can be done and must be done.
>
> (Tripp, 1942)

Like Ebenezer Howard, Alker Tripp was not content merely to point out what was wrong; he went on to demonstrate how matters could be put right. He suggested a hierarchy of roads, which may be compared with the recommendations of *Traffic in Towns*, (Buchanan et al, 1963, also known as the 'Buchanan Report') comprising:

- arterial roads – to standards almost up to those of the motorways of today and having similar restrictions as to use;
- sub-arterial roads – connecting the arterial roads to the local road system; and
- local roads – normal town roads serving the houses, shops and factories.

The areas bounded by the arterial and sub-arterial road network would be in the form of a precinct or neighbourhood with the front of the buildings facing into the precincts. Like Howard, he thought that a town road system should be of the radial and ring form. Whether these imaginative ideas could ever have been put into practice to transform a whole existing town is an open question but, for redeveloping a large area devastated by enemy bombing, they presented an attractive proposition.

Tripp's book was perhaps the strongest diatribe of the day against the slaughter taking place on the roads, and it had the merit of specifying constructive solutions to the problems. The second edition brought up to date in 1950 was an admirable state-of-the-art document, a textbook of road planning, layout and even construction methods. It did not fail to point out that in building a new town all the correct solutions (as Tripp saw them) could be applied.

Thus the 1930s drew to a close against a background alternating between threats of war and promises of peace, the number of vehicles was increasing rapidly and road casualties were at a horrifyingly high level. But measures to cope with the problems were being applied – driving tests, speed limits and pedestrian crossings had been introduced; many roadworks projects were in hand; and ambitious schemes such as the Mersey tunnel and Waterloo bridge were in progress.

With the outbreak of the Second World War, this progress was more or less halted. There was not much 'business as usual' in that war. Strict petrol rationing was introduced early on; the motor manufacturers and their components suppliers soon switched to war production; highway engineers transferred to airfield construction or similar employment. The Road Research Laboratory included amongst its wartime researches development work on Barnes Wallis' bouncing bomb. By the end of the war there emerged: men highly skilled in automobile and aeronautical engineering; a new thinking and experience in the production and use of heavy earthmoving plant; and engineers who had been in charge of airfield re-construction in Germany, including the use of concrete trains and other equipment formerly used on the Autobahnen.

Meanwhile in 1943 a Committee had been set up by the Minister of War Transport to consider the design and layout most appropriate to various types of roads in built-up areas 'with due regard to safety, the free flow of road traffic, economy and the requirements of town planning'. The Committee's Report made a timely appearance in 1946 providing guidelines on which the roads for all the first generation new towns could be based. It also touched on the needs of pedestrians, cyclists, equestrians and horse-drawn vehicles and upon the role of public transport. For twenty years *Design and layout of roads in built-up areas* (Ministry of Transport, 1946) was the most authoritative reference work for highway engineers, and in the new towns the standards set by the 'blue book' were carefully observed.

3   The twenty-eight British New Towns

At a general election soon after the Second World War, Winston Churchill was (in his own words) 'immediately dismissed by the British electorate from all further conduct of their affairs'. The new Prime Minister Clement Attlee appointed Lewis Silkin as Minister of Town and Country Planning and foremost among the successes of his administration was the passing of the New Towns Act 1946 and the Town and Country Planning Act 1947. One of Silkin's first moves was to set up a New Towns Committee, to draw up guidelines for the development of new towns, with the dynamic Lord Reith as chairman. The speed with which the Committee came to grips with its task, and produced three exemplary reports in only nine months, is legendary. Their final report dealt succinctly with practically every aspect of the setting up of a new town, with recommendations for agency, location, layout, communications, engineering services, public transport and so forth, right through to the programming and execution of the construction work. Extracts from the report, where it touches upon movement of all kinds within the towns, are given in Appendix 1. It is fair to say that the Reith Committee's recommendations drew heavily on the principles laid down by Ebenezer Howard, the experience gained at Letchworth and Welwyn, and the advice and persuasion of the Town and Country Planning Association.

The Minister immediately accepted most of the Reith Committee's recommendations and launched the first batch of new towns with commendable, if quite unusual, urgency. Even before the passing of the Act the Reith Committee was pressing for the establishment of a development corporation for a new town at Stevenage, and the Ministry of Town and Country Planning was working on a draft plan for the town. Stevenage, the first of the new towns, was designated in November 1946. Others of the first batch followed thick and fast; Crawley, Hemel Hempstead, Harlow, Aycliffe and East Kilbride in 1947; Welwyn, Hatfield, Peterlee and Glenrothes in 1948; Basildon, Bracknell and Cwmbran in 1949; and Corby in 1950. This was an achievement; for designation was not a simple automatic process. It carried the implication of acquiring much, if not all, of the land and property within the area, and it was only natural that the owners should rise up to a man in protest at the proposal. In many cases the local authorities too were opposed to the schemes. Innumerable consultations and all the processes of a local inquiry had to be gone through. So the making of fourteen designation orders in four years was good progress, launching this ambitious programme, which was also a remarkable act of faith.

The primary objective of most of the early designations was to relieve the over-large population of Greater London by bringing people away from the congestion and squalor that had worsened immeasurably as a result of air-raid damage and maintenance neglect during the war; to bring them to a new home with a garden; to provide a job in a modern factory or other workplace without the daily hassle of a long and tiring journey to work; and to give them (perhaps later rather than sooner) all the benefits of living in a well-planned country town. In this category were Stevenage, Crawley, Hemel Hempstead, Harlow, Welwyn, Hatfield, Basildon and Bracknell, the eight 'London New Towns' which, it was reckoned, would eventually absorb about 360,000 of London's 'overspill' population.

East Kilbride was to provide a similar overspill service for Glasgow, but the remaining designations had a different (and paradoxically an almost opposite) objective – to provide houses and to build up the population of several existing industrial development areas. These were developments that had sprung up in rural areas, yet were insufficient to support the facilities of a town. They were mainly single industry developments, such as the mining areas of Peterlee and Glenrothes or the gigantic steelworks of Corby, which needed more diversification of industry. Others were the more miscellaneous industrial developments that had been established at Aycliffe and Cwmbran.

Very few of the areas chosen were virgin sites, such as Harlow was for example, and as Lord Esher has pointed out: 'In an urbanized country like England we were bound to reach the realization that all the best sites for new towns had old ones on them.' (Esher, 1981).

Figure 3.1 Location of the New Towns

The tempo of the programme somewhat inevitably slowed down and was further checked in 1951, owing to the aversion of Winston Churchill's new administration to development corporations. The government's answer was the Town Development Act 1952,[1] which gave a more immediate boost to the Minister of Housing and Local Government's '300,000 houses a year' campaign by expanding existing towns. These developments were handled by existing local authorities.

The next New Town designation was Cumbernauld in 1955, in order to make further provision for people from Glasgow. No others were made until 1961, when Skelmersdale in Lancashire was designated, to help the slum clearance efforts in Liverpool and Manchester. This was the first new designation in England for eleven years. Livingston in West Lothian, Scotland, followed in 1962, and in 1963 a designation was confirmed in Dawley in Shropshire – the first new town in the Midlands. A vintage year was 1964, with Redditch, Runcorn and Washington. Irvine in Strathclyde Region followed in 1966 and, apart from the tiny Newtown development in mid Wales, designated in 1967, there were to be no more new towns in the pattern that had emerged in 1946 and which evolved during the ensuing twenty years.

In the more expansive late 1960s, Harold Wilson's government embarked on a more ambitious programme for six very large new towns – or new cities. Designation orders for Milton Keynes and Telford were confirmed in 1967 and 1968 respectively.

Milton Keynes comprised a huge area of 8,870 hectares (21,900 acres) a mainly rural site which however included the important town of Bletchley and a scatter of ten or more small towns and villages. It was intended to grow from an existing population of some 40,000 to 200,000 or more. In 1962 Buckinghamshire County Council, alarmed by current population predictions, had put forward a bold plan to the government. It wanted to protect its area of the Chiltern Hills in south Buckinghamshire by dedicating it to the Green Belt and to take powers similar to those of a development corporation to build 'North Bucks City' for 250,000 ultimate population in the north of the county in the area around Bletchley, into which the county's quota of new housing and new industry would be channelled. The county council had backed its proposals with some imaginative planning by its planning adviser, Fred Pooley – a main feature of the preferred plan being a monorail public transport system, linking together the numerous housing areas, the industrial areas and the proposed new centre. The concept was taken on board in *The South East Study* (Ministry of Housing and Local Government, 1964) and resulted in the designation of Milton Keynes and the appointment of a development corporation. In these circumstances the county council's role was reduced to normal county functions and consultants were engaged to prepare a fresh plan.

Almost as large as Milton Keynes was Telford's 7,788 hectares (19,243 acres) which absorbed the whole area of Dawley and took in Wellington and Oakengates as well. The plan was to increase an initial population of about 68,500 to an eventual population of around 220,000.

There were four further designations, all far removed from the earlier concept of a 'green fields' site. Each was based on a large existing centre of population and the projects were more akin to the expanded town concept than to that of new towns. However, the scale of the expansions was thought to be beyond the scope of municipal activity and it was decided to appoint development corporations. These towns were Peterborough, Northampton, Warrington and the conurbation of Preston, Leyland and Chorley which became known as Central Lancashire. The superimposition of a development corporation on the area administered by a powerful city or borough council, and the creation of a viable partnership between the two authorities, was a bold move, calling for enormous tact, consultation and co-operation. The function of Northampton and Peterborough was to take surplus population (but not jobs) out of the Greater London area and to attract fresh industrial development. Both Warrington and Central Lancashire were to relieve overcrowding in the north west and to attract new industry to the areas.

Several of the towns had a clearly defined secondary function. Thus, the Basildon planners had to contend with about 5,000 sub-standard bungalows and shacks strung out along 40 miles (64.4 km) of unmade

3.   *One of the grass roads at Basildon.*

21

4. Stevenage High Street in 1946.

roads that were grass tracks in fine weather but a slough of sticky London clay each winter. The development corporation's ancillary task was to tidy up this mess. 'At least', said one of the more cynical corporation members, 'we cannot make things any worse.' The same thing could not be said of some of the other designated areas, such as Bracknell, Harlow and Stevenage – pleasant countryside containing attractive and peaceful villages. Tidying up of another kind was needed at Peterlee, Glenrothes and Telford, where past mining activity had ravaged the countryside, leaving a legacy of unsightly shale heaps and potentially dangerous old mineshafts and workings. It was the same at Washington where, in addition, a huge spoil dump from asbestos workings had to be dealt with. Warrington and Central Lancashire both had important renewal tasks – in particular at the Risley Ordnance Depot at Warrington.

Some of the towns such as Glenrothes and Newtown were established to try to revitalise their economically depressed areas and establish growth points for diversified industry. Through the recession years of the early 1980s, most other towns – Livingston, Corby and Telford, for example – took on a similar role – wooing the small industrialist and trying to get things moving towards the long awaited upturn in the economy.

In studying the twenty eight new towns in the transportation context it may be helpful to classify them in some way, by trying to discern some common thread with which to tie together certain of the towns, for the purpose of study and comparison. A system of grouping that is often adopted, for general purposes, divides the towns into three categories, according to the dates of designation of the areas:

Mark I new towns: designated between 1946 and 1950
Mark II new towns: designated between 1955 and 1966
Mark III new towns: designated between 1967 and 1970

What, it may be asked, has the date of designation to do with transportation, in particular with the design of road systems? In fact Sir Frederick Gibberd described as 'futile any attempt to label types of towns by their road pattern' (Gibberd, 1953) and Dr. Stephen Potter has suggested that 'all that trying to group these designs into three or four pigeon holes achieves is a study of physical symptoms rather than what caused them to occur.' (Potter, 1976).

Yet this division into three generations of new towns is by no means irrelevant to the transportation scenario. Circumstances alter, ideas change and patterns evolve over time. The towns within each of the three respective categories were all started within a decade; in other words all started off with an equivalent level of transportation data and research findings, all were in the same era of highway design and construction technique, and all had a similar economic background. It is not surprising therefore to find many similarities in their solutions to

5.   *Colliery within the Washington designated area.*

Table 3.1
Particulars of the twenty-eight British new towns

Name of town	Type	Date of designation	Original target population	Revised ultimate population target	Primary Function
ENGLAND	Mark				
Stevenage, Hertfordshire	I	1946	60,000	80,000	Homes, employment and facilities for London overspill
Crawley, Sussex	I	1947	50,000	85,000	Homes, employment and facilities for London overspill
Hemel Hempstead, Hertfordshire	I	1947	60,000	85,000	Homes, employment and facilities for London overspill
Harlow, Essex	I	1947	60,000	80,000	Homes, employment and facilities for London overspill
Aycliffe, Durham	I	1947	10,000	45,000	Housing the workers on Aycliffe industrial estate
Peterlee, Durham	I	1948	30,000	30,000	Homes and facilities for Durham miners and to establish alternative employment
Hatfield, Hertfordshire	I	1948	25,000	29,000	Homes, employment and facilities for London overspill
Welwyn Garden City, Hertfordshire	I	1948	36,500	50,000	To support and continue the work of the Welwyn Garden City Development Company
Basildon, Essex	I	1949	80,000	130,000	Homes, employment and facilities for London overspill
Bracknell, Berkshire	I	1949	25,000	60,000	Homes, employment and facilities for London overspill
Corby, Northamptonshire	I	1950	40,000	70,000	Homes and facilities for steelworkers and to bring additional employment to the area
Skelmersdale, Lancashire	II	1961	80,000	61,000	Homes, employment and facilities for people from Merseyside
Redditch, Worcestershire	II	1964	84,000	84,000	Homes, employment and facilities for overspill from the Birmingham conurbation
Runcorn, Cheshire	II	1964	90,000	95,000	Homes, employment and facilities for people from Merseyside
Washington, Tyne & Wear	II	1964	80,000	80,000	Homes, employment and facilities for people from Tyneside and Wearside and to raise the quality of life in the north-east region
Milton Keynes, Buckinghamshire	III	1967	250,000	200,000	To integrate existing small towns and villages and establish a major new industrial city
Peterborough, Cambridgeshire	III	1967	160,000	150,000	To expand the ancient cathedral city into a regional capital city
Telford, Shropshire	III	1968	220,000	150,000	Homes, employment and facilities for overspill from the Birmingham conurbation and to tidy up derelict areas
Northampton, Northamptonshire	III	1968	230,000	180,000	To expand the large existing town
Warrington, Lancashire	III	1968	200,000	170,000	Homes, employment and facilities for overspill from south-east Lancashire and north-east Cheshire
Central Lancashire	III	1970	230,000	285,000	To co-ordinate the planned development of the area
SCOTLAND	Mark				
East Kilbride, Strathclyde Region	I	1947	45,000	90,000	Homes, employment and facilities for Glasgow overspill
Glenrothes, Fife Region	I	1948	55,000	70,000	To create a growth point for diversified industry in a new mining area
Cumbernauld, Strathclyde Region	II	1955	50,000	70,000	Homes, employment and facilities for Glasgow overspill
Livingston, Lothian Region	II	1962	100,000	90,000	Homes, employment and facilities for Glasgow overspill
Irvine, Strathclyde Region	II	1966	90,000	85,000	To revitalise existing communities
WALES					
Cwmbran, Gwent	I	1949	35,000	55,000	To house workers at local factories
Newtown, Powys	II	1967	11,000	13,000	To rejuvenate a rather depressed industrial area and establish new industry

common problems.

Nevertheless not all planning teams interpreted similar requirements in exactly the same way. Circumstances, too, varied from town to town and this, coupled with the views and theories of individual planners, resulted in differing provisions for the needs of the motorist, the pedestrian, the cyclist and for those relying on public transport. There were also different approaches to the important matters of road safety and the environmental aspects of the town. As with the similarities, these differences are more readily identified and evaluated if the basic division into Mark I, Mark II and Mark III towns is adopted.

This is not to imply that the precise form of the towns was fixed in all its detail once the original planning was completed, for all development corporations and their planning teams realised the importance of maximum flexibility. Thus, the ideas adopted in the Mark II towns were largely incorporated also into the later stages of the Mark Is. Yet a point was fairly soon reached in the developments when that most important transportation element, the main road system, was agreed by everybody and much of it was already constructed, after which major alterations presented great planning problems and involved great expense. Town centres too, when once laid out, were difficult to change in size or character. A Mark I town had to adapt as best it could to the new ideas and changing conditions of the 1960s but its basic plan, its transportation philosophy and much of its physical infrastructure had already been established for all time.

Table 3.1 summarises particulars of the twenty eight towns with their names, classification, dates of designation and an indication of the main function of each town. It also gives the target population for which the original master plan was prepared and the eventual population towards which development has proceeded, or is still proceeding.

The Reith report included guidance on the physical features to be taken into account in choosing a new town site. At least 25 miles (40 km) distance from London was recommended, or 10–15 miles (16–24 km) from other great towns (See Appendix 1, para 28). All the Mark I designated areas complied with these recommendations but, with the later designations, it became increasingly difficult to meet them.

Good road connections to the country's main road network were clearly of crucial importance to the well-being and prosperity of an industrial town. 'Access to an arterial road' was called for by the New Towns Committee and the Mark I towns were well located in relation to the trunk roads of the day. All the Mark I designations were of course made years before the construction of Britain's motorway network, and indeed before there was any certainty that the motorways would ever be built.

From a modest start in the mid 1950s, the motorway programme has not been without its setbacks. Shortage of funds, land acquisition difficulties and, not least, the fulminations of both conscientious environmentalists and of those, less worthy, who simply said 'no more roads', all contributed to delays and 'slippage' of the programme. Yet successive governments held on to the inter-urban motorways programme so that by the mid 1980s the basic network has been virtually completed.

This has been good news indeed for the new towns, most of which are well served by the motorway system. When the first stretch of the M1 motorway was opened in 1959, people in Hemel Hempstead reckoned that the motorway had 'put their town on the map'. From its earliest years Telford had felt disadvantaged by repeated postponements of the construction of the M54, its motorway connection with the network.

For the most part the towns now have easy access to at least one motorway – the Scottish towns are particularly well served. Redditch's road links will be improved by the completion of M40 and M42 while the London towns will benefit when the M25, the London outer orbital route, is fully opened. The proposed A1(M)/M1 motorway link will be of significance to Peterborough and of vital importance to Corby.

Following the designation of an area of land for a new town, the next step was to appoint the agency to develop it. The development corporations consisted of a chairman and about seven members, all serving part time. These were selected, in the case of the Mark I towns in England and Wales, by the Minister of Town and Country Planning.[2] Subject to consultation with local authorities, the Minister had reasonable freedom to pick whoever he wished to serve as chairman and as members of a development corporation. But it was not, as was sometimes suggested, just 'jobs for the boys'. The aim was to put together a mix of people with, between them, enough local knowledge, technical know-how, business acumen and managerial flair to set the pace and to keep the project on course. Thus, soldiers and sailors (or, more specifically, generals and admirals), politicians, businessmen, architects, engineers, estates surveyors (all of eminence in their callings), local councillors and residents of the area have all served time on development corporations and so helped enormously to shape the character of the towns. The list of the original chairmen alone contains illustrious names such as Lord Reith himself, Lord Beveridge, Captain R. L. Reiss, who had played a leading part in the development of the original Garden Cities; eminent architects such as Sir Thomas Bennett and Sir Lancelot Keay; Sir Ernest Gowers (who caused quite a sensation with his book *Plain Words)*, Sir Roydon Dash, previously the government's chief valuer and Lord Campbell of Eskan. Perhaps because of its diverse and non-political make-up, the development corporation idea worked extremely well.

A development corporation's first task was to appoint its key personnel. Head of the organisation was the general manager whose job was to co-ordinate and lead the team of chief officers who were in charge of departments. Planning and engineering were the departments mainly concerned with the transportation needs of the towns; other principal departments were architects, legal, finance and estate management.

The years just after the Second World War were vintage years for staffing the development corporations. Men and women just de-mobbed after an active and exciting war career, perhaps with high rank and glory, with new skills and an unsuspected flair for leadership, were looking for a change of direction. They had no inclination to return to that junior post at the town hall, the draughting table or the high street bank. The advertisements for chief officers and supporting staff for the new town projects, inexplicit as they were, seemed to hold some sort of promise of the excitement and adventure that they craved, and, for the married man, the prospect of a house to rent was at that time an important consideration. It was not a time for doubts about permanency or fears about pension rights. The development corporations of the Mark I towns were fortunate in the quality of the staff they recruited; the staff could see from the start that they were onto a fascinating exercise which, if successful, would develop into an immense and revolutionary development in planning, engineering, architectural and sociological terms. They were determined to make it succeed. They could be excused for thinking they had been thrown in at the deep end; for those were days of shortages; of food rationing, petrol rationing, accommodation hard to find. But when it came to building a town, they were short too of experience and precedent and even of the tools for the job. Frank Schaffer has related how General Rees went down to Cwmbran when he had been appointed as General Manager, borrowed a small room in the town hall and sat down to contemplate his instructions to build a town for 30,000 people. The sole assets of the Corporation were a pencil and a copy of the New Towns Act (Schaffer, 1970). Well, the Cwmbran Development Corporation's work is nearly finished and Cwmbran itself is now an attractive and thriving town of about 45,000 inhabitants. It is a similar story with the eleven other Mark I towns.

The Reith Report had stressed the need for teamwork and a remarkable degree of inter-disciplinary collaboration was attained, not just amongst the chief officers but right through the organisation. This was no mean achievement; it was almost a tradition that architects and civil engineers found difficulty in getting along together, and planners seemed to be unloved by everybody. Yet somehow in the new towns consensus was reached, collaboration of a high order achieved – helped by the close-knit organisation of the offices. This is not to say that all was sweetness and light; of course there were sometimes strong disagreements at chief officer level. But the general manager was there as referee and in the ultimate it was for the board to make the decision.

The early years involved intense activity for planners and engineers in survey, data collection and other research before anything could actually be built. This led up to the production of master plans carefully tailored to fit the target populations that had been set and future transport requirements as they were seen at that time. After this land acquisition was put in hand, programmes prepared and a start made on construction.

How was it all to be financed? The New Towns Act provided that the Ministry would make advances to development corporations which would be repayable with interest 'at such rate and over such period as may be approved by the Treasury'. In practice the repayment period was maintained at 60 years and the interest rate fixed, from time to time, in line with the rate charged by the Public Works Loan Board to local authorities for long term loans. The Act also empowered development corporations to make contributions to local authorities, sewerage authorities and statutory undertakers towards expenses in carrying out their statutory functions in connection with new town developments.

In appraising the British new towns we are studying a time span of forty years – years of remarkable change. Apart from the immense technological advances there have been so many social and economic changes; a general standard of living improving greatly in the 1950s and 1960s, reducing in the 1970s and followed by the recession of the 1980s; full employment in the fifties which gave way to massive unemployment; the surging power of the trade unions and the efforts of the Thatcher administration to contain it; inflation and in particular the steep rise in the cost of oil products; the benefits to Britain of North Sea oil and gas; the expected population explosion which somehow never quite happened and the increase in private car ownership that has gone ahead in spite of everything. These amongst other developments, affected every town and every person in the country. Naturally, the progress of the new towns, and indeed the character of the towns was in no way insulated from these influences.

It may be helpful to isolate the factors which made the greatest impact on the towns, and in particular on their transport policies.

These were:

- political considerations;
- control of budget;
- the birth rate; and
- proliferation of the private motor car.

These somewhat disparate factors have had far-reaching effects on the progress and the emerging character of the towns and of ease of movement inside them.

'Development Corporations' powers', wrote A. W. Thomas, the chief engineer at Hemel Hempstead, 'appear to be limitless; but in practice they are not'. (Thomas, 1965). How very true! Layouts could be planned and detailed designs prepared, yet before the first trench could be cut, the first brick laid, it was necessary to obtain approval, from New Towns Division of the Ministry, of the proposals themselves and of the expenditure involved – in addition to byelaw approval, or at least the agreement of the local authority. This routine was not too onerous for a straightforward proposal but anything at all out of the ordinary could start an inquisition! For a main road proposal the difficulty was compounded in that approval by the Ministry of Transport and the highway authority was also required; and too often imaginative schemes were frustrated by lack of funds.

There are no votes, it was often said in new towns, yet plainly all the political parties believed that there were plenty of votes in housing. In the early 1950s they were vying with each other to produce bigger and better housing programmes. When Winston Churchill was returned to power in 1951, his Minister of Housing and Local Government[3], Harold Macmillan, set about achieving a programme of 300,000 houses during 1953. So the pressure was on for builders, developers, local authorities and, not least, the new towns. No matter that building capacity was stretched to the limit, that standards were going down and tender prices up! This was the numbers game. The magic total was attained and that was what mattered. The purse strings too were loosening.

With more money around, the numbers of cars increased dramatically. 'Learning to live with the motor car' became a chief preoccupation of planners and citizens alike. The master plans came under frenzied scrutiny.

In the same period the 'population explosion' was taking place; ever since the war the size of families had been increasing, and nowhere more so than in the new towns. Immigration was also on the increase. In 1955 the population of England and Wales was forecasted as likely to be 46 millions by the year 2000, but following the 1961 census the forecast was revised to a staggering 66 millions. The demographers were saying that in five years' time there would be a shortage of schools, in eighteen years a shortage of universities and so on. Moreover the housing gap was widening. The trend was expected to continue and Hugh Wilson[4] calculated that to provide for the predicted growth would require the equivalent of a new town for 70,000 people to be started every seven weeks for the next forty years.

Pressure was greatest in the south-east of England where there was full employment, better pay and a kinder climate. *The South East Study 1961–81* (Ministry of Housing and Local Government, 1964) conveyed the message in stark terms. In the south-east of England, which for this purpose covered the area south of a line from the Wash to Dorset, it envisaged a population increase of some 3.5 million within a twenty-year period. It expected an overspill from London of about a million. Amongst numerous recommendations it suggested several possible sites for new cities (perhaps the first use of the term) and major expansion of all of the 'London' new towns.

Unlike so many others, this report generated some prompt action. In the New Towns sphere Milton Keynes, Northampton and Peterborough were launched while the development corporations of the eight new towns around London were asked to consider substantially higher target populations. This was a tall order. Because he had been given such a precise brief to work to, the new town planner had responded in similar terms. Neighbourhoods had been carefully grouped to the best possible advantage in relation to the town centre, to industry and so forth. The engineer had designed his sewers with precision and economy. Upping the population target was liable to upset all of this. But worst of all was the effect on the transport system. For whether the increase was to be achieved by higher density or additional neighbourhoods, or a combination of both, it was likely that at peak times the carefully designed roads would be over-loaded, the car parks inadequate. There would also be repercussions on the pedestrian layouts, cycleways and on the arrangements for public transport.

Nevertheless new population targets were established backed by revised master plans. The new targets are listed in Table 3.1 and, in the eight new towns within the South East Study area, they resulted in a proposed additional intake of 200,000 people. Other Mark I towns were nearly all expanded in the same way and some of the Mark II series also. So, many of the towns will finish up much bigger than originally planned.

Once building is substantially finished in a new town it is time for the development corporation to be wound up. The town will have huge assets but there will still be heavy loan repayments outstanding and a heavy maintenance commitment. Determining the actual point of 'substantial completion' calls for nice judgement, but, in practice, the winding up of development corporations is generally determined by political decision. 'It is easy', said Frank Schaffer

> to start a new town but much more difficult to stop it. Its very success generates fresh demands as industry expands and children grow up, marry and have families of their own.
>
> (Schaffer, 1970)

Construction was in practice stopped well short of the planned population total to allow for natural expansion to take place. Normal local authority functions, such as road maintenance and street lighting, should already have been handed over but authorities were sometimes reluctant to take on the maintenance of parks and landscaped areas which had been provided on a generous scale.

The Commission for the New Towns was set up in 1961 to take over the assets, liabilities and outstanding responsibilities from development corporations as they reached this stage of substantial completion. Crawley and Hemel Hempstead were transferred to the Commission in 1962 – somewhat prematurely perhaps in view of the considerable additional construction that has been required. Welwyn and Hatfield were transferred in 1966. Bracknell, Corby, Harlow and Stevenage Corporations have now been wound up and those of Runcorn and Warrington have been merged. Arrangements for transfer of the adminstration of most of the other towns are in train. This ends the period of induced growth, but it may be expected that the towns will continue developing in a normal manner. A drive around Bracknell for example will demonstrate that this is indeed happening apace.

Cumbernauld, the first of the Mark II towns, made an auspicious debut. By the late 1950s the impact of the increase of motor car numbers was pretty clear to all, and even recognised in the Ministries (had not Ernest Marples, the Minister of Transport, appointed Colin Buchanan to advise him on the problems of traffic in towns?). By this time there was confidence in the new town idea and more funds were available for infrastructure especially so perhaps in Scotland, where it somehow always seems easier to get money to build highways than in England. From Hugh Wilson and his team there emerged the first new town plan designed primarily for ease of movement, whether in a car or on foot, and for the avoidance of road accidents. The other Mark IIs also provided generously for the predicted increasing numbers of motor vehicles.

Of the Mark IIIs the Telford and Milton Keynes designated areas were similar to many of the Mark Is, but on a larger scale – they were mainly rural areas but with a number of existing townships and villages. The other four were quite different, being expansions of

31

existing important and long established towns. While the scale of the proposed expansion was beyond the resources of the existing local authority, it was clear that the installation of an autonomous development corporation would have been unacceptable. Therefore a partnership was arranged between the development corporation, the local authority and in some cases also the county council. The 'who does what?' question was then negotiated between the partners resulting in differing individual arrangements. For example, at Northampton the design and supervision of construction of the roads was done by the borough engineer, but they were landscaped by the development corporation; at Peterborough, design of the primary roads was undertaken by the development corporation's chief engineer but, when the contract had been let, supervision of the construction was the responsibility of Cambridgeshire County Council's engineer.

The publication *Traffic in Towns* (Buchanan et al, 1963) (more generally known as the Buchanan Report) caused a sensation with its stark exposition of the consequences of the motor age and its pragmatic suggestions of what could be done to maintain the viability and protect the environment of towns. Most of the material was already known to the engineers and planners of the new towns, in fact the Cumbernauld plan, which had preceded the Report by three years, is a classic Buchanan type solution. But the great value of the Report was in collecting together the bulk of the information on the subject and presenting it so graphically as to be comprehensible and valuable to people of all levels of technical knowhow. The Buchanan Report gave credibility not only to the Cumbernauld plan but also to the roadworks and bridgeworks proposals being put in by hard-pressed Mark I town engineers, hitherto held down by cost controls. Moreover, it paved the way for acceptance of the more elaborate highway networks yet to appear. The remaining Mark IIs were therefore also able to provide generously for the predicted increasing numbers of motor vehicles.

Looking back at the scene in the late 1950s and the 1960s, it seems like a golden age. These were the days of the Beatles and of Carnaby Street, of more or less full employment and comparatively stable cost of living; when prime minister Harold Macmillan told us we had never had it so good and moreover that if we hung on for another twenty-five years our standard of living would be doubled! The new towns' construction programmes were swinging along very nicely too.

Through the 1960s, while the remaining Mark II towns and the Mark IIIs were being launched, new towns were big news and no doubt all were expected to become money spinners – as several of the Mark Is already were. Contemporaneous as they were with the creation of the country's motorways, the Mark II and Mark III new towns were products of the motor age, and funding for the necessary highway infrastructure seemed to be fairly readily forthcoming. The opportunity was seized. In the early years of their existence the Mark IIs and Mark IIIs laid down what are arguably the best, and certainly the most comprehensive, urban highway infrastructures to be found in Britain. Those were heady days of confidence and good progress.

Yet they did not last long. By the early 1970s the situation had changed once again, influenced by the four factors that have largely governed the new towns and their transportation policies, namely, political considerations, control of finance, the birth rate, and the proliferation of the private car.

Take birth rate. Whatever could have happened in just a few years to alter materially the demographers' projections? The procreative urge of the postwar decade seemed to have burnt itself out; perhaps it was incompatible with the spirit of the sixties, the desire for more and better possessions – above all the motor car – and for 'keeping up with the Joneses'. There was also the universal awareness and fairly general acceptance of birth control practice, above all the contraceptive pill introduced in 1962 and seized upon with alacrity by married and unmarried women alike. This was a new and liberated lifestyle.

Following the 1971 census the existing population projections had to be scrapped and the sums done again. The forecast for the year 2000 was pulled back from 66 million to 52 million with far reaching implications for all forward construction programmes and most of all for the new towns.

Hardly had the population situation been reappraised when a new crisis broke. The Middle Eastern Sheikhs and the other oil-producing countries ganged up on the Western world and, almost overnight, the price of oil shot up fourfold with shattering effect. It was not just the extra cost of filling up the tank for the weekend. Shock waves reverberated through the whole economy, by then geared so completely to the use of oil and its derivatives. Because North Sea supplies were soon expected to come into production, Britain was better placed than most Western countries to withstand this price rise, but this was of little direct pecuniary benefit either to industry or to the man in the street. With traffic predictions already in confusion, owing to the new population projections, and with petrol prices rocketing would people cut down on their motoring activities? The coal miners, purveyors of Britain's main indigenous source of power, flexed their muscles, demanding a swingeing pay rise. There followed the miners' strike, power cuts, a three-day week, the fall of the Heath government and a hasty settlement by the new prime minister, Harold Wilson. This was succeeded by inflation, very high pay rises – and unemployment.

Yet another factor now emerged to menace the whole principle of new towns. The older and meaner central areas of the big cities were deteriorating sadly. So many families had moved away; generally it was the skilled and semi-skilled workers who had gone – either to new towns, expanded towns or elsewhere. Many small industries and businesses had moved out or closed their doors. The 'inner cities' looked derelict, the reduced populations were disproportionately high in unskilled workers and immigrants. Unemployment and unrest were on the increase. Inevitably the new towns were blamed for this situation. They were said to have been 'too successful; robbing the inner cities of their people and industries' – although in fact only about 10 per cent of the migration from the cities was into new towns. It was added, perhaps with more truth, that, with money getting tighter all the time, these new towns were getting more than their fair share.

This uneasy situation continued while Anthony Crosland was Secretary of State for the Environment, but when Peter Shore took over in 1976 the axe was not long delayed; it fell in a major speech he made at Manchester that year. The effects of his speech and subsequent announcements were far reaching:

- plans for projected future new towns then in the pipeline would be abandoned; a new town at Stonehouse, near East Kilbride, just started was to be cancelled;
- target populations were to be reviewed with reductions in some cases; proposals for revised master plans and larger ultimate population were likely to be turned down;
- dates were set for the winding up of most of the Mark I development corporations, the transfer of rented housing to the local authorities and of commercial and industrial assets to the Commission for the New Towns; and
- new priorities for housing allocation were to be geared to the needs of the cities rather than those of the new towns.

All this could perhaps be described as an appropriate curtailment of induced growth in the new towns. In some of the development corporations it was seen as the kiss of death. The abruptness and severity of these decisions had naturally affected morale, hitherto always so high in new town service. Professionals who had devoted most of their working lives to development corporation work now saw an early end to this career with no hope of transfer to another newly designated town. Some of the most highly valued people began to drift away. When in May 1979 Margaret Thatcher became prime minister little change was expected; it seemed unlikely that her new government would reverse the measures taken by Peter Shore. On the other hand it was not generally expected to exacerbate the difficulties under which the Mark I towns and the Commission were already labouring. Yet for certain Tory aims, made very clear in opposition, the new towns were sitting targets.

A central feature of the Thatcher government's policy was to draw back from public involvement. Housing programmes were slashed throughout the public sector and, in the new towns, this led to a slowing down of most building activity and a reduction of the target population of the Mark II and Mark III towns. Sale of houses to sitting tenants on advantageous terms, an innovation of the Heath government of the early 1970s, was quickly reintroduced to accord with the firm Tory commitment to encourage home ownership. Another policy that affected the government's attitude to new towns was the aim to cut down the number of 'Quangos' (quasi-autonomous non-governmental organisations), which had proliferated in previous administrations and were widely seen as providing 'jobs for the boys'. The development corporations were reckoned to be in this category.

The Environment Secretary, Michael Heseltine, dealt with all these matters deftly in one breathtaking package. Expenditure was to be drastically reduced in all New Towns and, in the Mark Is, any future capital expenditure was to be covered by the development corporations themselves by disposing of some of their commercial and industrial assets. The Commission for the New Towns was instructed to prepare a disposals programme and, no doubt at some future date, legislation will be introduced to give it a responsibility to dispose of all the assets.

There may be sound arguments to support the decision to wind down the activities of the development corporations so peremptorily and to dispose of their assets. However there may also be disadvantages in doing so. Premature exit for example from the new town scene of so many of the chief officers and staff has meant the loss of much local knowledge and expertise. It is in the gradual run down of a project that recording of information, statistics, as-constructed drawings and other feedback documentation are prepared and this is just one example of what may be lost by premature dissolution of a development organisation.

Luckily most major roadbuilding had been completed in the new towns by the time the cuts were imposed in 1976 for, in times of stringency, it is the more costly elements of highway construction which are omitted from proposals. A development corporation's house design can never be allowed to fall below a minimum acceptable standard; sewerage and sewage treatment must always be handled with rectitude. Yet it is curious that all the traffic studies, all the research into highway design, all the accident statistics and all the studies of pedestrian behaviour may be cast aside so readily. It is so easy to reduce a planned carriageway width, to substitute a round-about for a grade separation or a pedestrian crossing for an underpass, or to omit a cycle track altogether.

As subsequent chapters will show, the highway systems of the Mark I towns could perhaps have been even better – given more money, a better appreciation of the impending increase in the numbers of vehicles and an earlier knowledge of population increases. However in the Mark IIs and Mark IIIs the opportunity was there – and it was seized. Nothing was skimped. As a result there are in Britain a dozen or more towns equipped for the transport needs of the remaining part of the twentieth century and any foreseeable requirements of the next.

Notes

1 The Town Development Act, 1952 was the genesis of major town developments such as those which have been carried out at Swindon and Basingstoke.
2 The name of the Ministry has been changed from time to time and currently is the Department of the Environment, but the basic powers and responsibilities in respect of new towns have been mainly unchanged since 1946.
3 Note the change of name and emphasis: planning was 'out', housing 'in'.
4 Sir Hugh Wilson, at that time chief architect at Cumbernauld.

4 Towards a master plan

One of the first actions of a development corporation was to put in hand the preparation of a master plan. This was not a statutory requirement under the New Towns Act 1946 but was pinpointed as a basic need by the Reith Committee and was in any case the logical starting point of the whole project. The master plan was not, as was sometimes believed, a precise and inflexible statement of developments to be carried through regardless of circumstances. Alterations were bound to occur with detailed planning or policy changes and these sometimes caused trouble with land and property owners. This was why in some of the Mark II and Mark III towns, the plan was presented as the more tentative sounding 'Preliminary Planning Proposals' or 'Outline Plan'.

Many people thought of the master plan simply as the highly coloured map they had seen in the development corporation's office, and did not appreciate the huge back-up of research information which lay behind its preparation, or the rationale as explained in the master plan report. In fact the plan included data on ground survey, soils, geology, land terrier, regional influences, watersheds and existing land uses, together with outline proposals for locating the primary roads, residential areas, industry, schools and town centre; there were statements too on water supply and main sewerage, forecasts of future traffic, population trends and an outline of the landscaping policy.

Designers of the early towns were to a great extent feeling their way. There was sound guidance in the Reith Committee's Report, but on transport matters this was mainly by reference to *Design and layout of roads in built-up areas* (Ministry of Transport, 1946). At that time neither the Reith Committee nor probably anyone else had much idea of the nature of movement in towns of the future or the extent to which the private car would come to be the dominant factor in new town living. The Mark II and Mark III towns had a better chance to get it right with the benefit of much research by the Transport and Road Research Laboratory and others and with the experience of all the earlier towns to draw upon.

Summarising the philosophy of the planning process Sir Frederick Gibberd, who was responsible for the planning and much of the architectural design of Harlow, put it this way

> The design of a town – like the design of a car – is based on function. It has to work smoothly and efficiently. But, as with a car, we like a town to give pleasure to the eye, to be beautiful.
>
> (Gibberd et al 1980)

To continue the analogy, the working parts of a town, as of a car, are the things that move, that is to say the people, their cars and bicycles, buses and lorries. Smooth efficient working depends upon a good layout of roads with correctly designed junctions, car parks, footways, cycleways and public transport system. All these must fit coherently into the built environment of the town. However, the analogy must not be carried too far – for it is impossible in practice to design a town with the same certitude as a machine; a town is in fact more like an organism, in that change, unforeseen developments and decay are inevitable over time.

The guiding principle of the planners of the new towns was to provide a structure with a viable balance between the various elements of the town – not only after completion but also during the construction years. Balance was needed for example between population and employment, between various types of industry, between different socio-economic levels and between beauty and utilitarianism. That much was clear from the start. What was only dimly perceived in the early years was that a planned balance would also be needed to facilitate the way in which people could move around the town – a correct balance in planning for the various transport modes and, in particular, a balance between private and public transport.

The Reith Committee did not favour the engagement of a consultant to take charge of the preparation of the master plan, believing that the best results would be obtained from the development corporation's in-house team. The majority of the development corporations must have thought otherwise and thus many prominent names in the architectural and planning professions were brought into the new town orbit as consultants. However, in a number of towns, including Basildon, Bracknell and Livingston, the master plan was prepared in-house by the development corporation's chief architect/planner, and an inter-disciplinary planning team. Sir Hugh Wilson produced no less than five of the plans first as the chief architect/planner at Cumbernauld and subsequently as a planning consultant.

Table 4.1 records the person or firm in charge of the preparation and presentation of the original master plan for each of the towns. Revision plans were needed from time to time, for example to accommodate the increased target populations of the Mark I towns; revisions were generally carried out in-house and were not as a rule superintended by the original planner.

Table 4.1

Master plans
Chief Officer/Consultant

Stevenage	Ministry of Town and Country Planning
Crawley	Anthony Minoprio, Consultant
Hemel Hempstead	Sir Geoffrey Jellicoe, Consultant
Harlow	Sir Frederick Gibberd, Consultant
Aycliffe	Grenfell Baines Group, Consultants
Peterlee	Grenfell Baines Group, Consultants
Hatfield	Hon. Lionel Brett (Lord Esher), Consultant
Welwyn Garden City	Louis de Soissons, Consultant
Basildon	Noel Tweddell, Chief Architect, Basildon Development Corporation
Bracknell	E.A. Ferriby, Chief Architect, Bracknell Development Corporation
Corby	William Holford and H. Myles Wright, Consultants
Skelmersdale	Sir Hugh Wilson, Consultant
Telford	John H.D. Madin and Partners, Consultants
Redditch	Wilson and Womersley, Consultants
Runcorn	Professor Arthur Ling, Consultant
Washington	Llewellyn-Davies, Weeks and Partners, Consultants
Milton Keynes	Llewellyn-Davies, Weeks, Forestier-Walker and Bor, Consultants
Peterborough	Hancock Hawkes Partnership, Consultants
Northampton	Wilson and Womersley, Consultants
Warrington	Austin-Smith, Lord and Partners, Consultants
Central Lancashire	Sir Robert Matthew, Johnson Marshall and Partners, Consultants
East Kilbride	D.P. Reay, Chief Architect and Planning Officer, East Kilbride Development Corporation
Glenrothes	P. Tinto, Chief Architect, Glenrothes Development Corporation
Cumbernauld	Sir Hugh Wilson, Chief Architect, Cumbernauld Development Corporation
Livingston	P.G. Daniel, Chief Architect, Livingston Development Corporation
Irvine	Wilson and Womersley, Consultants
Cwmbran	Anthony Minoprio, Consultant
Newtown	Chief Architect, Cwmbran Development Corporation

The concept of neighbourhoods was firmly featured in all the Mark I town master plans. It stemmed from the writings of Sir Ebenezer Howard, whose sketch plan of Garden City showed six 'wards' (as he called them) separated by the six radial primary roads (Figure 1.1). This concept was adopted by the Reith Committee which, on the question of neighbourhood size, suggested that: 'something of the order of 10,000 is considered convenient, but there can be wide variations'. The Mark Is all followed this lead, although generally with smaller neighbourhoods of around 5,000 to 8,000 persons – about right to support a primary school, half a dozen shops, a pub and a community hall. The question of whether this arrangement detracted from the viability of the town centre and from people's sense of 'belonging' to the town as a whole is raised in Chapter 7. It was answered at Cumbernauld by Hugh Wilson. His 'compact' style of planning relied on good, direct pedestrian access to the centre which provided all the shopping and cultural facilities for the whole town. But for reasons to be discussed the idea did not catch on. Subsequent plans rejected the compact form, and neighbourhoods were back again – or something rather like them. They reappeared as residential 'communities', 'locations' or 'villages'; one development corporation referred to them as 'beads'; but the principle was pretty much the same.

The sites for the industrial areas, shopping centres, civic buildings, schools, churches, hospitals, playing fields and so forth were defined with some degree of precision on the master plans, as was also the primary road network.

The factors that combine to make a town beautiful are not easily defined. Gibberd wrote:

> The design of a town is not, as so many suppose, simply a matter of making plans – of 'town planning'. Its concern is with the quality of the environment, with the actual places or spaces, which result from a particular arrangement of buildings, landscape and roads.
>
> (Gibberd et al, 1980)

These factors in harmony make for a good townscape and the task of the planner is to ensure that this results. Otherwise, for all its considerable planning advantages, a new town might appear brash and characterless – lacking what Sir Hugh Wilson called 'depth in time'. (Wilson, *Skelmersdale Planning Proposals*). This is why all worthwhile existing buildings within the designated areas were carefully incorporated in the plans; it is why Peterborough will always bask in the glory of its Norman cathedral.

But how to make a road beautiful is more a matter of careful basic design than of cosmetic treatment. The engineer had painstakingly to ponder the design of his horizontal and vertical curves, for a smoothly flowing alignment is sometimes more important than strict economy of earthworks balance. The junctions necessary to handle traffic on the primary distributors needed great care, particularly the massive grade separations of the Mark II and Mark III towns, and it was in the design of the bridges and other structures that the engineers seized the opportunities of making valuable contributions to the appearance of the towns. The architect was meanwhile considering the massing and detailing of his buildings in relation to the roads, knowing that both were going to be viewed from each other for generations to come. 'Street clutter' (a term certain architects have been heard to employ), those essential road signs, street lighting units, name boards, litter bins and so forth had to be sympathetically designed. However it was impossible to omit any of these essentials just because they might not look attractive. The role of the landscape architect is crucial to the appearance of an established town, and it was recognised that his advice was indispensable right from the outset. No use bringing him in when it was all over – just to hide away the 'uglies'. Consequently a landscape report was always included as part of the master plan.

It can be seen that the new town planner was not in there all alone. He was leading a team of experts, each putting in a vital contribution. Nor did collaboration end there for the chairman and members of the development corporations kept a steadying hand on the tiller. The estates officer and finance officer expressed views, the county and district councils were consulted, even the statutory undertakers and many others; the views and advice of all were taken into account; and finally the master plan was ready for submission to the Ministry. 'I can't tell you', said one general manager, 'how many people have got to agree before you can do anything at all in a new town!'

Planning and developing these towns was a fascinating and rewarding task; perhaps it may have looked a fairly straightforward one, at least in the case of the 'green fields' sites, where the planning could be done all of a piece, worked out on the drawing board and translated in direct and orderly fashion onto the ground. In real life the scenario was rather different. For there were the changes, in many cases quite dramatic, of population targets; it required the skill of the juggler to keep the housing programme in line with employers' demands for labour; the piece of land most needed for development was often not available on time; some powerful industrialist required the whole of an employment area, upsetting all other plans for it; or conversely, a big company pulled out of the negotiations, deciding to build elsewhere. Financial approvals were sometimes held up; standards scaled down. And if ever things did go according to plan, there was usually some industrial action or else the British weather to upset the construction programme. It seemed that the only thing that could really be relied upon was the relentless increase in numbers of motor vehicles. But at the master plan stage of the Mark I towns even this was still unknown.

The suggestion made earlier that the master plan was not to be regarded as an inflexible statement landed the planner in something of a dilemma. The trouble was that, without the greatest care, planning tended to spell inflexibility. The more detailed and informative the planning, the more inflexible the result – which was not what was intended or required. One finished up addressing the same question as Sir Frederic Osborn, 'Can man plan?'

But don't shoot the planner! After all if he is given specific terms of reference to design a town for x thousand people he cannot be blamed for doing just that.

The need for flexibility was always recognised, although it is unlikely that anyone foresaw the extent of the changes that have actually taken place in the space of forty years. On Irvine New Town E. J. Prince wrote:

> The consultant may produce his report, planning proposals, basic plan, master plan or call it what he will, with whatever planning concept is the planning vogue at that time, but the real problem is just beginning. It is the responsibility of the development corporation to implement the plan to make it work, to fit the concept on the ground.

Perhaps the planner's chief skill is in lightness of touch and his principal tool the broad brush.

The plan for Bracknell was perhaps the worst affected by changing demands because the final population was more than double the originally planned ultimate population. The original master plan provided for four residential neighbourhoods grouped around a town centre, with two industrial areas – one in the east and the other in the west of the designated area. Each neighbourhood was to have a centre containing a school, church, community centre, convenience shopping, public house and so on, and each neighbourhood centre was to be located within easy walking distance of the residential development. However, with the expansion of the designated area in 1961–2, five new neighbourhoods were added together with one new industrial area. As the additional residential neighbourhoods were all situated to the south and south-west of the original designated area, the town centre, which was originally centrally located, was no longer so. Furthermore the original plans to enlarge and improve the existing High Street had to be drastically altered to accommodate the additional facilities required to serve more than double the population originally proposed.

The principle of public participation, which became so fashionable in the early 1970s, may have been cradled – it was certainly nurtured –

in the new towns. From the earliest days, development corporations took pains to explain their planning proposals to the general public, in particular to farmers and property owners within the designated area. This was usually done by personal approach by development corporation staff; and when planning proposals had reached an advanced stage it was customary to set up a public exhibition locally, with administrative and technical staff in attendance. There were also public meetings, sometimes chaired by the chairman of the corporation, at which the proposals were explained and debated. Misunderstandings were avoided in this way and occasionally a new idea floated at the meeting could be taken on board by the planners.

A phenomenon of the 1960s was the formation of innumerable local amenity societies and pressure groups throughout Britain. They generally came into being to protest against some specific proposal – usually a motorway or other road scheme. These societies were mostly started by a group of people who considered themselves to be adversely affected by the project or by country lovers 'appalled by the scale of the proposals and by the proposals themselves'. Environmental benefits to townsmen whose town would be by-passed and benefits such as quicker and safer motoring conditions were often ignored by amenity societies. The government did not attempt to resist the groundswell. With the publication of *People and Planning* (Ministry of Housing and Local Government, 1969) public participation became respectable, a recognised stage in the administrative procedures needed to get a project approved. It even became permissible to question the necessity of a scheme.

Public local inquiries, on the other hand, have always played an important part in the legislative system. When a new town was proposed, the Minister first consulted the county and district councils and other authorities concerned. Then he published details of the land it was proposed to designate. If objections were received, he normally held a public local inquiry. Again, when the master plan had been prepared and before it had been submitted to the Ministry for approval, a local inquiry was held to hear objections to the proposals. Further inquiries were subsequently held to hear objections to a development corporation's proposals, perhaps for major alterations to the master plan, for road schemes or for compulsory purchase orders.

The trouble with public participation is that so many of the participants are people with an axe to grind. Those who are satisfied with a proposal generally stay at home. Happily new towns were spared the extreme antics of local amenity society objections such as when the proceedings at a motorway inquiry were reduced to a shambles and to eventual abandonment; nor has there been anything like the long drawn out and colossally expensive Roskill Commission of 1969 which examined the proposals for the siting of a third London airport.

When all views had been taken into account, the master plan was submitted to the appropriate Ministry. The style of presentation of master plans became progressively more polished, more sophisticated, more competitive; each development corporation apparently trying to improve a little on its predecessor's production. One-upmanship? Perhaps to some extent. But as time went by there was more experience to draw upon, more research, more confidence, improved printing and publishing techniques and certainly more money to spend on the production and presentation. So the cyclostyled booklet and hand-drawn, hand-coloured set of drawings in triplicate of the Mark Is were succeeded by the highly professional, profusely illustrated glossies of Runcorn, Washington and the rest.

It was of great importance when preparing the master plan to ensure that the movement pattern for the town was developed in conjunction with the land use proposals and that consideration was extended to all transport modes – that is, to the road pattern in relation to private vehicles, and equally to public transport and freight traffic, and extended also to the footpath system and perhaps to cycleways as well. The relative importance of the transportation input was recognised in the earliest master plans but its significance had become even greater by the late 1960s when the plans for the Mark II towns were on the drawing board. The many aspects of transportation which contributed to the production of the master plan will be examined in subsequent chapters.

It seems appropriate at this point to take a look at one or two of the master plans – in particular their transportation content.

Mark I: the master plan for Basildon

The Basildon master plan submission of 1951, (Figure 4.1), prepared in-house under the direction of Noel Tweddell, the Development Corporation's chief architect/planner, was for a planned ultimate population of 80,000 within the large designated area of 3,160 hectares (7,800 acres).It comprised the plan itself, drawn to a scale of 12 inches to 1 mile; twenty-one back-up plans (mostly hand-coloured); and the technical report – a simple limited edition publication of some forty-five duplicated pages.

The report was nevertheless a thorough and informative package. After setting the historical background of that strange existing development comprising unmade roads (details in Table 4.2), small bungalows and shacks and the two substantial township centres of Pitsea and Laindon, the report then described the physical setting of

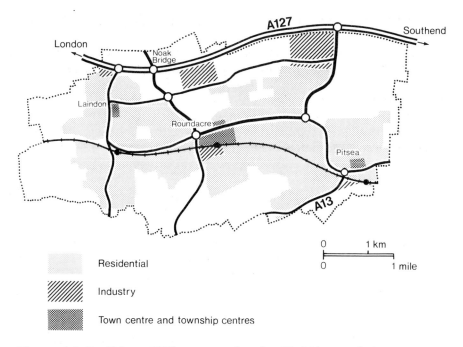

Figure 4.1 Basildon: 1951 master plan for 80,000 population.

the designated area – the main line railway bisecting the site, the two main roads sandwiching it in, the hilly ground of high landscape value in the south and the flat low-lying areas in the north which appeared uneconomic to drain. It went on to describe the existing services, such as they were, and the existing roads in the area, and dealt briefly with traffic flow and road accidents, bus and railway services and thereafter it examined the new town site in a regional context.

Table 4.2
Basildon: designated area: existing unclassified roads

Type of Road	Adopted (miles)	Unadopted (miles)
Macadam or concrete road with footway	5.63	0.40
Macadam or concrete road without footway	14.69	2.69
Builders' road (hardcore only) without footway	–	4.10
Grass track with footway	–	18.14
Grass track without footway	–	52.82
	20.32	78.15
Source: Basildon New Town Master Plan Technical Report, January 1951		

There followed a fairly detailed description of the plan's main proposals, starting with the roads there were proposals for 'living with' the A127 (London-Southend arterial road) and for diverting the busy A13 clear of the designated area; proposals for a new primary road system, with details of lengths, overall and component widths, bridges and the form that each of the principal junctions was expected to take. The five primary roads had the 'plan form of a wide letter H', and it was recognised that the busiest part of the traffic system was where three of these roads joined at a 'traffic circus near the town centre'. The extent to which the existing road pattern of the area could be incorporated into the plan was also discussed.

The proposals for new and extended bus services were perhaps necessarily rather sketchy at that early stage. There was a general statement that a network of footpaths would be provided to cover the whole town but that no independent cycleways were envisaged. There were to be nine neighbourhoods with housing at a density of 30–50 persons per acre, two industrial areas – both on the north side of the town – and a new town centre sited midway between the built-up areas of Pitsea and Laindon. Finally there was a landscape report contributed by the consultant landscape architect.

A revision of the master plan, in 1966, demonstrated how this large designated area could, without too much difficulty, accommodate the required enlargement of the town to 130,000 population.

Mark II: the master plan for Skelmersdale

Thirteen years later, in 1964, the Skelmersdale 'basic plan' was produced. Inevitably this was a more polished presentation than the Basildon master plan, the 80 page report was accompanied by a volume of 35 maps. The plan (Figure 4.2) was prepared by Hugh Wilson, as consultant planner, in association with the chief officers and staff of the development corporation and, like Basildon, was for an eventual population of 80,000. The amount of survey carried out was impressive. Searching enquiries were made into climatic conditions, industrial trends, retailing and so forth.

The preamble discussed the general requirements of new towns and set out a good deal of statistical information concerning population, employment and so on in some of the larger British towns and in the Mark I new towns. From these, data projections were made to derive values for Skelmersdale at various stages of population growth. With the M6 motorway some 3 miles (4.8 km) away to the east, the main physical constraints to the planning of this town were:

● the existing population of about 8,000 mainly in Old Skelmersdale and Upholland;

- the River Tawd valley running north-south through the area; it was unsuitable for development because of flooding and ground conditions;
- the steeply sloping land on the east side of the town, which was unsuitable for building.

Skelmersdale was the second of the so-called compact towns, casting aside the neighbourhood concept and aiming for a fairly high density in the residential areas, mainly 60–70 persons per acre – not as high as Cumbernauld but well above that of the Mark I towns, or indeed of subsequent new town developments. Industry was grouped into three main areas, well spaced out on the perimeter of the town. The principal shopping area was located centrally, just to the east of the River Tawd, so that 'the majority of the people living in the main town

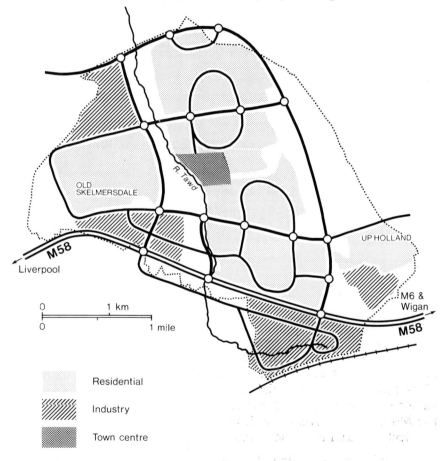

Figure 4.2 Skelmersdale: 1966 basic plan for 80,000 population.

area will be within ten minutes' walk of the shops as will also be a proportion of the people living on the eastern side of Old Skelmersdale'. The site of the town centre presented certain development difficulties because of its steeply sloping western edge and three gullies crossing the site. The submission put forward 'for further investigation' two alternatives – both on the basis of vertical separation of vehicles and pedestrians. A separate section of the report contributed by the landscape consultant described, amongst other things, the proposal to develop a parkland valley along the line of the River Tawd to form a landscape spine across the centre of the town, in association with school sites, playing fields and the town centre.

People's perception of personal mobility had changed enormously in the thirteen years between the production of Basildon's master plan and Skelmersdale's. Car ownership had trebled and forecasts from the Transport and Road Research Laboratory had made it clear what further increases lay ahead (See Appendix 2). Transportation studies were all the rage in the early 1960s and a fair degree of sophistication had been reached. So it was natural that the Skelmersdale master plan report should include a thorough analysis of the traffic situation by the development corporation's chief engineer with forecasts related to conditions in the year 2000.

However the master plan did not go overboard with its highway planning, as might conceivably have happened in that period. The primary roads were shown in the form of a sensible grid pattern at about 1.6 km (1 mile) spacing with grade-separated junctions, and the secondary distributors took the form of loop roads giving access to the residential and industrial areas. There were two access roads (but no through route) to the town centre car parks and service roads.

The plan attached great importance to the provision of a separate system of footpaths so that, from the housing areas, people on foot would have the most direct routes possible to the central area, schools, churches and so forth and the most direct route between one residential area and another; it was intended that the footpaths would have grade separated crossings of all principal traffic routes. The main footpaths were indicated 'in principle' on the plan. As for bicycle usage there was a somewhat grudging recognition of the possible need for 'some fairly direct routes between the main industrial areas and secondary schools and the residential areas'.

The proposals for local bus services appeared to rely on some re-routing of the regional services 'in such a way as to provide for both the local and regional traffic'. In short, Skelmersdale appeared to have succeeded in the contemporary aim of the sixties, in planning for complete mobility – but for just as long as you had constant use of a car! If you did not – and your trip exceeded the distance you were prepared to walk – it looked as though you might come off rather badly.

Mark III: the master plan for Peterborough

This cathedral city was to be expanded into one of the largest of the new towns. The master plan for Peterborough, published in 1970, was a beautifully illustrated document with all the emotive appeal of a 'This England' wall calendar. The nature of the planning task was seen as differing from that of the Mark I and Mark II towns, not only in its much larger scale, but also in other respects, for instance:

● it did not set out to be a new self-contained community but as additional development, to complement and revitalise the old, and

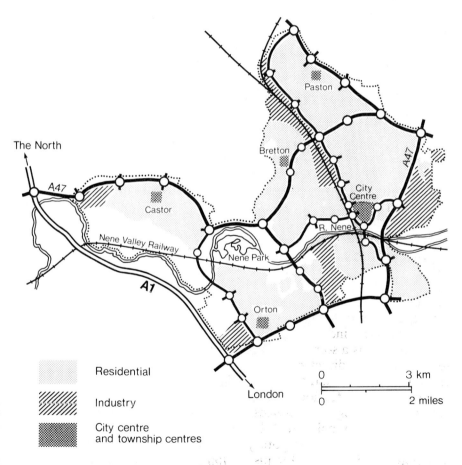

Residential

Industry

City centre
and township centres

Figure 4.3 Peterborough: 1971 structure map for 160,000 population.

to enable it more efficiently to fulfil its function as a regional centre;

- the expansion was not considered as a finite project but as a rapid acceleration, over a specified period of years, of an established and continuing process of growth; and
- initial development would not, as in the earlier towns, need to rely on an act of faith by enterprising industrialists as the city already had its own rapidly expanding industries with a fine export record and an urgent need for more labour.

The master plan (Figure 4.3), prepared in-house by the development corporation in close consultation with the Huntingdonshire and Peterborough County Council and the Peterborough City Council, was derived from a draft basic plan prepared earlier by Hancock-Hawkes, planning consultants. The population target by 1985, the expected end of the expansion period, was arrived at thus:

1970 population	88,000	
Natural increase	9,000	97,000
Intake population	70,000	
Natural increase	20,000	90,000
Expected 1985 population		187,000

The main features of the designated area were:

- the built-up area as it existed in 1970;
- the River Nene winding its way from west to east across the site;
- the main Kings Cross to Edinburgh railway line running south to north through the middle of the city with Peterborough station in the city centre; and
- an elongated industrial area alongside the railway.

Four new townships, each with a population of about 20,000, were planned to the north and west of the city, each having its own important shopping centre. The townships were to be divided into neighbourhoods but no detailed planning, such as the size of the neighbourhoods, was included. Each township was to have an industrial area.

While in general there were few proposals affecting the older parts of the city, it was made clear that the centre itself:

> must undergo the decisive stages of its transformation into a regional centre . . . without sacrificing anything that is valuable either in its existing fabric or in its characteristic quality.
>
> (Peterborough Development Corporation,
> *Greater Peterborough Master Plan*)

The landscape report was prepared in-house and is understandably eloquent about the concept of the 800 hectares (2,000 acres) Nene Park stretching:

> right across the designated area from the unspoilt open country, rich in antiquities, alongside the A1 in the west to the south-eastern corner of the city centre. Along the way there should be a gradual transition from informal, dispersed recreations to organised sports and team games, so that intensity of use increases as the city centre is approached. It is this that will make Greater Peterborough the prototype of a new form of regional development at once urban and rural, expressly designed for an age of motorised travel and increasing leisure activity.
>
> (Peterborough Development Corporation,
Greater Peterborough Master Plan)

Planning for maximum mobility, the Peterborough proposals really seemed to have all the right ingredients. For example:

- to facilitate the quick and easy movement of people and goods, even at the busiest times of day, between homes, workplaces and centres of social and commercial activity;
- to operate a fast, frequent, reliable and comfortable public transport service within easy reach of every home, workplace, service centre and main recreation area;
- in the interests of economy to spread the expected traffic load as evenly as possible, so as to avoid any need for costly dual three-lane carriageways and even more expensive three-level inter-sections;
- to build safety into the system by such measures as diverting through traffic well away from the city centre, keeping industrial traffic out of the new townships and insulating old and new neighbourhoods from all traffic that has no business in them; and
- to provide in the new townships (and wherever else existing development allowed) a separate system of footpaths and cycle-tracks.

It sounded excellent on paper but how could it be put into effect? The new primary road network was greatly influenced by the existing road pattern, in particular by A1 (the Great North Road) which abutted the south-west boundary of the designated area, and A47 leading westward to Leicester and eastward towards Great Yarmouth. Accordingly, the resultant pattern of primary roads did not fall readily into any stereotyped pattern; it comprised 48 km (30 miles) of dual two-lane carriageway roads of near motorway standard, with a limited number of two-level interchanges.

The master plan attached great importance to encouraging public transport. It included sections of independent bus track, and elsewhere it gave the buses privileges, such as priority at intersections during the peak hours, exclusive access to the innermost parts of the central area, provision by the development corporation of bus shelters and lay-bys and so forth. The idea was to get the newcomers accustomed from the start to using the bus service – in particular for the journey from their home to the city centre.

The planners proposed a comprehensive system of independent footpaths in the new townships on the most direct routes possible to give access from homes to the local shopping centre, schools and pubs and from one residential area to the next with grade separation at the road crossings. Cycleways were often to be provided alongside the footpaths and of course the potential for walking and cycling in Nene Park was not overlooked.

The constraints on planning referred to earlier dictated an urban area of curious form. Yet a viable plan was produced with the new townships satisfactorily related both to the old City and to Nene Park.

It is evident that to an increasing extent between 1945 and 1970, new town planners, and the engineers and others who brought the plans to life, recognised that land use and transportation were jointly the principal and essential elements of a successful town and that transportation in this context comprised not merely the main road provision, but also the networks of footpaths and cycleways, public transport policy, road safety measures, car parking policy, the overall townscape and the quality of the environment.

5 The transport input

The transport section of each master plan was prepared in accordance with the beliefs and conditions of its time. In consequence major variations are discernible in particular between Mark I and Mark II towns. To describe and compare the facilities for movement in the towns it is helpful to adopt some standard terminology. In the 1940s and 1950s no one worried much about such standardisation. Terms such as main road, feeder road, principal road, spine road, town road, collector road and so forth were used somewhat indiscriminately. Similarly, footway, footpath, pedestrian way, pavement and so forth might mean the same thing or something different – depending upon who was talking.

Of course there are more important reasons than just convenient nomenclature for adopting some form of hierarchy of roads. In modern urban conditions it is important to exclude all motor traffic from residential areas – except that which needs to go there. Additionally both cross town and through traffic should, if possible, have free-flow conditions on roads from which the pedestrian is virtually excluded. The 'Buchanan Report' (Buchanan et al, 1963) dealt with this by first dividing town roads into two categories, access roads and distributors, and then subdividing the latter into primary distributors, district distributors and local distributors. It compared the system to the trunk, limbs, branches and finally the twigs of a tree. The same classification was adopted in *Roads in urban areas* (Ministry) of Transport, 1966), which also included a note on the role of each class of road.

Table 5.1
Categories of roads in new towns

Category	Function
1. Primary distributors (or primary roads)	These comprise the primary network. They are used by traffic entering or leaving the town and for the longer distance movements within the town.
2. District distributors (or district roads)	These distribute traffic from the primary roads to the residential, industrial and shopping areas.
3. Local distributors (or local roads)	These distribute traffic from the district distributors, penetrating into the residential, industrial and shopping areas.
4. Access roads	These give direct access to the houses, garages and so on from the local distributors.

Table 5.2
Definition of ways in new towns reserved for classes of use other than by motor vehicles

Type	Definition
Footway	Associated with and approximately parallel to the carriageway on any of the four road categories.
Pedestrian way (or Footpath or Walkway)	Independent of the road system, providing segregation from vehicular traffic and direct access for pedestrians to schools, shops, bus stops etc.
Cycletrack	Provided as part of the layout of primary or district distributors in certain new towns.
Cycle lane	A part of the carriageway reserved for the use of cyclists only.
Cycleway	Independent of the road system, often associated with pedestrian ways.
Bus lane	Part of the carriageway reserved for the use of buses only; sometimes a contra flow lane on a one-way road.
Bus road or "Buses only" track	A length of road reserved for the use of buses only.
Busway	A continuous track reserved exclusively for buses.

The road pattern of Cumbernauld, planned some years before the Buchanan Report, was conceived on a hierarchical basis, and the principle was automatically adopted in the planning of subsequent towns. Even in the Mark I towns the same classification can be made to fit reasonably well, although sometimes the distinction becomes blurred in the middle. The four categories of roads as referred to in this study are summarised in Table 5.1. The other facilities provided for movement in the new towns are defined in Table 5.2.

Reference has already been made to four transport modes. These were derived from a longer list of methods of personal mobility in and around new towns:

- walking
- pedal bicycle
- motor bicycle
- driving a private car or van
- as a passenger in a private car or van
- goods vehicle
- taxi or other hire car
- bus
- coach
- train
- tram
- trolley bus
- rapid transit

The last seven are public transport of various kinds.

Not all of these methods needed special, or separate, consideration in new towns and some needed no consideration at all. Car passengers made no separate demand on the transport system. Light vans, taxis, hire cars and motor cycles could be included with private cars since their requirements in highway terms were similar. Trams were more or less obsolete in Britain when the new towns started, and trolley buses were also disappearing. Railways, in view of their independent infrastructure and monopoly management, were largely beyond the sphere of influence of a development corporation. Rapid transit, the modern counterpart of the tramway, was considered by a number of development corporations but, doubtless for economic reasons, none felt able to initiate its provision. This reduced the list to five forms of movement:

- walking
- cycling
- private motor vehicle
- bus
- goods vehicle

Goods vehicles ranged from medium-sized vans to the largest

juggernauts. The latter constituted the criterion for both the geometric and the structural design of roadworks and of bridgeworks and were incidentally seen as an environmental menace in the towns. However they were the 'odd one out' on this list. In a given land use pattern freight transport made a relatively fixed demand on the road system. Planning could influence the transport mode of people travelling, for example, to and from work; but not much could be done about the carriage of goods due to the lack of any reasonable alternative freight transport mode. The Reith Committee believed that the railways would have an important role in the new towns, but it soon became clear that, on the whole, sending freight by rail was neither convenient nor competitive. This left for detailed study the four transport modes which relate to movement by people in towns – walking, cycling, the private motor vehicle and the bus.

Walking and cycling are environmentally the most acceptable modes of movement in towns. They do not give rise to noise or smell, and the risk of accidents is negligible except to the extent that the walkers or cyclists come into conflict with the motor vehicle. Their necessary infrastructure is comparatively modest, but within their range, admittedly somewhat limited, they both give virtually complete accessibility. Of course they are both limited in their scope by the physical ability of the individual; they are not for the very young, the very old, the infirm or indeed for the lazy. It is coping with the motor vehicle – its size, numbers and environmental disbenefits that has, over the years, been a main preoccupation of the designers of the British new towns; indeed it is central to the theme of this study. The provision made in the new towns for these four transport modes will be considered in some detail, since their relative importance has been evaluated quite differently in the various towns, both in regard to transport and to land use structure. In a perfect world there would be full provision and freedom of choice between the modes, trying to give more or less equal mobility to everybody. However throughout the post-war period the private car has increasingly taken over in the towns of Britain while public transport has declined. Yet,

> The car driver is in the minority in this society and his dominance and the consequent impact this has on the transport system can be considered as an aggregate disbenefit to society as a whole in utilitarian terms. The motorist absorbs huge amounts of society's capital, consuming its energy, its land, adapting its built-up areas, creating noise, pollution, general inconvenience and a hazardous environment . . . the car has created a spatial pattern that reduces mobility for the rest of society.

> (Mooyman, n.d.)

A harsh judgement? Perhaps so. Certainly it was the new towns that had the best chance to contain the onslaught of the motor car; we shall see to what extent they have succeeded.

During the lifetime of the towns a whole new science, a new profession, that of transportation planning has emerged and it has grown up hand in hand with, and to a large extent dependent upon, the computer. The travel prognoses used in the master plans of the Mark I towns may seem simplistic by the standards of today; they were prepared manually with painstaking thoroughness and with only the aid of a slide rule. This method of working soon became obsolete once computers were introduced.

In the 1960s traffic studies were the 'in' thing and, fuelled by the predicted population explosion and increasing car ownership, they produced alarming forecasts of town traffic – it was generally assumed that the demand for unrestricted use of cars had to be met and that road building on an enormous scale would follow on from the studies. Perhaps in those more spacious days it all seemed realistic. Some existing towns seized their chance, building massive new urban roads – very successful in keeping the traffic flowing, but often detrimental to a city centre environment and damaging to the well-being of the pedestrian, the cyclist and the prospects of the local bus service. The Mark II new towns sailed in, as later described, on this flood tide to produce some of the best primary distributor systems in Britain.

But within little more than a decade it was all over. As a Government document of 1976 put it:

> The Government have now decided to limit the growth of public expenditure in the interests of higher exports and investment generally. This requires first a painful re-appraisal of the priority to be accorded to transport as against the competing claims of housing, education and the social services, and secondly a ruthless re-examination of transport expenditure to ensure that it is actually (which many critics doubt) achieving the social and economic ends in view.
>
> (Ministry of Transport, 1976. Reproduced with the permission of the Controller of Her Majesty's Stationery Office)

And a House of Commons Select Committee Report on urban transport planning advocated investment in public transport and demolished the theory that the motor car should be established as the universal mode for the journey to work.

The usual method of forecasting future traffic in an area, or on a particular road when the Mark I towns were being designed, was to measure the existing traffic flow, make an allowance for future development in the area and then scale up the resulting figures to cover the predicted increase in vehicle ownership up to the design year –perhaps twenty years ahead. This procedure worked satisfactorily in an established town but had to be modified in the case of new towns because existing traffic within a designated area was usually quite insignificant in relation to the traffic pattern of the town when developed. The principal input in the new towns had to be derived from a study of the planning data, and then a suitable addition made for through traffic. Designers of the first towns were feeling their way, drawing on the experiences of existing towns and the findings of research establishments. Those responsible for the later ones had the benefit of the experience gained in the first batch of towns, better information from the research organisations and all the advantages of the computer. So the degree to which these processes were carried out, the degree of refinement at the various stages, differed between the largely intuitive networks adopted in some of the Mark I towns and the highly sophisticated synthetic transportation forecasting technique adopted in some of the Mark IIs and Mark IIIs.

Traffic flow is usually taken to mean the number of vehicles, or of passenger car units, passing a given point in one direction within a time of one hour. Peak traffic flow is of course the 'rush hour', so familiar to people who live and work in large towns the world over. And it is perhaps obvious that the peaks occur during the journey to work period each morning and the return journey in the evening. There is usually also a secondary peak with different characteristics around central areas at the busiest shopping times. The main reason for traffic congestion at these peak times is undoubtedly the huge numbers of private motor vehicles used for the journey to work and for shopping trips, but matters are often exacerbated by contributory causes, which can be identified as:

- overlarge towns;
- too many jobs in too few locations;
- inadequate roads and, more particularly, inadequate road junctions;
- work starting and stopping times not spread out;
- through traffic using the central road system; and
- insufficient car parking space so that cars are cruising to find a vacant space and adding to the congestion.

A main objective of the designers of new towns was to avoid traffic congestion with its dangers and frustrations and wastage of time and money while providing an economical road network. They were not always entirely successful.

Take the size of the towns. The development corporation's brief stated an ultimate population target. The master plan was prepared to this, or to some adjusted, agreed population target. Table 3.1 indicated in how few of the towns was the ultimate population target held. The ironical fact was that the expansions occurred in the Mark I towns whose road systems, with mainly at-grade road junctions, were the least able to stand it. The Mark II and Mark III towns, with their generous grade separated junctions, were the ones which mostly had their population targets reduced and their programmes curtailed.

As regards the location of the towns' industry, most of the designated areas had a trunk road close at hand, and it was customary in the early towns to plan for the factories to be grouped into one, or perhaps two, locations on the extremity of the town, close to the trunk road. This arrangement led to heavy tidal traffic concentrated on only one or two distributor roads. The implications of this were better understood when the Mark II and Mark III plans were prepared with perhaps half a dozen or more main areas for industry spread about the town. Other potential causes of traffic congestion are further discussed in subsequent chapters.

Advances in the method and accuracy of transportation studies between 1945 and the early 1970s are well illustrated by the reports included in the new town master plans. In the case of the Mark I towns, the design year (usually about twenty years ahead) and a tentative road network (as a rule several alternative networks were put forward for testing) would already have been decided upon and the subsequent steps, described here in rather simplified terms, were as follows:

1   Each neighbourhood (or other convenient unit) was considered in turn, to estimate the number of workers it would house in the design year.
2   Each industrial area and other main employment centre was considered, to arrive at the number of job opportunities.
3   Subject to any special conditions it was assumed that the personnel would be distributed among the available jobs *pro rata*.
4   An assumption was made as to the level of vehicle ownership in the design year. A further assumption was made as to the extent to which private motor vehicles would be used for the journey to work; and the likely extent of walking to work, cycling and going by bus were all considered.
5   From these data the modal split for the design year was predicted.
6   Making due allowance for commuting by car (both into the town and outwards), for freight traffic movements and for through traffic, a forecast was made of the total movement during the journey to work period relative to the design year.
7   As the total movement was likely to be spread over two or three

59

hours it was then necessary to derive the peak hour flow. (In most of the towns it was found that the peak hour flow was about 60 per cent of the work journey total and that the heaviest traffic was generally during the return journey *from* work, usually on Friday evenings.)

The Mark II and Mark III designers generally adopted the current Transport and Road Research Laboratory traffic forecast figures coupled with observation in the earlier new towns. A trip end model was used to establish the details of the journey to work trips; the modal split was applied to this matrix of trips and the results factored up to allow for other trips taking place at the same time. Finally the assignment of the traffic to the network was carried out, adjustments to the network made, and the whole system retested as necessary.

Clearly the traffic prognoses were relying upon a number of assumptions, one of the most important – and the most teasing – being the future level of car ownership in the respective towns (and, more significantly, the level of actual car usage for the work journey). The Transport and Road Research Laboratory publications showed that in 1960 there was a total of some 94 million vehicles of all kinds in Britain and that ownership of private cars averaged 0.11 cars per person over the whole country. Their forecasts envisaged an increase of car ownership to about 0.35 cars per person by 1980 and to 0.43 cars per person by the year 2010. This was part of the input for the design of most of the Mark II Towns' road systems.

So far it has not happened as forecast. From 1973 when the price of oil rose rapidly, it was evident that the predicted car ownership levels would not be reached. The Transport and Road Research Laboratory's forecasts were revised downwards in the short term although, from the year 2000 onwards, the Laboratory held to its original forecasts. Extracts from the Transport and Road Research Laboratory's reports and revision reports of forecasts of numbers of vehicles in Great Britain 1970-2010 are given in Appendix 2 and of car ownership in Appendix 3. In 1973 also, the much lower national population projections appeared, leading, as we have seen, to reduced population targets for the Mark II and Mark III towns. Most of the primary roads and junctions were already built; the remainder were in many cases redesigned on simpler lines or deleted from the plans altogether.

However, this chapter is about the transport input to the master plans as originally conceived, and the foregoing discussion may serve as an introduction to the examination of the traffic studies for:

Crawley
Cumbernauld

Runcorn
Washington and Milton Keynes

Crawley

Crawley provides a good example of the type of traffic study made in the early days of the Mark I towns. In a comprehensive traffic report of 1951 the development corporation's chief engineer reviewed:

● all available relevant local statistical data;
● the experience of a number of towns in Britain and their post-war development plans; and
● current government recommendations on, and research into, traffic capacities, junction design, car parking demand etc.

(McIntosh, 1951)

All the town's industry was to be concentrated in one main area in the north-east corner of the town and the principal shops and business zone were all to be in the centre. So it was fairly easy to define the routes that would be used on the journey to work; but there was no hard evidence to indicate what the modal split might turn out to be. The chief engineer reached these conclusions:

● most people would walk to work if it took them no more than 10

Table 5.3
Crawley: industrial population within the various zones of distance from work

Neighbourhood	Zones					Total industrial population
	I	II	III	IV	V	
West Green	–	–	880	470	–	1,350
Northgate	280	840	–	–	–	1,120
Three Bridges	60	650	460	–	–	1,170
Southgate	–	–	–	1,250	830	2,080
Pound Hill	–	70	700	610	–	1,380
Tilgate	–	–	–	–	1,220	1,220
Gossops Green	–	–	–	180	1,020	1,200
Ifield Green	–	–	260	1,200	260	1,720
Langley Green	–	850	560	–	–	1,410
Town Centre, etc.	–	–	350	–	–	350
	340	2,410	3,210	3,710	3,330	13,000

Source: Report on traffic conditions and volumes within the New Town.
Notes: It was assumed that the estimated industrial population of 13,000 was split amongst the neighbourhoods in proportion to their total population.

Based on an original master plan for 50,000.

minutes;

- quite a large proportion were prepared for a 20 minute walk; an equal number might favour the bicycle; and
- the whole of Crawley would be within a 20 minute cycle ride of the industrial area, and within this range a majority might choose to cycle.

(McIntosh, 1951)

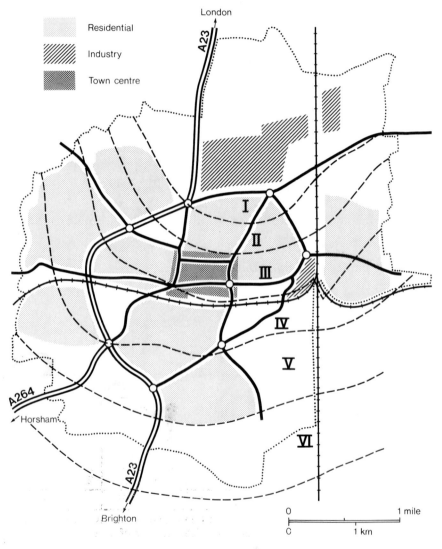

Figure 5.1: Crawley journey to work: zones of distance from main employment area.

A plan was prepared (Figure 5.1) showing the designated area divided into zones according to the journey time from the industrial area. The eventual industrial population of each zone was established (Table 5.3) and the percentage modal split was forecasted for each zone (Table 5.4). The design year was not stated but, since the town was assumed to be fully built, the year 1960 (or thereabouts) was probably envisaged.

It is now clear that the alternative figures for car usage (shown within brackets in Table 5.4) were nearer the mark than the main

Table 5.4
Crawley: journey to work: modal split

Zone	Duration of journey		Percentage			
	Walking	Cycling	Walk	Cycle	Car	Bus
I	10 mins	3.3 mins	70	25	5	–
II	20 mins	6.7 mins	40	45	5	10
III	30 mins	10 mins	20	50	10(20)	20
IV	40 mins	13.3 mins	5	50	20(40)	25
V	50 mins	16.7 mins	–	50	20(40)	30

Source: Report on traffic conditions and volumes within the New Town.
Note: The figures in brackets indicated the ultimate percentages for cars which it was thought might occur at a later date than those for other forms of transport. For design purposes the ultimate for each form of transport was used.

Table 5.5

Crawley: journey to work: mode of travel to the industrial area
Crawley Development Corporation's 1951 perception of the likely traffic demand at c. 1960

Zone	Walk		Cycle		Car		Bus	
	%	Persons	%	Persons	%	Persons	%	Persons
I	70	238	25	85	5	17	–	–
II	40	964	45	1,084	5	120	10	241
III	15	482	45	1,445	20	642	20	642
IV	–	–	35	1,299	40	1,484	25	928
V	–	–	35	1,166	40	1,332	25	833
		1,684		5,079		3,595		2,644

Notes: With an assumed car occupancy of 1.5 the number of private cars for this journey was expected to be 2,400. The number of buses required was estimated at 50.

Based on an original master plan for 50,000.

forecasted figures so, using these together with the population statistics (Table 5.3), a further table (Table 5.5) can be derived to demonstrate the expected journey to work traffic to the industrial area. Even so, thirty years later the forecast makes curious reading in regard to the large number of people expected to cycle to work and the small number expected to travel by car.

This process was repeated in respect of the town centre workforce. The two results were aggregated and additions made for freight traffic, commuting (inwards and outwards) and for through traffic. It was then possible for peak traffic flow diagrams to be drawn and the road network of the draft master plan to be tested. Road widths were considered and designed with plenty of spare capacity, although with, what might now be thought, inadequate attention to the capacities of the junctions. To cope with the anticipated heavy cycle usage, a comprehensive system of cycleways was envisaged in the Crawley master plan. Cycle movements were analysed, similarly to those of motor vehicles, peak flow diagrams made and the proposed cycle network tested.

The Crawley study was, in 1951, a valuable state-of-the-art treatise on the movement pattern for a new town, and it provided the basis for a classic example of the radial and ring primary road system.

No one could have expected the initial travel prognosis for the early new towns to hold good for all time and it was not long before plans were being urgently re-appraised in the light of increased population targets, higher housing densities and other planning changes – most important of all in the light of increasing car ownership. A new look was therefore to be expected in the master plans for the Mark II towns, and this was plainly to be seen in the first of them – the plan for Cumbernauld.

Cumbernauld

One of the stated objectives of the Mark IIs was 'to come to terms with the motor car' and at Cumbernauld the means of curtailing its 'domination' were identified as:

- to introduce an identifiable hierarchy of roads;
- to provide free flow conditions on the primary distributors;
- to provide ample parking facilities;
- to facilitate complete freedom of choice of transport modes;
- to adopt high densities in the residential areas so as to make the town more compact in line with the current fashion for greater urbanity; and
- to secure the maximum possible segregation of pedestrians from moving vehicles.

64

Were these aim achieved in Cumbernauld? The essence of the plan was to get away from the so-called 'garden city concept' of the Mark I towns. The neighbourhood principle was abandoned, housing densi-

Table 5.6
Cumbernauld: summary of design assumptions

Design year	2010 AD
Car ownership	0.4 cars per head
Car usage factors for both intra-town and inter-town trips	0.722 cars per worker
Car usage factor for commuter trips to Glasgow	0.40 cars per worker
Proportion of workers commuting out	40 per cent
Directional breakdown	West 75 per cent South 10 per cent North 15 per cent
Proportion of jobs filled by workers commuting in	40 per cent
Directional breakdown	West 20 per cent South 40 per cent North 40 per cent
Average family	3.2 persons Average number of workers per family 1.5
Journey to and from work	
Distribution of work journey	morning peak 60 per cent of total trips evening peak 60 per cent of total trips
Assumed modal split	Walkers 5 per cent Public Transport 10 per cent Car Drivers 64 per cent Car Passengers 21 per cent
Commercial vehicles as proportion of peak hour flow	7 per cent
PSV as proportion of peak hour flow	1½ per cent
Car passengers: intra-town trips	0.33 passengers/car
commuter-in trips	0.33 passengers/car
commuter-out trips	0.15 passengers/car

Source: Cumbernauld Traffic: a Cumbernauld Development Corporation Report: 1967.
Note: These design assumptions were part of the input to the computer programmes used for the Cumbernauld traffic analysis and assignment.

ties were relatively high and everyone was supposed to live within about 10 minutes' walk of the centre. The idea of a hierarchy of roads was, as previously mentioned, basic to the Cumbernauld plan. Also fundamental in the planning was the requirement of free-flow conditions at all times on the primary and district distributor roads.

The derivation of Cumbernauld's 'new look' road network is of some interest and importance. As at Crawley it was the peak hour of the journey to (or from) work that presented the most severe traffic conditions. The initial steps in the traffic prognosis were similar to those taken at Crawley. *Cumbernauld Traffic* (Cumbernauld Development Corporation 1967) explained that the original, intuitively planned, primary road network had been of the radial and ring road type (similar to some of the Mark I towns) with three radials

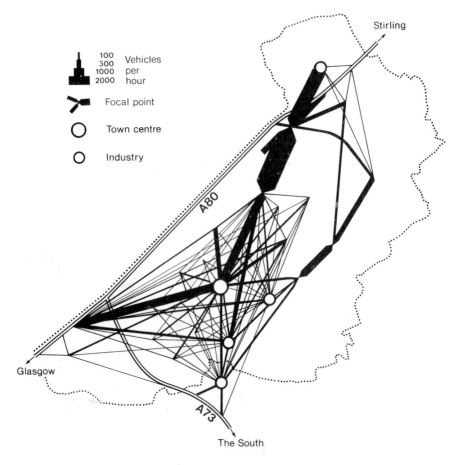

Figure 5.2: Cumbernauld: desire line diagram.

connecting the town with the A80 and A73 trunk roads and giving access from the north and south and west; an inner ring road circled the central area; and an outer ring running around the hilltop served the residential areas. A desire line diagram was drawn (Figure 5.2) and, using the design assumptions given in Table 5.6, the traffic assignment showed that, in the design year, the junctions on the inner ring road:

> would all need to be multi-level junctions to handle the high traffic volumes generated by unnecessary conflict of desire lines during the work journey peak.

At this point the Cumbernauld designers made a complete break with usual procedures; they had decided these conflicts were unnecessary and they would try again. The desire line drawing was used to produce an 'ideal' road pattern which, when adjusted for considerations

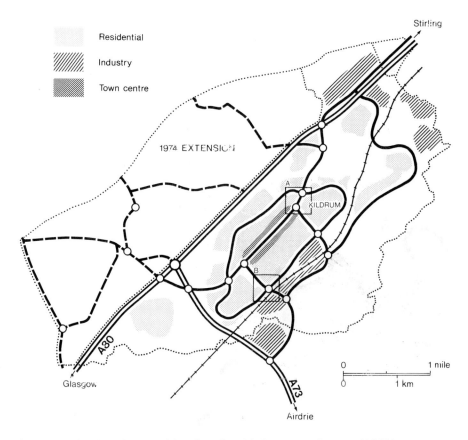

Figure 5.3: Cumbernauld: plan for 50,000 population (1959).

imposed by the topography and planning diktats, led to the adoption of a fresh plan (Figure 5.3), which was a considerable departure from the original, and of quite different character from any of the Mark I towns. The inner ring road disappeared and most of the traffic which would have circulated around the central area was assigned to the primary distributors, with grade separated junctions adequate to handle it. Potential congestion around the central area, or alternatively the building of costly multi-level junctions was avoided. 'The great interest of the case,' said the Buchanan Report, 'is that it was the first example in this country of a serious, systematic attempt to elucidate the relationship between activities and traffic.' (Buchanan et al, 1963).

But what of freedom of choice? And in particular what of the bus services? The implications of the Cumbernauld solution will be further discussed in the next chapter. Meanwhile consider the transport planning of another Mark II town – one which, more than any other, set out to provide a planned balance between the use of the private car and public transport.

6. *Cumbernauld: grade separations.*

Runcorn

Professor Arthur Ling's master plan for Runcorn broke with tradition by providing a continuous public transport route serving the whole town quite separate from the highway network. The concept, illustrated in Figure 5.4, comprised:

- a public transport route in the form of a figure eight threading its way through the residential and industrial areas, so that nearly everybody would be within about 460 m (500 yards), or five minutes' walking time of the nearest public transport stop; and
- a ring expressway with connection to the M56 motorway just south of the town and across the River Mersey towards the M62 motorway and Liverpool. The expressway also took the form of a

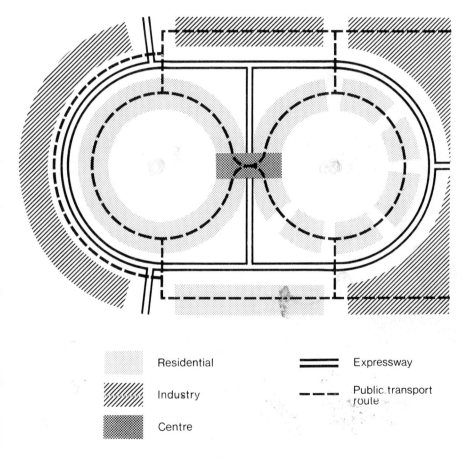

Residential   Expressway

Industry   Public transport route

Centre

Figure 5.4: Runcorn: diagram of transport structure.

figure eight, encircling the residential areas and with the industrial areas on the outside of the rings. The north-south cross-town connection gave direct access from all areas to the town centre.

The expressway system (Figure 5.5) was designed on the basis of a traffic prediction model developed from the employment and residential densities proposed for the various areas of the town, supplemented by predictions of growth in regional traffic and vehicle ownership. Adjustments were made to the model for the expected effect on traffic generation of the separate public transport system. The basic input was as set out in Table 5.7.

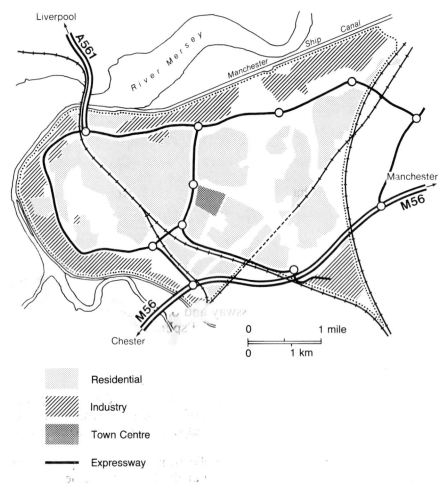

Figure 5.5: Runcorn: the expressway: 1966 proposal.

Table 5.7
Runcorn: design of Expressway: basic input

Design year	1996
Population of the town	100,000
Working population	44,000
Work places in major employment zones	39,950
Work places in residential zones	2,500
Workers without fixed work places	1,500
Workers commuting into Runcorn	12,000
Workers commuting out of the town	12,000
Car ownership	45 per cent
Car occupancy	1.5 workers per car
Source: *Runcorn New Town* Runcorn Development Corporation 1967	

The master plan seems to have been greatly concerned to establish the modal split, as between private cars and public transport, and there was a good deal of discussion on this subject in one of the plan's appendices. The aim was to achieve a 50:50 split between the two modes. However it was recognised that to achieve this some 15 per cent of people who had a car available for the work journey would have to choose to go by public transport. The engineers recognised that this might not happen, so they worked to two differential strategies:

- for the design of the public transport track the calculations were based on a modal split of 50 per cent car travel and 50 per cent public transport; and
- for the design of the expres   other all-purpose roads, the calculations were based on a modal lit of 85 per cent car travel and 15 per cent public transport.

This design method may have seemed rather extravagant; indeed the whole concept of an independent public transport track must have been scrutinised critically in the Ministries. Yet the development corporation felt confident that the cost of providing the track would be offset by consequent savings. This aspect is further discussed in Chapter 10.

In its preoccupation with the public transport versus private car controversy, the master plan, so fully explicit on many aspects of the Runcorn traffic situation, did not concern itself much with those people who could be expected to walk to work or those who might get there by bicycle. But this must not detract from the wholehearted commitment to the important role of public transport so evident in the plan for Runcorn. For these were the years when the motor vehicle was at its most virile, its most assertive stage, when every authority – whether town, county, or regional – seemed to be commissioning a transportation study to try to solve the problem posed by the proliferation of the motor vehicle, on the general assumption that, with enough wide roads and spaghetti-like junctions, the problem would disappear, yet ignoring the advantage which might have been gained through the encouragement of public transport. This line of thought can be discerned in some of the Mark II and Mark III towns, where the studies carried out for the master plan consisted of estimating future traffic – and this seemed to mean exclusively trips by motorised vehicles – and devising a highway system accordingly.

Washington

To a greater or lesser extent all new town planners respected the interdependence of the transport network and the distribution of land uses; these were generally considered contemporaneously and developed in step with each other. Nowhere was this discipline acknowledged more firmly than in the master plan for Washington. The planners' philosophy was expressed in this way:

> Various considerations have led to a new picture of a desirable urban pattern. Instead of thinking of the town as composed of a number of elements – industrial estate, housing estate, central area etc. – each circumscribed by a fixed boundary and connected together by a communications network custom-built for the purpose, the town is now seen as a rather more complex, overlapping structure. The emphasis in design is away from division into separate compartments and towards the creation of a structure for the town which will allow the various functions to adjust to social and economic change and which will encourage diversity of opportunity for its residents.
>
> (Washington Development Corporation, 1966)

What this meant in practice was (amongst other things): residential units known as villages in groups of three or four within a grid of primary roads; and industrial areas well spread out around the perimeter of the town, with direct access from spur roads off the primary road system.

The traffic consultants, Freeman, Fox, Wilbur Smith and Associates, tested seven different networks and recommended a system of

72

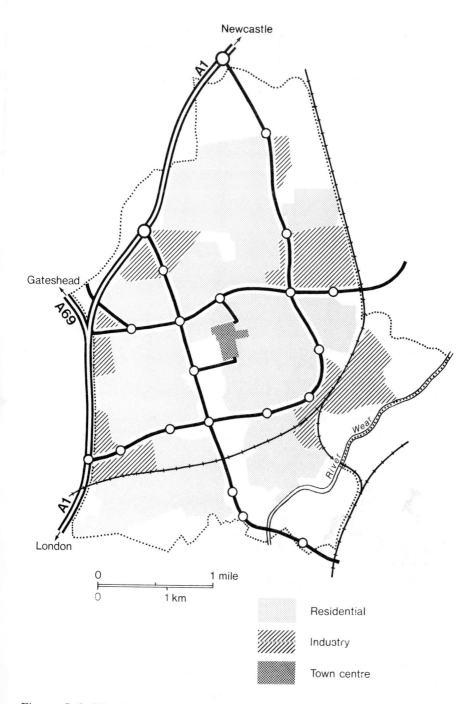

Figure 5.6: Washington: primary roads.

7. *Washington: grid road and junctions.*

roads consisting of:

- a grid of primary distributors at about 1.6 km (1 mile) spacing, high capacity roads, with all interchanges grade separated and having three junctions with the A1 trunk road (now the A1(M) motor-

Plate 1 Primary and secondary distributor roads

(a) Pattern of roads at East Kilbride.

(b) Basildon: a primary road.

(c) Approaching the town centre at Glenrothes.

(d) Skelmersdale: a primary distributor.

(e) Peterborough: one of the parkways.

(f) Washington: grid roads.

Plate 2 Primary roads and junctions

(a) Hemel Hempstead: a surface roundabout junction.

(b) Hemel Hempstead: 'The Plough' roundabout.

(c) Telford: the expressway.

(d) Telford: Hollinswood interchange.

(e) Grade separation at Cumbernauld.

(f) Cloverleaf intersection at Livingston.

(g) Northampton: grade separated junction.

way), which forms the western boundary of the designated area;
- 'secondary spur' roads, connecting villages, industrial areas and the main shopping centre to the primaries; these were located midway between the primaries so that together they formed a 0.8 km (½ mile) grid;
- secondary distributor roads for movement within the village and between neighbouring villages; the layout of these to be such as not to encourage short cuts across the town;
- development roads providing access to houses etc.

The distributor road system is illustrated in Figure 5.6.

There was a pedestrian network covering the whole designated area planned on a 0.8 km (½ mile) grid. These inter-village walkways were to pass under or over the primary roads at the quarter points of the primary grid.

Probable future car ownership levels were estimated in relation to the land use pattern, and a mathematical model was used to simulate the likely pattern of car driver trips in 1981 and in the 'horizon' year. Goods vehicle trips were allowed for by appropriate percentage additions. Some of the design assumptions are given in Table 5.8 and the resulting evening peak hour traffic flow diagram for 1981 is at Figure 5.7.

Table 5.8
Washington: road design basis: data and assumptions

Design years	1981 and 'horizon year'
Car ownership 1981	0.35 cars per person
'horizon year'	0.45 cars per person
Average number of households per village	1,400
Average household size	3.25 persons per household
Generation of work trips	1.9 per day per car-owning household
Car driver trips as percentage of work trips 1981	65 per cent
'horizon year'	75 per cent

Compiled from information given in *Washington New Town Master Plan and Report* prepared by Llewellyn-Davies, Weeks and Partners for Washington Development Corporation, 1966.

Of all the new towns perhaps, it was Washington that was of and for the motor age. The need for a public transport service was acknow-

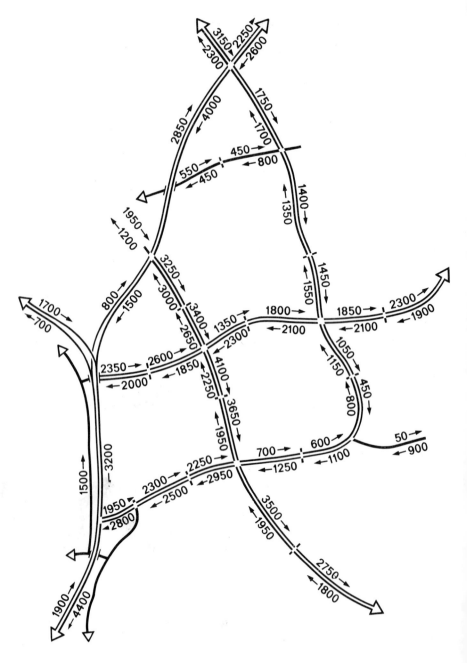

Source: Llewellyn-Davies, Weeks and Partners, 1966.

Figure 5.7: evening peak hour traffic flow diagram (vehicles per hour).

76

ledged in the description of the master plan:

> It is obvious that public transport will be a necessity while car ownership remains relatively low, and even in the long term public transport will have an important role to play. This arises partly from the needs of many individuals in the population, who for one reason or another will not be able to use cars, but also from the general transportation problems of the urban region as a whole. In order to ensure that reasonably economic bus services can function it is necessary to plan the town so as to bring the population easily and naturally to a limited number of focal points connected together by reasonably short bus routes and this has been done.
>
> (Washington Development Corporation, 1966)

Yet public transport did not figure in the traffic analysis, and the road system did little to facilitate bus routeings or favour an efficient passenger service. However, in implementing the plan, to assist bus operations the development corporation pioneered a system of bus-only links, enabling buses to enter the core of residential, industrial and commercial areas.

The inter-village walkways on their regular ½-mile grid were a feature of the plan. Being straight and intersecting at right angles, these walkways did not set out to provide particularly direct routes to points of attraction 'but', claimed the master plan report, 'they will give a recognisable frame of reference and help people to visualise the town as a whole'. (Washington Development Corporation, 1966). So walking was recognised in its own right as a transport mode to be catered for. Not so cycling. As in the other Mark II new towns the master plan took no cognisance of this humble, unmechanised method of propulsion.

What was noteworthy about the Washington plan was the way it succeeded in sticking to the stylised grid pattern of the roads and walkways, yet disposing the land uses – residential units, industrial areas and so on, to good effect. But, in the idiom of the sixties, it was a one-mode plan – designed pre-eminently to serve the needs of the motorist.

Milton Keynes

From the Llewellyn-Davies stable came also the plan for Milton Keynes. Its transportation system was aimed towards the following six goals:

- optimisation of accessibility between traffic generating and traffic attracting land uses;
- maximisation of freedom of choice between private and public

transport modes through conscious planning to avoid congestion and the provision of a competitive form of public transport;

- provision of good quality public transport from the beginning to provide service for both captive and choice patronage;
- flexibility to:

    (a) expand in a manner complementary to the expansion of land development;
    (b) respond to possible alterations in the form which the plan may take over the period of its development;
    (c) accommodate a diversity of trip orientations; and
    (d) accommodate probable changes in transport technology;

- co-ordination of local and regional transportation facilities; and
- segregation of conflicting movements and modes and, by corollary, integration of movements and modes at points of interchange.

> (Milton Keynes Development Corporation, 1969).

One of the first steps in the evolution of the plan was to analyse the volume and direction of movement at peak travel time. It was established that this would be in the journey to/from work period and, by testing a number of possible land use forms, it was considered that the most economical arrangement in terms of movement was a plan which featured a very large number of medium and small employment locations, distributed fairly evenly throughout the designated area with some concentrations of employment at the centre. This was adopted as the preferred land use form.

This plan was evaluated by dividing the city into zones and allocating population and employment to these zones. Journey to work trip patterns were then determined:

> respecting the goal of freedom of choice in location of work place and residence, and these were translated into the trips which could be expected to take place during the peak period.
> (Milton Keynes Development Corporation, 1969)

The assumption was made at this stage that car usage might account for 80 per cent of all peak hour non-walk trips. This exercise was repeated for an alternative land use form, which was then rejected in favour of the more dispersed pattern of the preferred form.

Examination of the desire line diagram led to the adoption of a grid type system of roads: 'because it combined good general accessibility for the dispersed land uses of the plan with a high degree of flexibility to adapt to growth and change'. (Milton Keynes Development Corporation, 1969). But what should be the size of the mesh? Should it be a widely spaced grid with fast roads and multi-level interchanges say a 1.6 km (1 mile) grid as at Washington, Livingston and Irvine, or a smaller grid with roads and intersections at ground level? The consultants' recommendations and the decisions taken are discussed in the next chapter.

Crawley re-visited

Some hard evidence on the performance of a Mark I town road system thirty years on can be found in a consulting engineer's report (Dick et al, 1976) to assess the transportation implications of a proposal to expand the shopping floorspace in Crawley town centre by about 50 per cent. (Commission for the New Towns, 1976). Traffic surveys made in April indicated that, at that time, there were no significant traffic problems.

The report does not facilitate a direct comparison with the predicted journey to work situation at Crawley given earlier in this chapter, since it relates to shopping trips. Even so, the modal split (Table 5.9) is of interest – in particular the small amount of cycle traffic compared with that which was envisaged at the planning stage. The extensive system of cycleways then proposed was never constructed.

Table 5.9
Crawley: modal split of journeys to and from the town centre 1976

Mode	Percentage of Trips (Pedestrian Interview Survey)	Percentage of Trips (Employment Survey)
Car Driver	42.53	47.22
Car Passenger	13.94	15.74
Bus	16.27	10.01
Walk	20.98	18.97
Cycle	2.26	3.47
Train	2.57	3.95
Other	1.45	0.64
Source: Crawley town centre traffic study: Alastair Dick and Associates		

No attempt will be made here to summarise the report. The salient conclusion was that, on the assumption that the full expansion proposals were carried to completion and that the whole development was trading successfully, the existing road system would, with relatively small alterations and improvements, satisfactorily serve the likely level of traffic until 1986.

6 The primary road system

In over half of the new towns the primary road network, which emerged from the calculations and assumptions discussed in Chapter 5, can be identified as slotting into one of three patterns – radial, grid or linear. These towns are listed in Table 6.1. In the other towns the pattern tended to be more individualistic, lending support to the views expressed by Sir Frederick Gibberd (Gibberd, 1953) and Dr Stephen Potter (Potter, 1976) concerning the difficulties of categorisation.

Table 6.1
Basic form of primary road system

Mark I	Stevenage	Grid
	Crawley	Radial
	Harlow	Radial
	Basildon	Radial
	Corby	Radial
	Aycliffe	Radial
	Peterlee	Radial
	East Kilbride	Radial
Mark II	Skelmersdale	Grid
	Washington	Grid
	Runcorn	Linear
	Redditch	Linear
	Livingston	Grid

	Irvine	Grid
Mark III	Milton Keynes	Grid
	Peterborough	Linear
	Northampton	Radial

In fact the only strong trend is that discerned in the Mark I Towns towards the radial pattern, which was of course the general form of most existing towns in Britain; it was the form suggested in the Reith Report and moreover it accorded well with the neighbourhood concept which seemed to be almost mandatory when the Mark I towns were being planned. This is not to say that these Mark I plans were copperplate versions of the radial pattern. Still less did they remain so through the construction years. Variations were introduced for many reasons, such as the influence of the existing regional roads, other local features and the particular land use requirements of the town. Let us now look at some of the primary road patterns as they went into the master plans.

Crawley

The clearest example of the radial pattern was at Crawley, where five radials converge on the centre and there is a complete ring road at about 1.2 km (¾ mile) radius. Half of this ring road was fortuitously already in existence, being the dual carriageway Crawley bypass of 1937. Four of the nine neighbourhoods were contained inside the ring; the others, and also the one and only industrial area, were just outside it (Figure 5.1).

Harlow

A somewhat relaxed attitude to highway planning seems to have been taken at Harlow. 'The main roads', wrote Sir Frederick Gibberd:

> were to run in open landscape and were inseparable from landscape design. They were not regarded as simple ribbons taking the shortest distance between two points imposed on the landscape . . . probably as a reaction against current thinking, the Master Plan contained no section on road design as such.
>
> (Gibberd et al, 1980).

But can the function of a town's highway system really be written down to this extent? It must certainly be conceded that at Harlow, aided by the virtual absence of existing roads and of any physical problems, the simple Y plan of primary distributors could hardly have been improved upon.

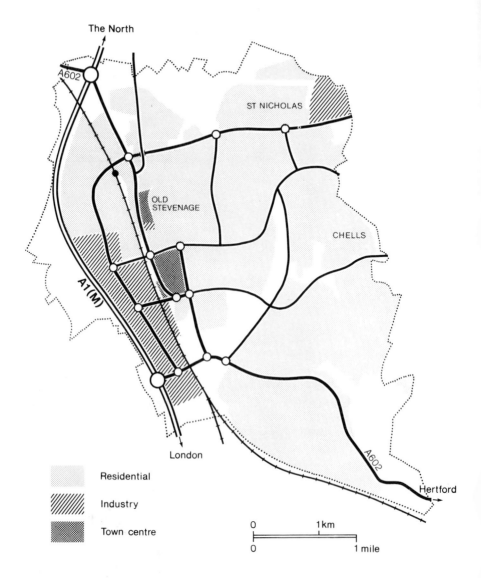

Figure 6.1 Stevenage: road pattern.

Stevenage

The original master plan for Stevenage (Figure 6.1) was in preparation in the Ministry of Town and Country Planning even before the New Towns Act reached the Statute Book in 1946; it might have been expected to embody all the suggestions of the Reith Committee. In many respects it did so, but not in the important matter of the primary road pattern. This evolved basically as a 1.6 km (1 mile) grid reticulating the seven large neighbourhoods and the one large industrial area. It reflected the strong north-south alignment of both the Kings Cross-Edinburgh main railway line and the Great North Road, A1 (now A1(M)), on the western boundary of the designated area. The grid road pattern in Stevenage seems to have been twenty years ahead of general highway planning thought; but the trouble with this particular layout was that in addition to the trunk road and the railway station, nearly the whole of the town's industry was at the extreme west of the town with the new town centre close at hand. Inevitably this led to a disproportionate build up of traffic on the roads in the west of the town, in particular during the journey to and from work. Today that seems so predictable. Yet, in 1946, planning was for a town of only 60,000 people and the modal split for the journey to work assumed that only 16 per cent of workers would be car drivers or passengers. Small wonder that some of these roads are now over-loaded in the rush hour.

Cumbernauld

The evolution of the primary road pattern for Cumbernauld (Figure 5.3) was noted in the last chapter, but it is worth examining its rationale as presented in the Development Corporation's *First addendum report to the preliminary planning proposals,* which appeared in 1959. In that edition of the plan the development was still confined to the south-east side of the A80 trunk road. (With the subsequent raised population target and lowered densities, it was extended to the north-west side.) The transport objectives established at the outset of the preparation of the plan were retained in this report and, as far as the primary roads were concerned, the plan was entirely successful. For the motorist Cumbernauld is a very good town; but, as for freedom of choice, the internal bus service came in for constant criticism, and the excellent footpath system, according to Dr Stephen Potter:

> had not proved as successful as was hoped, as the physical constraints of the site (hilly, steep, wet and windswept) both discouraged walking, and prevented the town being built at the densities proposed, so the proportion of non-walkable journeys thus increased. As a result, Cumbernauld, far from being the most pedestrianised new town in this country, became one of the most dependent upon motorised forms of transport.
>
> (Potter, 1976)

This criticism seems a bit strong. A survey by the development corporation's chief engineer in 1981 of the number of people entering and leaving the centre and their transport modes (Table 6.2) showed that about 43 per cent of the total were on foot – it was almost the same proportion as that of people travelling by private car. The survey also indicated that the number of people walking had increased by 21 per cent when compared with a previous similar survey of September 1978.

Table 6.2
Cumbernauld: number and transport mode of people entering and leaving the town centre

	Tuesday 8.9.81	Friday 11.9.81	Saturday 12.9.81
Total movements by people (in and out) during survey hours	44,406	52,918	52,617
Total by taxi	621	1,502	1,135
Total by bus	5,615	6,581	5,312
Total by foot	22,320	21,789	19,782
Total by car	15,850	23,046	26,388

Source: Cumbernauld development corporation traffic survey 1978-81 final report: (Cumbernauld development corporation, 1981).

Skelmersdale

In common with Livingston, the Skelmersdale plan (Figure 4.2) was a clear example of the grid pattern of primary roads with a spacing of about 1.6 km (1 mile) between the roads. The plan evolved from the examination of some sixteen alternative road patterns. It had two north-south roads connected at the southern end to the proposed A506 trunk road (which was subsequently built as the M58) and thence to the M6 motorway. One of these north-south roads took a line through the middle of the town, just east of Old Skelmersdale, parallel with the Tawd valley; the other ran close to the eastern boundary of the town. Some of the industrial areas, and also the existing built-up areas of Old Skelmersdale and Upholland, lay outside the grid, but this was unobjectionable as all crossings of the primary grid were grade separated. The secondary distributors were mostly arranged as loop roads, virtually forming a number of linear systems connecting the residential and industrial areas. This layout facilitated the planning of a particularly direct main footpath system, routed quite independently of the roads and, as at Cumbernauld, this was central to the 'compact' town concept.

84

However, the vogue for these high density, compactly arranged towns was short lived. It was true that Cumbernauld and Skelmersdale had succeeded, where the Mark I towns had possibly failed, in providing for the full predicted end-of-century traffic and in giving shorter and safer pedestrian access to work places, schools and shops. Yet high density housing had not proved very popular with the customer and perhaps inevitably, densities had to be brought down again.

There was also by the 1960s a realisation in planning departments that something was amiss in all the master plans to date, despite efforts to meet the demand of the motorist and to provide safe and attractive walkways. Even looking ahead to the time when car ownership reached saturation, it was clear that a considerable number of people would, on occasion, need to make journeys when there was no car available to them. Yet bus services in most of the towns were inadequate to satisfy the need. It was now believed by some that, if public transport could provide a cheap and much improved service, it might gain many converts from amongst motorists – not to mention cyclists and pedestrians – as well as benefiting those who did not have the use of a car. Moreover in the Mark I towns a change in this direction might obviate, or at least postpone the need for costly junction improvements. This was the new scenario.

All the development corporations to date seemed to have assumed that bus services would automatically appear and attain a tolerable level of service as had happened over the years in established towns. In the event, the high-minded statements on public transport in some of the master plan reports were revealed as little more than pious hopes. It was clear by the mid 1960s that public transport needs must in future be far more definitively integrated into master plan proposals.

Runcorn

The call was answered in some of the Mark II towns by adoption of the linear plan. A unique example was Runcorn with its figure of eight independent public transport track (Figure 10.2) threaded through the residential communities, the industrial areas and the main shopping centre while the separate, less direct expressway was routed around the perimeter of these areas (Figure 5.5).

Redditch

The Redditch solution was a more relaxed version of the linear principle than that of Runcorn. The primary road system was on new routes and its form owed something to the radial principle, with a full cloverleaf interchange at the centre, and something also to the grid

8. *Irvine: district distributor road approaching a bus-only route bridge.*

pattern. But the most significant feature of the layout was a linear route for public transport. Where possible this utilised the old main road system of the area, in particular the A441, Evesham to Birmingham road. As at Runcorn the route formed a figure of eight linking the residential and industrial areas and the town centre like 'beads', as the *Redditch New Town Planning Proposals* put it, 'threaded on the string of the public transport system'. (Redditch Development Corporation, 1967). Private and commercial vehicles could penetrate into the various districts on the same road as the buses – but only so far; they could not pass through from one district to the next as the bus was able to do. (Figure 10.3).

The Redditch plan provided an excellent system of primary roads as well as good routes for public transport. With an independent network of footpaths for direct access to the principal points of attraction, this plan went most of the way towards full mobility for everybody.

The role of public transport at both Runcorn and Redditch is discussed more fully in Chapter 10.

Milton Keynes

The plan for Milton Keynes was awaited with keen anticipation following the interest shown in Fred Pooley's studies for the public

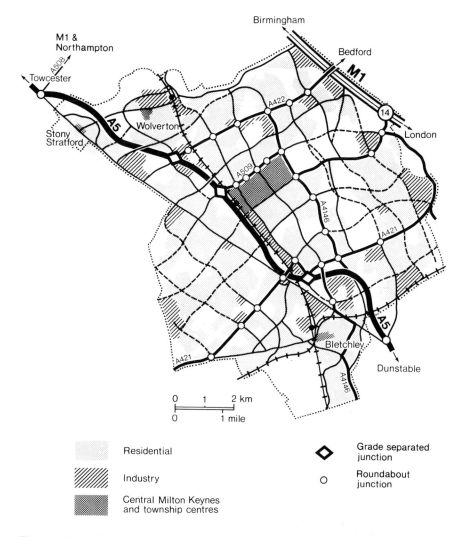

Figure 6.2 Milton Keynes: road pattern.

transport-orientated North Bucks City, with its proposed monorail.[1] (Buckinghamshire Dept of Architecture and Planning, 1965). The zenith of new town transportation planning techniques was possibly reached in the studies for the plan for Milton Keynes, yet there is no great degree of sophistication about the resultant road pattern (Figure 6.2). It should be remembered however that, by the early 1970s, money was less readily available, cost/benefit studies were the order of the day and the propaganda of the 'anti-roads lobby' was having some effect.

The transportation consultants, Peat, Marwick, Kates and Company, had as guidelines the six transportation goals as listed in the previous chapter. They settled on a grid system of roads at approximately 1 km spacing – since this would permit grade-level crossings for most intersections and could be provided at lower cost than a more widely spaced grade-separated system. The spine of the system was a new urban motorway, 16 km (10 miles) long, traversing the area from south-east to north-west. This was a diversion of the A5 trunk road, bypassing townships and villages such as Bletchley and Stony Stratford. It was seen to be of great regional importance and, coupled with the A508, was intended to absorb much of the medium-distance traffic generated by Milton Keynes, thus relieving the M1 motorway of additional pressure due to the new city. The junctions at either end with the original A5 route were just outside the designated area boundary and there were additional connections with the primary distributors of the grid at three grade-separated interchanges. The former route of A5 across the area survived as one of the grid roads, shorn of its classification number, but still bearing the proud, historic name of Watling Street.

The master plan proposal consisted of a ground level road system with intersections for the most part controlled by traffic signals, and with grade separations only at the junction with A5 and where needed to give additional capacity on some of the primary routes.

It had avoided extensive and costly road spaghetti – the hallmark of the Mark II towns – and had acknowledged that time-separation in the form of traffic signals could be something more than a tool for remedial traffic management. This plan provided an economical and flexible road system which was reckoned to be virtually congestion-free. A disadvantage of such a network was that all the roads appeared to be equal even though some (the classified roads) might be rather more equal than others.

But what became of the public transport goals? Did the plan promise good quality public transport of a competitive form? These matters are discussed in chapter 10, but the short answer is that the grid road system did preclude advantageous bus routeing, and laybys, located on the perimeter of the 'squares' (villages) meant too long a walk by people living on the far side of the village. Nothing came of the consultants' idea of traffic signal control at the surface intersections. With the 'right-hand rule' by then in vogue, the development corporation's chief engineer substituted roundabouts at all at-grade crossings.

It is perhaps ironical that the last word in new town primary road patterns – as represented by Milton Keynes, although so different in concept and derivation, bears more than a passing resemblance to that of Stevenage, which was the first of them all.

An advantageous feature of most primary roads in new towns is the generous overall width. Even in the Mark I towns they were nearly all designed as dual two-lane carriageways with ample grass verges which provided scope for landscape design and additional width which could be used for carriageway widening when needed in the future. It may be wondered how such extravagant layouts were ever sanctioned by the Ministries in those austere early years. In fact at the time they were not seen as being all that extravagant; land was bought by the development corporations at what today seems a knock-down price. Initially a single carriageway was generally provided and the remainder of the overall reservation was laid out as grass verge, or other landscaping, the maintenance of which did not then seem the daunting expense that the respective highway authorities are facing today. But trouble began when a development corporation had the temerity to press for both carriageways to be constructed initially. The Ministry of Transport and the highway authority (the county council) were then likely to point out that a three-lane single carriageway had nearly as much capacity as dual two lanes and was much cheaper; so some towns were lumbered with the unsatisfactory 30 feet or 33 feet wide single carriageway for one or more of their primary roads.

The generous verge widths no doubt contributed to the 'prairie planning' taunt. Yet how sensible it was to leave so much scope for eventual widening; the second two-lane carriageways have now mostly been provided, allowing, according to a Department of the Environment *Technical memorandum H9/76*, (Department of Environment, n.d.) a peak hourly flow of some 3,000 vehicles per hour in one direction (see Appendix 4). If that order of flow is reached, there will still be the facility in some of the Towns to widen to dual three-lane carriageways – provided that the junctions will stand it. This is usually the problem.

It was at the road junctions of the Mark I towns that difficulties were most likely to arise when the traffic increased. Generally speaking, these junctions had been designed to comply with the recommendations of *Design and layout of roads in built-up areas* (Ministry of Transport, 1946), and there were examples of T-junctions, Y-junctions, baffle-Ds and so forth; few if any of the new road junctions were designed for traffic signals control. At an intersection of primary roads a roundabout was nearly always favoured; design by the weaving angles method resulted in a large central island 100 feet (30 m) diameter or more to provide free-flow conditions through the junction at a speed of some 24 kph (15 mph). It worked well until the junction became overloaded. When the rule of 'give way to traffic from the right' (the right-hand rule) was applied to these roundabouts, there was opportunity to increase the traffic throughput by increasing the number of lanes at some (or all) of the entry points and by reducing the size of the island. The 'right-hand rule' changed the whole principle of roundabout design. For future junctions, the size of central islands could then be greatly reduced even, in some cases, down to mini-roundabout standard.

In the few cases in the Mark I towns where there seemed to have been serious underdesign of a junction this could usually be traced to a combination of those familiar reasons:

- greater than anticipated increase in the level of car ownership;
- increased target population especially in the Mark I towns;
- tight financial control at the time when the roads were designed; and
- impracticability of leaving enough land to convert a surface roundabout to a grade-separated layout.

All four of these factors applied to the important Roundacre intersection, adjacent to Basildon town centre. Even in the early 1950s the development corporation accepted that grade separation was needed here; yet the idea was rejected out of hand in the Ministries and an alternative solution had to be adopted, comprising a huge six-way surface gyratory. This had little chance of coping with the work journey traffic load in the wake of high car ownership, the large increase of planned population and the considerable through traffic. At Hemel Hempstead the Plough roundabout was similar in size and shape to Roundacre and subject to similar, if less formidable, problems.

With the Mark IIs, as we have seen events were quite different. The pendulum may indeed have swung rather too far for it now seems unlikely that the predicted traffic flows will be attained by the design year; it is understandable that Washington, Skelmersdale and Livingston, for instance, are sometimes thought to be 'over-roaded'. Perhaps that is no bad thing. Roadbuilding is for the long term; a prediction for twenty years ahead is still relevant, even if the numbers are reached only after twenty five or thirty years. Consider too how relatively cheaply these roads were built. It can hardly be said that this, or indeed any of the infra-structure laid down at this period, needs further justification.

A slight cutback can be discerned in the plans for the Mark III towns, although the Telford primary network is more akin to Mark II ideas. However the plans for Northampton, Warrington and Peterborough show a little more restraint and in Milton Keynes, as we have seen, it was decided that by closing up the grid of distributor roads to an average spacing of 1 km (0.6 miles) it was possible greatly to reduce the required number of grade-separated junctions, resulting in an appreciable net saving of cost.

So should plans be made for an ultimate which may never be reached or for the economical solution which may not suffice in the long term? When the traffic builds up, the cost in money and environmental terms can be immense – the same familiar problem which has to be faced in the central areas of older towns up and down the country.

Roundacre at Basildon exemplified the problem. A report by consulting engineers in 1973 appraised three alternative proposals, but they all involved demolition of completed buildings, were very costly and entailed extensive viaducts and slip roads. The development corporation refused on environmental grounds to contemplate such dominant construction alongside the mainly low-rise town centre, although a palliative scheme of widening and adjustment of the layout on lines suggested by the consulting engineers achieved some improvement.

The original layout at the Plough roundabout at Hemel Hempstead gave rise to traffic delays and in 1973 the Transport and Road Research Laboratory co-operated with the Borough and County Council authorities in experiments to increase the capacity of the roundabout, while preserving the carriageway outline and the amenity of the attractively landscaped central island. Several alternative arrangements were tried out and monitored. In the final version the one-way circulation was changed to two-way traffic around the central island with a mini-roundabout opposite each of the six entries. Thus a driver approaching the junction had the option of turning left or right according to the direction he wished to take, and according also to the traffic situation at the junction as he saw it. The system depended upon strict operation of the right-hand rule which was perhaps not universally understood at that time, and when the system was introduced experimentally it was with some misgivings. But the frequent accidents predicted by some people did not occur. The experiment was judged a success, and the layout was made permanent, resulting in some 16 per cent increased capacity through the junction. What at first seemed a revolutionary idea is now accepted as commonplace and the same principle has been applied in other towns in Britain.

In the Mark IIs and Mark IIIs are to be found many examples of grade-separated layouts varying from the simplest up to the full cloverleaf interchanges of Redditch and Livingston. The sixteen grade-separated junctions as planned for Telford are shown diagrammatically in Figure 6.3. (As a result of revised planning when the population target was lowered, only ten of these junctions were built

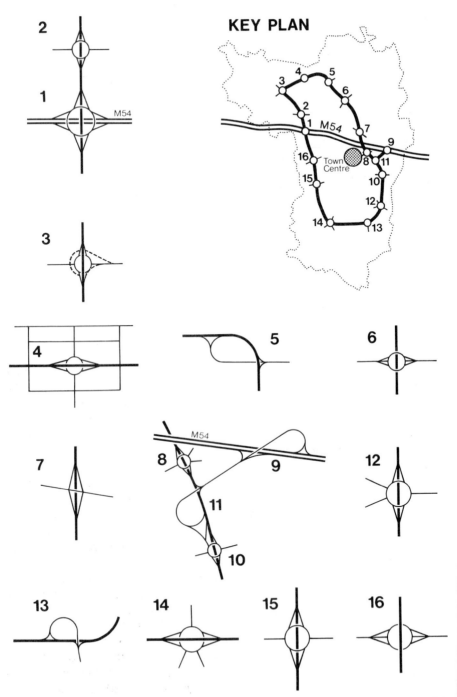

Figure 6.3 Telford: primary road junction arrangements (1970 proposals).

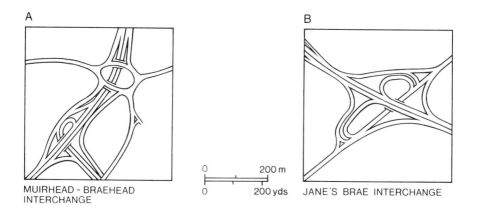

A

MUIRHEAD - BRAEHEAD
INTERCHANGE

0   200 m

0   200 yds

B

JANE'S BRAE INTERCHANGE

Figure 6.4 Cumbernauld: two of the interchanges (for key see Figure 5.3).

with grade-separation). Two of Cumbernauld's elaborate grade separations are shown in Figure 6.4.

A junction type rarely seen in the British new towns is the cross-roads controlled by traffic light signals – so much a part of the urban scene in all older towns. Perhaps the reason is that signals were considered to be a tool of traffic management; to install them on new layouts was almost to admit that something went wrong with the road planning. They are found of course in the older parts of those Mark III towns, which are really major expansions, such as Northampton, Peterborough and Warrington. Signals were installed in Runcorn wherever a local distributor crossed the Busway track, and these were programmed to give priority to the bus; but where primary roads crossed the track there was always grade separation. Similar provision was made at a number of locations in Peterborough. Milton Keynes would have been a forest of columns and coloured lights if the transportation consultants' original proposal, to control every surface grid road crossing by phased signals, had gone ahead, but in the event, apart from one or two junctions in the central area, there are no traffic signals in Milton Keynes.

Many of the new primary and some of the secondary distributor roads were planned in a regional context to form part of the principal road system of the particular county, and so to have classification potential. There was not much argument about this and most of the Mark I towns were able to reach agreement with their county council as to classification values. Some of the development corporations assumed, naively as it turned out, that the county would bear the cost of provision of these main highways – assisted by substantial government grants (75 per cent in the case of Class I roads) to which, as highway authorities, they were entitled. Any corporation that thought this was badly mistaken. Argument about the allocation of costs went on for years. But the building of the towns could not wait and the development corporations were obliged to go ahead, to get the roads built, and to pick up the bills – of course without the benefit of the government grants, which were only available to highway authorities. The corporations were left in a pretty weak bargaining position.

The best attempt to resolve the problem was embodied in the Stevenage Formula[2]. Hertfordshire County Council accepted that the corporation as developer was only liable for the construction of a 'byelaw road' in terms of width, gradient and construction detail; also that the restriction of access appropriate to classified roads meant that the roads had virtually no intrinsic value for development. It worked out that the development corporation would be left with about 40 per cent of the cost of the classified roads, with the proviso that the corporation would in addition provide land reservation sufficient for the full ultimate width of the roads.

The Stevenage formula was applied in all four Hertfordshire towns and was also taken as the basis of agreements between some of the other towns and their respective county councils. It was a far better deal than Harlow or Basildon managed to negotiate after seemingly endless discussion with Essex County Council.

Following the reorganisation of local government in 1974, existing arrangements made for allocation of classified road costs, like so much else, were discontinued. They were replaced by new cost-sharing agreements, within guidelines prescribed in Department of the Environment circular 53/76, (Department of the Environment, 1976) extracts from which appear in Appendix 5. The guidelines put the negotiations between development corporations and county councils on a firm basis. They established that the development corporation would finance the new town roads initially and that the county council would be expected to make a contribution each year based on a percentage of the annual loan charges incurred by the corporation.

By way of conclusion, it seems fruitless to attempt a detailed appraisal of the respective road patterns planned for the various towns, to compare their merits – even within the more restricted groupings of generation or of pattern type. This is because each town had its particular problems to overcome, its own parameters, differing location, size, terrain, land use requirements, traffic predictions and so on – all of which make meaningful comparison virtually impossible. However in broad terms it can be concluded that:

● the radial road system, the familiar and traditional arrangement of provincial towns in Britain tends to break down under present-day traffic conditions if the radials converge in or near the central area. Moreover it is not generally suitable for very large towns. In the new towns it has adapted well to late twentieth century traffic: public transport routeings can be conveniently integrated into a radial town by a ring road for the bus passing linear-fashion through the residential and other areas. The pattern does not adapt particularly well to the provision of a system of independent footpaths and cycleways.

- The grid pattern can be made to fit any size of town but is more suitable for a large town; however a very large town tends to present the driver with locational difficulties and the principles of road hierarchy sometimes break down. The pattern provides great flexibility in land use within the grid squares. There is inflexibility however in trying to phase roadbuilding in with other development; to leave out sections of road until required for adjacent developments results in an unsatisfactory loss of route continuity for the motorist; and
- the linear pattern, as modified for new town use, has proved very successful and can be particularly helpful to the planning of public transport routes.

What is certain is that, with all the differing parameters and imponderables, there can never be a clear-cut or preconceived primary road pattern for any new town development project.

Notes

1 Fred Pooley, was Country Architect and Planning Adviser, Buckinghamshire County Council.
2 The Stevenage Formula was evolved by George Hardy who was Chief Engineer of Stevenage Development Corporation from 1947-63 together with the County Surveyor of Hertfordshire.

7 The residential areas

Until the end of the Second World War, the roads that served new housing areas were almost invariably constructed to comply with the byelaws of the relevant local authority. They had to be if it was intended that the authority should take them over and maintain them in the future. Between the wars there had been variations between one local authority and another, but by 1939 byelaws were pretty well standardised. Local authorities themselves had of course always complied with their own byelaws and this was part of the reason why pre-war council housing estates up and down the country were indistinguishable from each other, stereotyped and, in a word, dull; depressing if on a large scale. The vast out-County housing estates of the London County Council, such as Harold Hill, bear sufficient testimony.

If there was no immediate intention of asking the local authorities to adopt the street, it was of course possible to provide only (say) a 10 feet (3 m) wide carriageway and a single footpath – the sort of thing that was sometimes done in the two Garden Cities – or, indeed, no paving at all as at Pitsea and Laindon within the site of Basildon new town. Even then the actual land allocated to the street – between the fences (if there were any) – was nearly always laid out at the prescribed width.

However, immediately after the war the street byelaws were suspended and standard widths laid down for the various categories of estate roads. These too were fairly rigid. Local authorities could no doubt have relaxed their requirements to some extent in the new towns but would seldom do so – for the development corporations were not in the early days, very highly regarded and the conclusion was that they should be made to toe the line like everybody else. The local authorities, were of course strictly correct, merely enforcing the standards laid down by the Ministry. Discussions might have dragged on and on; but the development corporations were under pressure to make a start, to show something on the ground. The architects were desperate. They hated the 12 m (40 feet) standard width road with its frontage development, fast moving traffic, danger to pedestrians and children, noise and fumes. They longed to bring some interest, something more adventurous, into their layouts. Yet they were made to obey the rules. Some development corporations waged a running battle with the local authority, trying to get a relaxation of the requirements in the interests of environmental improvement and economy; and sometimes it lasted for several years. Government guidance appeared in 1953 when it was stated:

> It is common to find culs-de-sac constructed as if they were local roads, but a distinction can, and should, be made between a local road which has to be constructed to meet all traffic needs and a road serving a limited purpose in a housing precinct.[1]

But it was not until 1964 that the Ministry of Housing and Local Government issued *Notes on new streets byelaws* which stated:

> The impact of growing car ownership on the pattern of living in residential areas, and the need to make the fullest use of available building land, are both factors which are likely to stimulate new forms of housing layout and neighbourhood design. The Minister is most anxious that the necessarily somewhat rigid character of *New Streets Byelaws* should not militate against the adoption of layouts which do not conform closely to the byelaws for new streets but which are designed to secure better vehicular movement and pedestrian safety. . . . The Minister trusts that Local Authorities will also use their power to relaxing byelaw requirements under Section 160 of the Highways Act 1959 to facilitate other forms of layout not covered by the byelaws.
> (Ministry of Housing and Local Government, 1964. Reproduced with permission of the Controller of Her Majesty's Stationery Office).

Saddled as the Mark I towns were at the start with byelaw-type restrictions, what tactics could the architects and engineers devise to avoid the monotony of the traditional housing estate? One device was to get away from the dead straight road; nearly all the towns opted for a gently winding horizontal alignment – there are good examples at Crawley and at Hatfield – and the effect was often enhanced by utilising the undulations of the site. On the sloping ground of the hill or valley towns, such as East Kilbride and Cwmbran, dramatic effects were sometimes achieved by exploiting the contours.

There were opportunities also to do something with the space between the road and the houses, for in most of the towns front gardens were 'out' and this area was available for landscaping. It meant that the development corporation was taking on the burden of maintaining these areas both for itself and its successors. Some tenants may have wished for their own front garden and the added privacy that it gave, but the majority were pleased to avoid the trouble of looking after it. There were a few examples of front gardens being provided, for example at Welwyn and Hemel Hempstead, but not many. Having this space to 'play with' was a great help in designing attractive layouts because, provided the building line was not encroached upon, the set-back and orientation of terrace housing could be varied considerably and to good effect, as can be seen for example at Crawley and Hemel Hempstead. Varying the set-back from a quite narrow verge up to the size of a small village green, as was done at Basildon, could produce

9.   *Traditional road layout at Harlow.*

pleasing results.

The potential of the cul-de-sac was quickly appreciated and it was featured extensively in the plans for the earliest housing developments in many of the Mark I towns. Compared with 'ribbon developing' a normal byelaw through road, the cul-de-sac was economical and offered more scope for variety in the siting of houses; in the absence of through traffic it provided a quieter, more private environment.

If the cul-de-sac was originally a short, straight length of dead-end road, in the new town version it was often of considerable length, curved and with right-angle turns and junctions so that, in plan, it resembled a stem with several sprigs (Figure 7.1). The resulting arrangement of houses was often appealing in its informality. A more formal version was a square of terrace houses, the 'stem' in this case splitting to form a loop road around a landscaped green, as can be seen at Harlow, for example.

Although the Buchanan Report (Buchanan et al, 1963) and the idea of a rigid hierarchy of roads were still many years ahead, it was always seen as necessary in the Mark I towns strictly to limit the number of accesses on to main traffic routes and, as far as possible, to keep these routes free of pedestrians. So in the residential areas, once it had been accepted that there was to be no frontage development on the distributors, it followed that the houses must either turn their backs to these roads or show an end-on view. The architects were then faced with the need to present an acceptable appearance for the benefit of the passing motorist, the bus passenger and the visiting stranger. But however good the rear and side elevations of the houses, it was necessary to screen the back gardens from view and in particular the washing hanging on the line. A see-through post-and-wire fence was of little use; generally speaking a 6 foot (1.8 m) close-boarded fence was provided, or a brick wall. Evergreen shrubs and hedges were visually the best, if rather longer-term, answer and the generous layout of most new town distributors usually provided ample verges for planting a good screen, so that the main road and its nearby houses were scarcely inter-visible. By the 1970s, to meet the growing emphasis on traffic noise attenuation, earth bunds between the highway and the back gardens were often incorporated in the layout, formed from surplus spoil from roadworks or building works within the town.

In the matter of housing density the architects for the Mark I towns found advice from:

- the current policy for local authority housing in Britain
- the writings of Ebenezer Howard and practice in the Garden Cities
- the suggestions of the Reith Committee

All these indicated a density of 12-15 houses to the acre (30-37 per

99

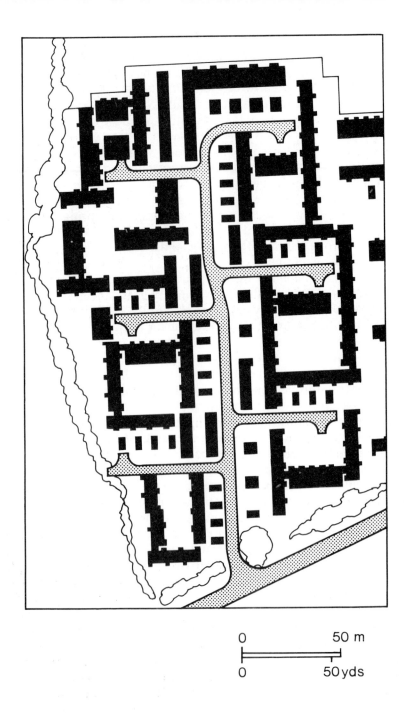

Figure 7.1 Redditch: exploiting the cul-de-sac.

10. Courtyard layout: a Bracknell solution.

hectare) and for the most part densities within this range were adopted in the early years.

This made for comfortable planning, with mainly two storey houses, a few single storey and the occasional block of low-rise flats. There were reasonably sized gardens at the back of the houses and landscaped areas in front. Within the architects' departments of the development corporations there was an urge to do something a little more adventurous. A block of high-rise flats – somewhat rare in Britain in those days – would, for example, have been welcome. But there was little chance of this; for these times were still austerity days. Building materials and skilled labour were short, and money was scarcer still. Wartime rationing of petrol for civilian use still applied and there was very little increase in the numbers of cars on the road. Yet it was obvious that car ownership would before long get back to pre-war levels and probably well beyond. There was considerable debate as to what provision should be made for garages and car parking in the residential areas. In theory there was nothing (not even a byelaw) to hinder the provision of direct access onto the road from a garage integral with the house. But except for the so-called 'higher income group' houses, this was not a practical answer, for by no means every householder would require a garage, and there was no way of ascertaining which householders would require one. Moreover a design density of 12-15 houses to the acre (30-37 per hectare) and the terrace housing that resulted from it would not have sustained this treatment. The answer was to provide garages in groups at what an estate agent might call 'a convenient remove' from the houses and, as to numbers, the Ministry cut short the debate by declaring that garages should be built at the rate of one garage for every twelve houses. In those days there was even a view held by some to the effect that people who lived in subsidised houses shouldn't own cars anyway! More about garages and car parking in Chapter 13.

Outside the new town circle, there was agitation in the architectural profession, a suggestion that opportunities were being missed, the houses undistinguished, the town too loosely knit. It was being put about too, though on somewhat dubious authority, that people accustomed to living in overcrowded conditions in London or other big cities missed the close neighbourliness of city life and resented the spaciousness of their new surroundings. The *Architectural Review* coined the term 'prairie planning', which caught on and somehow stuck as the new town image for quite a while, and J.M. Richards of the same journal passed judgement thus:

> a town is by definition a built up area whose role is to provide for a particular mode of living, a sociable place for people who want to live close together, and expresses itself as such through the compactness of the layout, through the sense of enclosure experienced within it and through being composed of streets. The new towns consist for the most part of scattered two-storey dwellings, separated by great spaces. Their inhabitants, instead of feeling themselves secure within an environment devoted to their convenience and pleasure, find themselves marooned in a desert of grass verges and concrete roadways.[2]

Inevitably, with a project that was new and looked like being a success, any story (especially if condemnatory) was picked up and kicked around by the press.

The neighbourhood concept too was being questioned as being too inward-looking – anachronistic in times of considerable and increasing personal mobility. It was all very well to design residential areas for architectural effect and it is always commendable to design economically and to build quickly. But to attribute the call for higher densities to the desires of the people living in the town, let alone those who would later occupy the higher density houses and flats, seemed illogical, if not worse. Did people really want to live closer together? At twelve houses to the acre the average garden size had provided little enough scope for the enthusiastic gardener and had surely not been excessive for those who did not want to grow anything at all.

There was no great demand for flats and, if the roads and verges had been laid out any less generously, the problem of car parking, serious enough in the earlier constructed neighbourhoods, would have been much aggravated. Cumbernauld, forsaking the neighbourhood principle entirely, started off with a relatively high proportion of flats to achieve its density of 26 dwellings to the acre, but this density was not sustained and there were no flats at all on later housing areas. Bracknell, in common with some of the other Mark Is, managed one block of high rise flats – it was a very fine one. Point Royal was a six-sided building of seventeen storeys containing 102 flats with parking for 90 cars in the basement. Completed in 1966, it was considered to be the most outstanding building in Bracknell; but it was never repeated. In some of the Mark II towns, Redditch for example, the development corporation set its face against building flats right from the start. The truth is that in Britain there is an indisputable general preference for the individual one-family house with a garden and, in general, there is a distaste for flats. That was the consensus; it was what the resident wanted and, apart from a few digressions along the way, that is what the New Towns have for the most part provided.

Yet early in the 1950s Harold Macmillan was calling for a programme of 300,000 houses a year. The new town corporations responded and, amongst other changes, housing densities were stepped up, with incidental beneficial effect on cost per housing unit of the estate roads and sewers.

The 1950s also saw a slightly more relaxed attitude to new town housing layouts on the part of most local authorities so planners were able to come forward with more adventurous proposals. They were under increasing pressure in several respects:

- Ministerial pressure to step up the New Town housing programmes;
- the clamour from the architectural press, which had fair support within the profession;
- the current increase in car ownership and startling forecasts for the future; and
- growing concern at the numbers of road accidents in towns in Britain.

These requirements were to be met with increased densities and a more systematic attempt to deal with the growing numbers of motor vehicles and a reduction in the conflict between pedestrians and motor traffic. It was a time of opportunity and some architects and planners were quick to seize it.

At Basildon, layout proposals appeared featuring a proportion of 'back access' type houses; the front door opening on to a footway and

11.   Basildon: courtyard design at Laindon.

to spacious lawns where a child could play in safety, away from roads and from motor traffic. The back door led into a small fenced garden and thence to a cul-de-sac, which provided vehicular access to the houses and to the lock-up garages. It was an initial and tentative step in the direction of the Radburn principle.

In subsequent Basildon layouts the theme was developed to give more complete segregation, and, meanwhile, other Mark I towns, including Stevenage, Harlow, Aycliffe, Peterlee, East Kilbride and Glenrothes, were also trying out the Radburn plan – adapted as necessary to suit their housing densities and local conditions. Basildon continued developing the theme to its logical conclusion and later carried out a comprehensive development of the Laindon East neighbourhood entirely on the Radburn principle and with pedestrian circulation as the primary consideration.

Laindon East neighbourhood (Figure 7.2) adjoined the Laindon township centre and comprised 725 houses and 137 flats at a density of seventeen dwellings to the acre (forty-three per hectare). Planned in 1964, it achieved a complete separation of pedestrian movement from vehicular traffic. A comprehensive system of footways served the whole neighbourhood, giving easy access to the primary school and to

104

the neighbourhood centre without crossing a road. Vehicular access was from five culs-de-sac, each with several branches which terminated in wide aprons for car parking and forecourts to the rows of lock-up garages. The small back garden of each house either gave direct access to one of these aprons or was connected to it by a short length of footpath. Garage provision was on a scale of sixty garages per one hundred dwellings, and there was car parking on the basis of one space for every dwelling. (27 September 1967)

An appraisal of the Laindon East development appeared in the

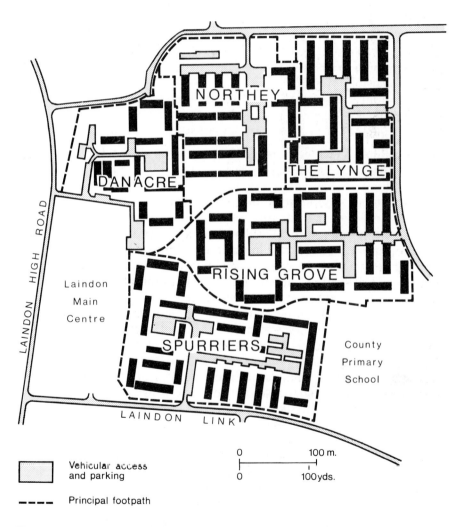

Figure 7.2 Basildon: Laindon East neighbourhood.

Architects' Journal at about the time of completion, and included these comments:

> . . . a significant example of a well handled medium density layout. It is full of interest and variety, and should when mature be a pleasure to live in. The problems of pedestrian/vehicle relationships have been surely handled throughout. . . . Pedestrian priority has been established as far as the demands of the engineer and Ministry of Transport road width requirements will allow. Progression through the pedestrian ways is already a stimulating experience. One passes from narrow passages into a series of differently sized and treated open spaces; vistas are continually opening and closing; glimpses down side routes frequently afford views of small squares and play areas. A sense of anticipation has been sustained throughout. Transition from vehicular to pedestrian routes has also been sensibly treated. At several points the cardinal sin of the separationists has been advantageously committed; play areas spill into parking areas, and why not? Dad can tinker with the car, while junior plays near at hand: neither constitutes a danger to the other.

Of course not every new town designer went all the way along 'the road to Radburn', although through the 1950s pedestrian/vehicle segregation was seen as the panacea for town traffic troubles. There were ingenious adaptations of the principle, tailored to the local requirements of each particular town. A favoured method was to have a loop road (usually to byelaw standard with two footways) threading through an area of several hundred dwellings and arranged so that some of the houses fronted onto the loop road; the remainder being in blocks end-on to the road with short footpath connections. Access to the backs of the houses and the lock-up garages was from culs-de-sac. This made for a more conventional layout, perhaps more acceptable to many residents (examples can be seen at Harlow, for instance). However it was less successful in solving the pedestrian/vehicle relationship and it did little to facilitate pedestrian movement to the primary school, the neighbourhood centre or the town centre. Moreover it was in many cases extravagant in overall road length and therefore in road costs. Such developments were often loosely referred to as Radburn layouts, for the term had become a sort of prestige symbol by the early 1960s.

Cumbernauld, the 'compact' town, first of the second generation towns, commenced its housing programme with the high average density of 64 dwellings per hectare (26 per acre). Looking at one particular housing area layout, that of Kildrum 3, there were six four-storey blocks of flats and about 200 houses. A loop road acted as a spine for the development with several culs-de-sac branching from it.

late 3 Residential areas

) Traditional street pattern at Harlow. . . .

) . . . Stevenage and . . .

) . . . Hemel Hempstead.

) Pedestrian/vehicle segregation: footpath access at Bracknell.

) Basildon: pedestrian access at Laindon East and

  . . . vehicular access and parking from cul-de-sac.

Plate 4 Residential areas

(a) Cumbernauld: footpath access at Kildrum 3.

(b) A more recent housing development at Cumbernauld.

(c), (d) and (e) The birth of the 'shared access' concept was at Runcorn's The Brow estate.

(f) Shared access at Cwmbran.

(g) A development at Irvine.

ate 5 Housing layouts of the 1970s

) Washington: shared access.

) Glenrothes: a development of the 1970s.

and (d) Washington villages.

and (f) Basildon: Noak Bridge village: return to
the traditional street pattern?

Plate 6 Residential: access to houses in the Mark III tow

(a) Milton Keynes: courtyard access.

(b) Formal arrangement at Peterborough.

(c) Looking out on Milton Keynes.

(d) Looking down at Central Lancashire's culs-de
    sac and footpaths.

(e) Traditional layout at Warrington.

(f) A Northampton square.

The flats were set in gardens with footpath access and their lock-up garages, close at hand and approached by cul-de-sac access roads, were arranged unusually in annular shaped blocks; the garage doors were on the inside of the ring and the paved circle in the middle served as forecourt and turning space. This interesting arrangement eliminated the visual effect of an ocean of cars surrounding the flats.

Most of the houses were in long terrace blocks – the longest comprising sixteen houses – mainly arranged end-on to the loop road with footpath access to the house. Access to the garages for these houses was direct from the loop road. The layout was simple and as uncompromising as that of Laindon East. But Kildrum was on a steep slope and the contours, coupled with the high standard of Cumbernauld landscaping now grown to full maturity, have combined to soften the stark outlines. It was an economical road layout.

Increased garage provision will have been noted in the layouts just described. The Ministry would not agree to a bigger proportion until 1956 when the provision was increased from one garage to twelve houses to one to eight. Thereafter the allowance was increased progressively; the layouts here described at Basildon and Cumber-

12. *Cumbernauld: footpath access amongst the heather.*

13.   Exploiting the contours at Newtown.

nauld were getting up towards one garage to each dwelling with parking spaces in addition.

For many years Radburn in more or less modified form was generally considered to be the most promising answer to the question of 'how to put the motor vehicle in its place and keep it there'. Even so it was not without its shortcomings. For instance, the simple matter of naming streets and numbering the houses in the streets became complex on a Radburn layout. Should the 'fronts' or the 'backs' be named and numbered? At Laindon East the five culs-de-sac were each given a name that applied to every house whose back door led to that cul-de-sac. So, arriving by car, it was easy to find the right cul-de-sac and not too difficult to find the right sprig and the right number. However locating the front door was another matter; it was necessary to study direction boards with a bewildering display of names and numbers. Thus a pedestrian visiting for the first time had greater problems than a motorist arriving at the back entrance. Yet who likes to have their guests entering via the kitchen? And at times of emergency, of sorrow or rejoicing, it is hardly satisfactory when the ambulance, the hearse or the bridal car are obliged to jostle for a place in the cul-de-sac. At Redditch street naming in Radburn type layouts was processed with commendable logic. Each individual length of cul-de-sac was given a distinctive name, the initial letters of the names running in alphabetical order. This helped identification – provided you knew the code.

It was all very well to say that the children could play at the front of the house, out of danger. But what if the grass was damp – which it usually was? And how could anyone keep an eye on the children from the kitchen, which was usually at the back of the house? In practice the children could be found playing in the tiny back garden, on the garage forecourt or inside the garage. Perhaps the quest for privacy had been overdone and housewives would have preferred to be nearer the action, to see more people and more traffic. With the breadwinner away all day and the 'family' car sitting outside the factory or office and with a bus service perhaps indifferent in the early years, it was small wonder that some housewives became bored, depressed, perhaps addicted to drugs. Their lack of mobility may have been hard to bear. Whether there were numerous such cases spread around the towns, or just one or two cases in one town, is not clear. Anyway some journalist dubbed it 'the new town blues', and this was taken up by the press in general and flogged mercilessly as a worthy successor to the 'prairie planning' taunt.

Irrespective of new town blues, the Radburn layout was being questioned. No one was denying the validity of Stein's and Wright's concept. Perhaps the real trouble was the high densities of the day; the original Radburn density had been about 17 houses per hectare (7 to the acre). Culs-de-sac and walkways, cars and garages did not merge into the landscape so happily at 17 or so to the acre. The result was very different. A radical reappraisal was needed and a new solution. This breakthrough occurred at Runcorn.

In 1964, under pressure to make an immediate effective start on house building, the Runcorn team opted for what might be called an 'off the peg' Radburn solution for their first housing area; it was a high density layout of 49 dwellings per hectare (20 to the acre). The resulting architecture and general arrangements were somewhat undistinguished and, perhaps for this reason, the Radburn solution was never repeated in Runcorn. Pedestrian/vehicle segregation, which had seemed so essential a decade earlier, was not fitting in very successfully with the one-car-per-family requirement of the 1960s. Could a 'front and back' road system be afforded as at Harlow? Did New Town residents really welcome those huge, amorphous culs-de-sac and aprons as seen at Basildon? In short, had the infrastructure for the motor car taken over so as to dominate the residential area after all? The questions did not end there. Had it been a false assumption that the pedestrian could be persuaded to use one side of the house only or were people in fact walking and playing and loitering around on the culs-de-sac and aprons? A further appraisal of the situation was required.

Starting from the premise that the cul-de-sac offered the most satisfactory means of access in a residential area, Eddie Jenkins identified three basic rules that should be applied to the cul-de-sac:

- *the system must be safe*
  Safe, that is, for all users of all ages, from the toddler of eighteen months escaping the attention of a mother deep in conversation or distracted by a crying baby to the semi-sighted octogenarian some of whom still regard the motor vehicle with awe and fear or even on occasions hatred.
  Safe for the older child on its first bicycle or the group playing football or hopscotch.
  Safe for the dreamer or dawdler walking home from school.
  All of these and many more will be present at some time in the cul-de-sac whether it is designed for them or not;
- *the system must work*
  The motor car must be allowed to penetrate to the curtilage of the dwelling. How many of us would accept as a good design a solution which made us walk 50 yards to our garage, however good the exercise might be for us. No blushing bride-to-be wants to walk in driving rain or a gale to a bridal car parked at the end of a pedestrianised court and even the dying have dignity and prefer the ambulance to come to the door.
  The bin lorry, the furniture van, the bread and the milk float, service and emergency vehicles, must all get close up to the dwelling. There must be adequate off-street parking and sufficient manoeuvring space; and
- *the system must be environmentally acceptable*
  It must be in keeping with the overall environment, it must not dominate the solution but must relate to it. The user should have a feeling of rightness whether travelling by vehicle or on foot, whether at work or at play.

(Jenkins, 1975)

It was clear that not all layouts based on the cul-de-sac were meeting these criteria. There was nothing to stop drivers reaching excessive speeds on the straight runs of the larger culs-de-sac; some residents could get the car no closer than about 46 m (150 feet) away from the house; and it was certain that not all housing schemes could be regarded as environmentally acceptable.

Yet how could the motorist be controlled? Not by curtailing his penetration into the residential area, for he wanted to be able to drive and to park his car close to the front door of the house. It was his speed that had to be controlled for, if he were driving alertly and at a speed of no more than 16 kph (10 miles per hour), conflict between his vehicle and anyone on foot, even a child at play, seemed very unlikely. It was no use trying to slow him down by putting up notices, for the average motorist is notoriously unlikely to obey a speed restriction for which he can see no reason relative either to the road geometry or traffic conditions. 'How', asked Jenkins, 'do we achieve an instinctive response from the motorist?'

Road geometry was in fact the key. For if the cul-de-sac was designed for low speed, if the road width, radii, sight lines and so on were designed thus, with only just about enough room for the furniture van to get through, then the motorist who lived there would naturally drive slowly in the area while the visiting driver would grope his way in with the feeling of entering a private place. That was the theory. It was put into practice at a site called The Brow, the second housing development in Runcorn. This steeply sloping site contained 370 dwellings at a density of about 37 dwellings per hectare (15 to the acre) and the designers set out deliberately to create a pedestrian dominated area (Figure 7.3). The site was served with local distributors from which sprang a number of short culs-de-sac, each giving access to several small courtyards, around which a half dozen or so houses were grouped quite informally. Very low traffic speeds were induced by varying the road width, short sections being a mere 9 feet (2.7 m) wide so that vehicles could not pass at those points. Small radius curves and short sight lines were introduced as a continual reminder of the need for slow driving. This created a feeling of being in a pedestrian scale environment and the 'small is beautiful' theme was carried through into the detailing of these shared access ways, for there was no kerb and no separate footway. Edges were delineated by special contrasting pavings, such as bricks or granite setts, and the planting, which has now grown to full maturity, helped to give this residential area particular privacy and charm. The independent footpaths were cleverly contrived to take advantage on this steep westerly slope of views across the Mersey estuary or of the castle ruin on the hilltop. As with all the Runcorn residential areas, the Busway, as described in Chapter 10, ran through the middle of the site, with a bus stop and pedestrian underpass crossing at the local centre. This was within five minutes' walk of all dwellings in the area.

Traffic volumes in The Brow appear to be surprisingly low. A traffic count referred to in Jenkins's paper (Jenkins, 1975) showed that on the western part of the site some 1,040 vehicle movements were generated by 206 dwellings on an average working day and that during the peak

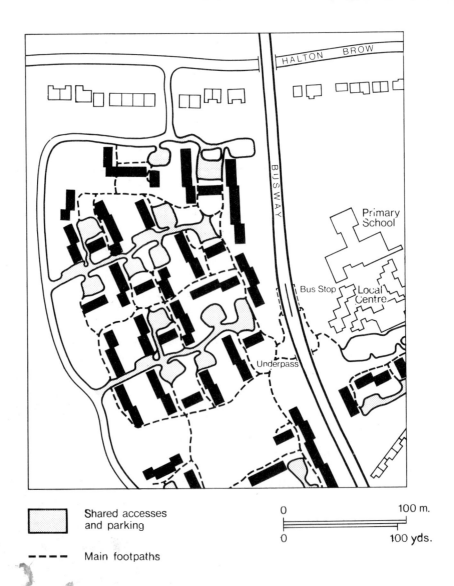

Figure 7.3 Runcorn: The Brow residential area (north-west corner).

hour only some 100 movements were generated. That is an average of 25 vehicle movements per cul-de-sac, or less than one vehicle movement every two minutes during the peak hour. Only fifty per cent of families owned a car when the count was taken, but, even if this car ownership were doubled or trebled, traffic would still be light and its effect both on pedestrians and on the environment would be unchanged.

112

However there is no doubt that, in evolving a design so different from the prevailing fashion and in getting it so right at the first attempt, collaboration between architect, engineer and landscape architect of a specially high order was achieved at Runcorn. The Brow was one of the most innovatory influences emanating from the new towns. When it was being designed, in 1966, the local authority was still working to the *New streets byelaws* adopted by the council in 1926 and was unwilling to relax these byelaws for fear of creating a precedent. In fact the plans were rejected, although the council willingly appreciated the merits of the design. The development corporation went ahead with the construction, completing it in 1968, and, in the event, the roads were adopted by the local authority without any difficulty.

There was a certain truth in the criticism implied in the extract from the *Architects' Journal* quoted on page 106. Application of the standards in *Roads in Urban Areas* (Ministry of Transport, 1966) to residential areas had tended to produce designs slanted too much towards highway design at the expense of other considerations such as environmental factors and local architectural character. So in this respect also The Brow was a breakthrough. Its significance was in demonstrating an alternative, more relaxed method of coping with the proliferation of the motor car. Its simple treatment, reactionary in a

14.   *Runcorn: shared access at The Brow.*

15. Washington: shared access.

way, was welcomed by many for its complete break with the regimented layouts of high density Radburns. It stirred great interest in architectural circles and set the pattern for future planning, not only in Runcorn but in other new towns and elsewhere throughout Britain. Figure 7.4 shows an example of Washington's solution to the shared access concept.

Essex County Council and Cheshire County Council both produced architectural design guides in 1973, and the latter contained much of the experience gained by the Runcorn development corporation on The Brow. Four years later the Department of the Environment published *Design Bulletin 32*, (Department of the Environment, 1977) which was also produced in consultation with the designers of The Brow and other Runcorn schemes.

At Basildon, one of the new neighbourhoods, added to the master plan when the target population was increased, was Noak Bridge, which lies to the north of A127, the London-Southend Arterial Road. Its rural setting and segregation from the rest of the town suggested development in the form of a self-contained village. A curving High Street in the form of a loop road was taken through the middle of the site joining the various parts in the straightforward village tradition with a footway either side, and some of the houses were brought forward to the back of pavement allowing rather larger back gardens than is usually possible. Off the High Street there were courts, squares

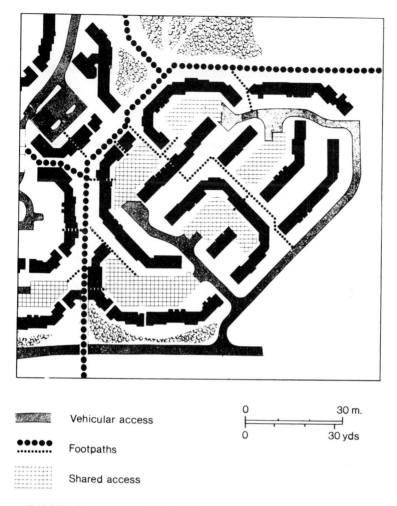

Vehicular access	
Footpaths	
Shared access	

0   30 m.

0   30 yds

Figure 7.4 Washington: residential area 'mixer courts'.

and greens. The formality of much new town housing architecture was abandoned here in a quite deliberate decision to adopt a pastiche style. The elevations of the houses were immensely varied in terms of roof line, fenestration, facing materials and colour. The development probably owed much to the influence of the Essex design guide, seen by some as a move back to the traditional. Certainly the terraces of cottages appear to be very much in the style of Essex vernacular architecture, with the addition of some unexpected features such as Dutch gables. The architecture and layout is generally agreed to have resulted in a village environment of great charm and character. It seems that, just as fashion in clothes sometimes looks back to an earlier epoch, so too with residential area layouts and with house designs.

In the early years most new town houses were built by the development corporations, all for letting and with the benefit of the government subsidy; a very small number were built privately to owner requirements or by housing associations. This approach has changed greatly over the years. Private development, mainly speculative, has been permitted and indeed encouraged more and more and, with a less pressing housing need, the development corporation's role has been reduced until in the 1980s the surviving corporations' programmes for housing have been reduced to a trickle while, even during the recession, many speculative builders' schemes have helped to keep the overall programmes alive. However the arrangements for the provision of access roads and other infra-structure have not been much affected. The land was sold to the developer as a freehold and subject to a very detailed development brief. This set out the development corporation's overall proposals for the area with which the developer must comply, together with detailed conditions covering the layout of roads and footpaths, parking, pedestrian safety, standard of architectural design, landscaping and so forth; in some cases the infrastructure was already provided by the development corporation as part of the deal.

Home ownership has been greatly encouraged by each of the Conservative governments since 1970. Local authorities and the new towns have been able to sell houses to the council house tenants on advantageous terms. Alternatively the tenant can part-purchase his house while continuing to pay rent, but at an appropriately reduced rate. One of the results of this policy has been that the development corporation has shed the responsibility for, and control of, house maintenance. One house in a block might look tatty when the rest are newly repainted. Individual features might appear – a new front door or a pergola perhaps – a source of pride to the new owner, joyfully doing his own thing – but anathema to the architect.

But perhaps these homely touches are the sort of things that help to give a lived-in appearance, to what might otherwise have seemed to remain for all time a 'new' town.

Notes

1 Source unidentified (HMSO, 1953). Reproduced with permission of the controller, HMSO.
2 From an article by J. M. Richards in an edition of *Architectural Review*.

8 New town shopping

New town shopping facilities, like the highway systems, can be considered on a hierarchical basis: town centre, township centres, neighbourhood centres, neighbourhood sub-centres, corner shops, and mobile shops. In most towns, in addition to the central shopping area, there is a shopping centre for each neighbourhood or district or village, and there are 'corner shops' scattered around.

However, it was the planning of the central areas of the towns that presented both the greatest opportunity and the greatest challenge. To the resident, the town centre represents the weekly shopping spree, the night out at the cinema or theatre, dance hall or restaurant; it is where he goes to pay his rent and rates and gas bill; where the summer fair is held and the carol service around the Christmas tree. To the villager, who drives or comes into town by bus once a week, it is his sole port of call; it reflects his image of the whole town. The success (or failure) of the town, in terms of social wellbeing and prosperity, is bound up with the degree of success of the centre – attracting people from a 12 mile (20 km) radius or more, rather than seeing the town's residents set off to spend their money elsewhere. The town centre brings together several disparate functions. First and foremost are the shops. It is also the seat of local government, police headquarters and so on and there are banks, insurance companies, building societies, library and museum. It is a main recreation centre: the theatre, if there is one, will be here, as will the cinema and, perhaps, a leisure centre.

How does the designer set about undertaking this heavy responsibility? How can he ensure a successful town centre? Fine architecture? Landscaping? Sculpture? The most important requirement is to get the transportation element right – ease of circulation: convenience of access if arriving by car or bus: ease of parking the car or bicycle; and most of all the facility to walk around the centre in safety and comfort, perhaps pushing a pram or a trolley-load of groceries; to be able to pause awhile, to sit down and watch the pageant of movement and colour is also a considerable attraction.

Until the Second World War, shopping habits had changed little in a hundred years or more. It had been the era when 'the customer was always right'. The shopkeeper valued his customers and tried hard to keep them. The fortunate minority with a carriage, or later a motor car, would presumably have their order taken in the street, and one of the errand boys would straightaway load up the purchases, or deliver them promptly to the house. Every provincial town had its 'High Street', where most of the important shops were situated and where the motorist could draw up outside the shop he wished to visit leaving the car there for as long as he liked. After the war, these comfortable arrangements revived in some towns – but not for long. Change was in the air, due largely to the increasing number of private cars. Although the Reith Report had not anticipated great changes in the years ahead it had advocated shopping streets capable of taking four lines of traffic to allow short term kerbside parking. It had also envisaged short pedestrian shopping streets and covered arcades – but only 'as a possibility'. (See Appendix 1, paras 144-6).

So, in the late 1940s, design of the Mark I town centres was put in hand – mostly on the 'High Street' principle. Corby with its considerable existing population and need for facilities was first off the mark with its wide straight vehicular shopping street, terminating one end in the market square and with civic buildings at the other end – a composition that somehow shrieked of post-war austerity. The original plans for Bracknell, Peterlee and Aycliffe were cast in a similar mould and so indeed were those for East Kilbride and Cwmbran, although the last two were soon changed.

In a town that already had a flourishing and attractive business centre, like Crawley, it was natural to capitalise on this; so the fine old High Street, with its short-term car parks in the middle and delightful mix of small shops, banks and other offices, private houses and a splendid old coaching hostelry, was retained. The stores, principal shops and supermarkets were all located in new streets, and these again were vehicular streets, providing for short-term parking.

If ideas were changing it was because of changing circumstances: first and foremost with the impact of the motor car in its increasing numbers, demanding greater parking facilities; and, secondly, with the

118

16. *Bracknell town centre roads and car parks.*

direct and the knock-on effects of a state of full employment, which led to a general reduction in the services offered by the shopkeepers: a cutback on house-to-house deliveries, for example, and the advent of the supermarket with its push trolleys and do-it-yourself service arrangements. To the new town planner the vehicular High Street was already an anachronism; to the shopkeeper it still seemed a traditional necessity. Hemel Hempstead came face to face with this dilemma. As at Crawley the town centre was to be based on the existing shopping street but in this case considerable re-development was involved, and, as Frank Schaffer described:

> Two alternative outline plans were prepared for the new centre, one straddling the valley in a compact square, the other down the valley in a long street. After much discussion and pressure from the Ministry – at that time among the strongest supporters of the Multiple Shops Federation in their opposition to any serious departure from tradition – the long street won and the opportunity to build a really modern centre at Hemel Hempstead was lost for ever.

> (Schaffer, 1970)

On one side of Hemel Hempstead's vehicular street there is a traditional parade of 'High Street' shops; on the other are pedestrian precincts containing the smaller shops, the banks and the market

119

square. There may still be some who would argue that Hemel Hempstead is all the better for its vehicular shopping street where, with a bit of luck, a car can sometimes be left for a few minutes at the kerbside. But vehicles in shopping streets produce noise, pollution, congestion and a constant fear of accidents, particularly for the elderly and for shoppers with young children. Pedestrian shopping gives a cleaner, quieter atmosphere. In pedestrian ways there is every incentive to wander across from shop window to shop window, without having to run the gauntlet of lines of moving and parked vehicles.

The breakthough came at Stevenage, where it was decided to go for an all-pedestrian shopping centre. The development corporation was resolute in this intention until strong pressure from its estates advisers and from the trade lobby obliged it to waver. Support came in the nick of time when Hertfordshire County Council, the then urban district council and local residents' associations weighed in to support the pedestrian scheme. Ministry approval was obtained and from then on there was no looking back.

Stevenage town centre is on a rectangular site with public buildings to the west and south and the shopping centre on the east side (Figure 8.1). The main pedestrian route is from north to south, a total length of about 420 m (1500 feet) but divided into three sections, the middle section is Queensway, which opens out into the pleasant Town Square where there are more shops; two further malls run eastwards at right angles to Queensway. This arrangement of buildings left rectangular plots at the rear which provided service roads to the shops in the form of loop roads, with public car parks within the loops. As in most towns, the original proposals for providing public car parks proved insufficient, so multi-storey parks had to be built in some of the car parking areas. Although the car parks are not seen from the precinct, they are very close at hand, reached through passages between the buildings. The bus station is centrally sited adjacent to the town square and the railway station is on the west side of the centre. The town's footway and cycleway systems lead through under-passes right into the centre; cycling is not allowed within the precinct but there are plenty of cycle racks available. The paving generally is to a light specification as it does not have to carry traffic, although provision had to be made for the vehicles required to maintain the services and for the fire engine and ambulance; a strengthened route for these vehicles was clearly identified as part of the pavement pattern.

It was not long before the success of the pedestrian scheme became obvious. There was no loss of trade, as the shopkeepers had predicted, and no drop in values as the estates advisers had feared. Stevenage quickly attracted attention as the first wholly pedestrian centre; it became the most visited project in Britain and received international

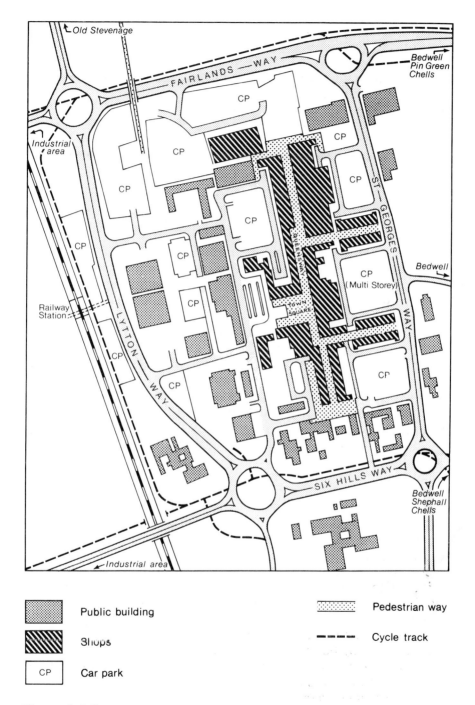

Legend:

Public building

Shops

CP — Car park

Pedestrian way

---- Cycle track

Figure 8.1 Stevenage: town centre.

acclaim. It set a new trend in this country and sent the designers of other Mark I towns scurrying back to the drawing board.

Even in the most rapidly developing new town the centre did not need to be designed and built all in one piece. This would have been economically unsound. It had to develop incrementally, as dictated by the demands of the growing town, and this often provided the opportunity to think again, replanning to accommodate updated ideas and changing needs. Initial planning therefore should always have been for maximum flexibility to allow for enlargement perhaps where target population increases had to be accommodated. On the positive side it was sometimes possible to turn this situation to good account, improving the layout in line with more mature ideas. The vehicular main street at Corby for example was pedestrianised and the overall layout improved in the process of enlargement. Crawley shopping streets were later all pedestrianised with the exception of the original High Street; and at Harlow's commanding centre, 'The High', tall imposing square blocks now flank all-pedestrian shopping malls.

This is not to say that perfection had been achieved – the British weather for example plays tricks on new towns as it does elsewhere. Those long pedestrian ways somehow contrive a wind tunnel effect in rough weather, even though there is more protection than in most other towns. Summer brings the full benefit – seats and shady trees, space for the children to run about. Each town has its particular charm and special features – the much-photographed bronze sculpture 'Mother and Child' by Franta Belsky in Town Square, Stevenage, Maurice Lambert's interpretation of the same subject that is Basildon's water sculpture, to say nothing of the Victorian bandstand at Crawley.

Car parking provision was fairly generous in most Mark I town centres, falling short of requirements, under the 1984 demand level, only on rare occasions, such as the pre-Christmas rush. But what if you came in by bus? Practically all the local and regional bus services have been brought into the centre and most of the towns now have a bus terminal. Bus terminals and car parking are examined more fully in chapters 10 and 13 respectively.

The Stevenage model was by no means to be the last word on town centres for new towns. Hugh Wilson produced a bold plan for Cumbernauld, first of the Mark IIs, which may be said to have taken town centre design into the third dimension. Two-level shopping had been tried in a modest way, for example at Basildon, but the plan for Cumbernauld comprised one vast building on eight levels, the ground level being given over entirely to transport functions. The access road passed right through the middle, and branching from it were the service roads and car park accesses. Up above were the shopping

122

decks, offices, public buildings, health centre, sports centre, hotel and all the rest, on the top floors were a restaurant and a number of penthouses. For the size of town, this was probably the largest and most comprehensive town centre yet for, with no neighbourhood centres and hardly a corner shop planned, the centre was designed to serve all shopping and social needs. This centre, in its commanding position on the hilltop, was a landmark for the whole surrounding countryside; it was a landmark too in the concept of pedestrian circulation and amenity. So, whether shoppers entered after a walk up the hill from home or after travelling by car or by bus, an escalator, lift, staircase or ramp took them to whichever level was required. Once inside they were completely insulated from the weather, while doing their shopping or other business in comfortable, air-conditioned warmth. However, on calm days there were plenty of terraces with outstanding views for miles around. The landscape architect was given a fresh challenge: instead of the usual indigenous species, the planting in this town centre consisted of tropical trees and desert flowers.

This interesting structure at Cumbernauld, somewhat reminiscent of

17.   Road system, Busway and multi-storey car parks seen from the air at Runcorn's 'Shopping City'.

18. *Date palm trees flourish in the indoor town square at Redditch.*

19. *Grosvenor Centre, Northampton: controlled environment shopping.*

the terminal building of an international airport or of an ocean liner, started a new trend in town centre design, which was followed and further developed in the town centre plans of the other Mark II and the Mark III towns, while in the Mark Is, when further shopping provision was needed, this too often took the form of chunky blocks giving indoor facilities and comfort.

Runcorn centre, known as Shopping City to distinguish it from, and avoid overt competition with the old Runcorn town centre, is another example of the multi-level shopping complex. As at Cumbernauld, the lowest level was given over to motorised transport – approach road, regional bus terminus, and access to surface and multi-storey car parks (of which there are four). Above this there were two decks of shops and offices. Inevitably the Busway (described in Chapter 10) makes its presence felt in Shopping City. Two bridges lead the track across to enter the centre at fourth floor deck level. So, from the bus stop you go down, by escalator or otherwise, to the shops on decks below.

One might wonder what had become of the traditional town square in such a changed shopping environment, whether it had disappeared along with the High Street and the kerbside parking. Not so. At Shopping City it was located at first floor level and extended right up to the glazed roof. Here, as in the other contemporary new towns, it served the traditional purposes – for meeting people, chatting, sitting around amongst shrubs and trees and sculpture, for public meetings, exhibitions, the Christmas carols and so on – but with everything in all-weather, air-conditioned comfort.

The quality of materials used in Shopping City and contemporary town centres was remarkably high – terrazo paving, marble facings for the shops – a far cry from the early towns when General Manager and Chief Engineer would turn up at the Ministry to plead the necessity for a few granite kerbstones or a more expensive street lamp. Perhaps it was because those early towns were built so cheaply (or so it now seems) that they succeeded so notably and, because they succeeded, that the Mark IIs were able to proceed with such confidence and panache. It should be remembered too that considerable investment in some later shopping centres was made by estate developers or pension funds, working in partnership with the development corporations, while at Northampton the splendid Grosvenor Shopping Centre was provided, without any development corporation involvement, by Grosvenor Estates in partnership with the Northampton County Borough Council.

An extremely interesting town centre development was that at Peterborough with its established character of a cathedral market town and the mediaeval street pattern of its historic core. It was made clear in the master plan that 'the old will not be subordinated to the new'.

Cathedral Square had for long been the crossing point of two trunk roads so a first requirement was to build an inner bypass road. After this, an ambitious scheme of pedestrianisation was embarked upon, pavements being extended right across the old carriageways eliminating all kerbs; trees and shrubs were planted along these pavements and seats, flower tubs, kiosks and the like disposed about them for shoppers' pleasure and convenience. The paving and other works, largely completed in 1984, were carried out with sensitivity. The master plan explained that the city centre would have to undergo the decisive stages of its transformation into a regional centre:

> It must accommodate shopping space doing three to four times as much trade in constant value terms, nearly twice as many people working in shops, commercial offices, hotels and other leisure facilities; and three to four times as many cars parked in multi-storey buildings that will take up almost as much land as all the new shops, offices, entertainments and cultural provisions put together.
>
> Yet all this can be done without letting the centre overflow the physical boundaries to the east, west and south that now identify it as a separate, compact entity and without sacrificing anything that is valuable either in its existing fabric or in its characteristic quality.
>
> (Peterborough Development Corporation, n.d)

The Queen Street renewal area covered 9 hectares (22 acres) and was bordered on three sides by the old main shopping streets and on the fourth by the new principal road access to the city centre. Queensgate shopping centre (Figure 8.2) now occupies this site. There is pedestrian access to the centre from all three of the old shopping streets, in which most of the old buildings have been retained. The centre has two main shopping levels and includes a large department store and numerous other major stores – all household names. Goods deliveries are at basement level. On the fourth side there is access from the new bus station, the terminus for all local and regional services, multi-storey car parking for 2,000 cars and a pedestrian bridge linking Queensgate with Peterbrough's Inter-City railway station. Great care has been taken to integrate Queensgate with the main shopping streets and the older surroundings of the city. Its exterior is finished in fine materials – Clipsham stone to match the cathedral, handmade brick, tinted glass and lead mansard roofs. The interior is inviting and colourful; there is plenty of natural light and the centre is climate-controlled. Queensgate won an accolade as European shopping centre of 1983 from the International Shopping Centres conference in Monte Carlo.

This sophisticated level of pedestrian shopping brought fresh opportunities and experience to development corporation engineers of

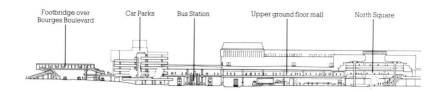

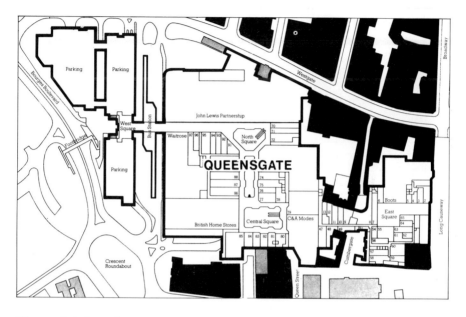

Figure 8.2 Peterborough: Queensgate Shopping Centre.
(Plan at upper shopping level).

a kind seldom encountered on highway or municipal engineering projects. For example, there was the structural design of these large multi-storey complexes, in most cases undertaken in-house. Also the numerous service installations monitored, as at Queensgate, in the central control room by a microprocessor-based data system, into which is fed information about the fire alarm, security system, carbon monoxide monitoring equipment, heating and ventilating equipment, lighting systems and car parks situation. At Queensgate the state of all these services is presented on video while a teletype printer provides a record of the information. These are utilised for the economic running of the system, analysis of faults, alarm conditions and energy conservation.

The largest, and arguably the most luxurious covered centre of all is Central Milton Keynes. Ignoring the multi-storey vogue, the shops are all at ground level, reached from tall, glass-walled twin arcades which

20. Refurbished, pedestrianised and landscaped – the old Main Street in Irvine.

seem to go on for ever. They are paved and lined with polished travertine and lavishly furnished with exotic trees and shrubs. Not for Central Milton Keynes the gimmicky clock or garish mural; there's a certain refinement which even the fascias of the multiple shops seem to respect. It is one of the largest centres of its kind in Europe, as well as being one of the most attractive and convenient; with very easy access and ample car parking provision, the centre has a particularly strong regional draw.

At the other end of the town centre shopping hierarchy are open markets. A few towns such as Bracknell, Northampton and Peterborough were established market towns with flourishing cattle markets; which continued to operate even though they had little relevance to new town development. However the idea of the street market one or two days a week seems to have caught on in most of the towns. They were encouraged by the development corporations as an asset in the early years and have since become established as a permanent and popular feature. The development corporations mostly allocated and paved a market square with semi-permanent stalls and, in some towns, Warrington for example, a covered market was provided.

Where a designated area already included a substantial township, the decision as to whether to expand the existing centre or start afresh in a new and perhaps more logical situation was one of the most important decisions a development corporation was called upon to make. The scale of an existing small town High Street may have had little relevance to the grand design of the new town centre; yet economics and local susceptibilities would not have permitted its demolition, and, if happily there were some fine period buildings, these were clearly of priceless value giving built-in distinction and character to the new centre. Crawley has already been noticed in this context, and it was the same at Bracknell, Northampton, Peterborough and others.

At Redditch, the old shopping area lay astride the A441 road and was a long way from the centre of the designated area. As the master plan put it:

> The image of Redditch is that of a ridge town with its centre on a hill, the plateau with the existing centre and the church spire forms a landmark for the surrounding countryside and for much of the town. It is important in any new town to exploit the qualities of the site; in Redditch this should be done not only by respecting its fine woodland character but also by taking advantage of the dominant site available for the centre, a site which seems to be inevitable from every point of view. It is the established focus for the existing town and the hinterland and its development would do much to ensure integration of new and old.
>
> The fact that the location will be geographically off-centre in the Designated Area is no disadvantage since it is well related to the town road system and to the town and country bus services and it contains the railway station. Any growth of the town to the south should be related to the bus routes and primary roads and thus have good access to the centre.
>
> (Redditch Development Corporation, 1967)

A bypass of the A441 was constructed forming part of the ring road around the Redditch centre; the old roads inside it, including the A441, were or will ultimately be pedestrianised. The new pavements and landscaping in the vicinity of the church have been particularly well conceived.

Some towns adopted the alternative course. At Harlow there was no problem – the old village was very small and near the perimeter of the designated area. The old shopping area at Stevenage was largely preserved and skilfully extended as the centre for Old Stevenage neighbourhood – a sharp and interesting contrast with the new town centre.

At Hemel Hempstead, although the new town centre was completed many years ago, there remained, adjoining its northern end, the original High Street containing St. Mary's Church and the old Town Hall, with little else of any architectural distinction. But here was the traditional shopping street which still appealed to many. By the late 1960s its shops were mainly of a specialised kind – antique shops for instance – and inevitably the street had become seedy and run down, sitting in the shadow of its glittering new neighbour. The development corporation wished to bring life back to this part of the town, and sought the advice of the Civic Trust.[1] The Trust made it clear that what was required was a co-ordinated programme embracing housing, new uses for existing buildings, a new retail drive, and so forth. The development corporation, local authority and the shopkeepers themselves all collaborated with the Trust to achieve these ends and to give to the area a general 'facelift'. Unnecessary signs and other clutter were removed, tasteless advertising obliterated, the faded facades refurbished and redecorated to a co-ordinated plan. Better lighting and improved landscaping were introduced and the car parking arrangements regulated. The visual improvement was dramatic and a new lease of life was given to this old shopping street. The trouble with an improvement like this is that after a few years it needs doing all over again.

Like Redditch, Runcorn started off with an important existing town centre, that was geographically off centre. The master plan spelt out a number of advantages in a proposal to extend it, but also recited a list of disadvantages of the site. Only one alternative location was put forward by the planners as worthy of detailed consideration. This was a large clear site in the middle of the designated area. The master plan claimed eight advantages for this site, four of which were transport-related:

- the site was large enough to accommodate the necessary large-scale roadworks without compromising the function of the other elements;
- the town centre in this position would be at the centre of the town and hence entail the shortest journey for the majority of the population;
- the site was at the best possible location on the projected rapid transit system being at the crossing of the 'figure of eight'; and
- there was no other major traffic generator in the vicinity of the site, so that the central area traffic would not conflict with traffic associated with other parts of the primary road system.

(Runcorn Development Corporation, 1967)

The decision to build a new, more central shopping complex must have required considerable courage. However Shopping City was designed and carried out so well that there can now be few doubts about the correctness of the decision. Meanwhile the old centre was given a fresh character as a district centre through a programme of renewal and rehabilitation. It still retains the town hall and various town functions.

Parking in the new town shopping centres was designed to be plentiful and readily accessible. The centres of the Mark I towns were planned to have surface car parks, but these have already proved inadequate and have to some extent been augmented or replaced by multi-storey blocks. In some of the Mark IIs and Mark IIIs, such as Redditch and Peterborough it was intended from the start that nearly all parking would be in multi-storey blocks; yet Milton Keynes was able to allocate sufficient space to accommodate the whole of its huge parking requirement at ground level.

Each new town succeeded in providing colourful, lively and safe shopping conditions in the town centre; yet the centre could be a desolate place in the evenings when, by the time the shops shut, everyone had scurried home. It was easy to pinpoint the reasons for this:

- the increasing draw of television and, more recently, of home videos and computer games had influenced people to stay at home in the evening;
- the spread of lawlessness had deterred some people from venturing out at night;
- the amount and quality of public entertainment had declined; and
- with generally increased mobility it seems to be the country pub that draws the crowds rather than the newer, more pretentious, in-town establishments.

The problem was not confined to new towns. It arose increasingly in established towns throughout the country. Yet most established town centres did comprise a mix of shops, offices and houses, and traditionally, many of the shopkeepers live 'upstairs'; so, even at night and on Sunday, the centre was peopled to some extent. In new developments, where the emphasis was on multiple companies and on lock-up shop premises, there was a real danger that the centre would die when the shutters went up.

There seemed to a number of the development corporations to be a good case for introducing some housing into the town centre. At Basildon an additional residential area was added immediately adjacent to the centre and a fifteen-storey block of single-person flats was erected within the town square itself. In Mark II towns specific provision was made at the master plan stage; Redditch, for example, planned for a population of 3,400 within the centre. The decision called for a fresh approach in terms of access and car storage. For the up-market type of housing in town centres, the residents expected a

131

good approach to their front door and exclusive parking or garaging; they were not content to take their chance on the public car park nor to approach their home through the supermarket service yard. Skelmersdale had the same idea, allowing in the master plan proposals for some 8,000 people living in the centre itself. However the plan was not carried out in this form, the size of the town centre having been greatly reduced, with large contractions at both the north and the south ends. The land thus released has been used for residential development which, to some extent, has helped the desired effect of peopling the centre when the shops are shut; and of course the arrangements for accommodating residents' cars are now no different from those of other residential areas.

Most of the new towns have a shopping centre for each neighbourhood and there are 'corner shops' scattered around. Exceptionally there are other categories so that the full hierarchy is:

- town centre
- township centres
- neighbourhood centres
- neighbourhood sub-centres
- corner shops
- mobile shops

Cumbernauld as previously noted eschewed the neighbourhood concept; in theory at any rate there were no subsidiary centres or 'round the corner' shops; in its original concept the town was planned so compactly and conveniently that everyone could go, usually on foot, into the centre for day-to-day requirements as well as for major shopping. Skelmersdale too was developed on similar lines. However other towns had a subsidiary centre for each of their areas whether known as neighbourhoods, districts, villages or whatever – for simplicity these local centres are all referred to here as neighbourhood centres. Their size and content varied greatly according to the population they served, their distance from the town centre and other factors, all of which were weighed carefully in the commercial balance by the corporations' estates departments and then 'humanised' if necessary by the planning teams. There were a vast number of these local centres throughout the new towns, many having considerable charm and character. As to their content, a basic mix would include grocer, greengrocer, butcher, baker, newsagent, chemist – perhaps ten units in all – a post office and a pub, sometimes a church and a community centre. The neighbourhood centre was always on a vehicular road, though not always a through traffic route, it always had a bus stop, whether the bus ran on the public road or, in the case of Runcorn, on a special track. Ample car parking space was a necessity, although car park size was underestimated on some of the earliest developments. The neighbourhood centre was naturally at the nodal point of the pedestrian system and, if there was a cycleway, it too passed through the centre.

Existing village or township centres often served as partially ready-made neighbourhood centres; Stevenage and Harlow have already been noted. Telford and Milton Keynes had several townships and villages within their designated areas whose centres were utilised in this way.

Here and there were instances of neighbourhoods being rather too large for the neighbourhood centre to serve, so a sub-centre was introduced on similar but more modest lines to the neighbourhood centre.

Yet another category – township centres – were introduced in some of the larger towns, where some neighbourhoods are remote from the town centre. They were much the same in size and character as the central area for a small new town. The prime example is Peterborough where the expansion was planned as four, later reduced to three, townships, each centre having its supermarket and most town centre facilities (Figure 8.3). Within the Basildon designated area Pitsea and Laindon each had an existing rather sub-standard, though commercially viable, centre. There was a strong tradition of shopping at these points which it might have been unwise to curtail; the long east-west axis of Basildon meant that outer developments resulting from the big target population increase were remote from the central area. At the town centre itself there were constraints that made it impracticable, especially in respect of roads and car parks, to extend in any direction other than upwards. These were reasons behind the imaginative and almost fortuitous conversion of these two rather tatty shopping areas into important township centres. At Laindon an elevated pedestrian way sweeps in from the residential areas to the first floor shopping mall, the whole of the ground level being given over to access roadway, service roads, car parks and public transport.

The 'shop around the corner' is the successor to the traditional village store selling a wide range of goods; within easy reach of everyone and often with extended opening times it frequently plays an important part in the social life of the residential area, and there is generally a small car park or convenient lay-by.

Finally, it may seem strange that the mobile shop should ever have been deflected from its usual course around the villages in favour of town life and new towns at that. Yet, in the early days of the towns, particularly those on green fields sites, it did fulfil a very useful role. With the best will in the world the development corporation was not as a rule able to provide new shopping facilities until a reasonable

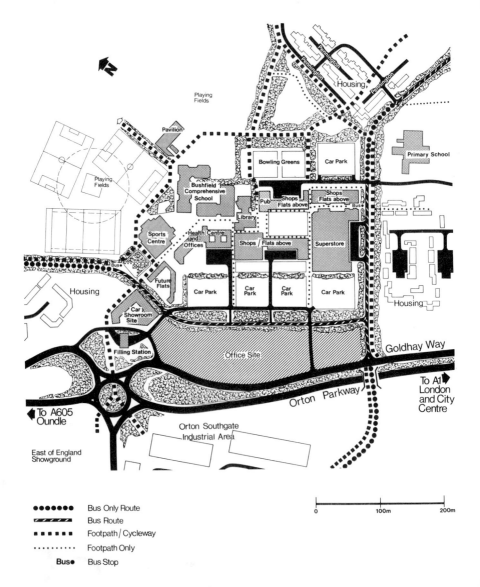

Figure 8.3 Peterborough: Orton township centre.

number of houses had been built, so in the meantime it was a great boon to have a mobile vanman calling around. The requirement did not last long. Once the new shops opened the mobile shopman was soon forgotten – although he sometimes turned up again as the shopkeeper in the neighbourhood centre or corner shop. The only business on wheels that looks like surviving in the towns for all time is

134

that of the ice-cream vendor.

Note

1 The Civic Trust, 17, Carlton House Terrace, London, SW1Y
   5AW.

9 Industry and employment

Following the Industrial Revolution manufacturing industry was traditionally located in areas where raw materials were easily accessible. Thus steelmaking was carried on where ironstone deposits and coal were available and the cotton industry, which was dependent upon imports, was established close to the Lancashire seaports. After the Second World War a totally different set of criteria were used to locate new industrial centres. These were to be cited primarily, as in the case of the new towns, in relation to the large cities and the national transport structure. This change had already been envisaged by Ebenezer Howard who made it clear in his thesis of 1898 (Howard, 1898) that the old idea of 'dirty industry' was no longer valid, that power supplies for future industry could all be by electricity, and that siting in relation to the prevailing wind was immaterial. Schematically his factory area took the form of a ring encircling the built-up area of Garden City. The Reith Report, on the other hand, uncharacteristically had nothing to say on the subject of siting industrial areas. Some of the Mark I towns, Welwyn, Stevenage and Bracknell for example, had their main industrial area adjacent to the railway to allow a facility for sidings – but easy access to the regional road system was seen as more important and the Mark I master plans tended to provide only one, or perhaps two, industrial areas strategically located as near as possible to an arterial-type road. What was not realised in those early days was the effect of this arrangement, when coupled with high car ownership, on the journey to work. It became, as we have seen, a serious problem in the 1950s and 1960s.

When it was decided to enlarge the Mark I towns, the planners had taken this message to heart, siting new areas for industry on the other side of the town. And naturally the Mark IIs and Mark IIIs catered for greater dispersal of industry right from the start. The Telford plan, for instance, had four principal industrial sites well spaced out around the perimeter, each with advantages for particular types of industry. In addition, there were a number of smaller areas for workshops, small manufacturing units and service industries. The Washington plan had six principal industrial areas well distributed around the perimeter of the town, approximating to Howard's theoretical concept. Redditch had eight main areas scattered about the town, well arranged to minimise any build-up on the primary roads and junctions during the journey to work. The Milton Keynes strategic plan contained a much larger number of employment sites.

The movement away from heavy industry has been a matter of concern to many in Britain. Consider just one example – steel production. While world demand is reducing, more countries have acquired the means of production and are equipped with more up-to-date plants. It can be no surprise that the British steel industry has so often failed to compete. Several British steelmaking plants have closed down including that at Corby New Town. With other heavy industries the story is the same. It is not a cheerful story. Among the very first to warn of the seriousness of this trend was James Bellini, writing in 1981 he put it this strongly:

> For more than a century, British manufacturing has been in decline. Its quality of product has fallen, its capacity to invent new ideas and carry them through to the market has slipped steadily . . . factories have decayed and the machinery inside them has taken on the appearance of an enormous inventory of industrial relics.
>
> (Bellini, 1981)

New town designers saw from the start that the old 'smokestack industry' was declining in importance. They saw their role as providing the conditions in which light industry could flourish. Nevertheless it was a shaky start; as the Mark I development corporations laid down the infrastructure of their first industrial areas, it seemed like an act of faith. Where were the industrialists rash enough to invest in such a chancy development? The difficulty was compounded by the attitude of the Board of Trade, whose duty it was to issue the industrial development certificate necessary to enable a new factory project to go ahead. Far from encouraging an industrialist to move into a new town, the Board perceived its function as steering him away from the towns (at any rate from those in the south-east) towards the areas of worst unemployment, such as the north-east, Scotland and Northern Ireland. Eventually these problems were overcome and, by the mid 1950s and through the 1960s, a great deal of industry was attracted into the towns. The difficulty then was often to build houses fast enough to accommodate the workers required for a surge of new factory openings.

Nearly all the top names in British industry are to be found in one or another of the new towns and there is an impressive number of companies of international parentage. But these new town industrial areas are not just about top companies or mammoth factories. They were equally suitable for smaller concerns and have been particularly successful in attracting new industrial enterprise. The development corporations have encouraged this by building blocks of small standard factories as a speculative venture. A single unit could be rented on advantageous terms and equipped as a small workshop, perhaps producing components for one of the 'big boys' on the same estate. The concept was perhaps a forerunner of the Thatcher government's policy in the early 1980s of encouraging the setting up of new small businesses – the sort of enterprise an employee made redundant might start, utilising his redundancy money and a loan from the bank. The 'nursery' factory was a good place to start and there are plenty of examples of such an enterprise expanding into a second standard unit and finally into a purpose-built factory on the same estate. Even through the years of recession several development corporations have continued the building of standard factories with confidence.

21. *Redditch: standard factories: access and parking.*

138

Plate 7   New town shopping

(a) General view of town centre at Glenrothes.

(b) Hemel Hempstead: a traditional high street.

(c) Stevenage: the first all-pedestrian centre.

(d) Central Milton Keynes: the open market.

(e) Irvine new town's shopping mall spans the River Irvine.

(f) Inside Queensgate shopping centre at Peterborough.

Plate 8 Access for industry

(a) Central Lancashire – the M.6 motorway runs alongside this employment area.

(b) Road layout for a Northampton factory area.

(c) The Genesis building at Warrington's Birchwood Science Park.

(d) Milton Keynes – the Volkswagen headquarters in its lakeside setting.

(e) Unit factories at Washington.

(f) An industrial estate at Glenrothes.

22. *Warrington: Birchwood Science Park: extensive surface parking areas.*

A significant and increasing proportion of new town industry features the new high technologies – electronic, automated, data-based industries. It was perhaps only natural that many of the factories for new and advanced techniques would come to the new towns. Take the way things are going in Central Lancashire. This largest of all the designated areas includes the towns of Preston, Leyland and Chorley – important centres of manufacturing industries in the nineteenth century. Despite the decline of the textile trade and other traditional industries, Central Lancashire still retains a strong engineering base, and there is now a remarkable concentration of high technology companies engaged in electronics, telecommunications systems, robotics and space research. There has also been a steady increase in the service and distribution fields.

It was Warrington New Town that introduced to Britain the concept of the science park – now emulated throughout the country. In the early 1970s the development corporation, recognising the importance of maintaining a diversified industrial and employment base, set up the Birchwood science park as an area reserved for established and new growth high technology businesses. 'We saw as the move into the next phase of development', said Tom Walsh, the development corporation's chief engineer, 'the necessity to provide a new type of environment – one that would be efficient for the new generation of high technology companies while strictly a straightforward venture'.

(Walsh, T., 1983). The location of Warrington satisfied the essential criteria, being within easy reach of both Manchester and Liverpool, of four technological universities and of an international airport. It also offered through its location in the county of Cheshire, excellent motorway links and a choice of housing both within the town and within easy commuting distance in the pleasant rural countryside beyond.

Of the first twenty-eight companies operating at Birchwood, the main product areas were computers and computer peripherals, instrumentation and nuclear business. The 'Genesis' building at Birchwood, which Walsh described as 'a factory for intellectuals', illustrates the philosophy of advanced thinking. It is typical of the facilities currently available in the New Towns for high technology enterprises.

As so little use is made of the carriage of goods by rail the dispatch of industrial products is almost entirely dependent on the road system within the town and in the region. While new town manufacturers are not in the business of heavy industry, many of their products involve the use of the largest goods vehicles. These were important considerations when locating the industrial areas and preparing the layouts and specifications for their roads. There was also increasing use of air freight dispatch for such products as small, but costly, electronic components.

To facilitate the movement of heavy goods vehicles in and out of the industrial areas, and to relieve traffic congestion in the journey to work, road layouts in the industrial estates have always been on a generous scale. A simple grid of straight, wide roads was the norm, and this sort of conventional and formal layout made for well-shaped factory plots. Yet there is nothing conventional or dull about new town industrial estates. Whether you visit the original and immediately successful industrial area at Crawley, one of the first to be built, or those at Milton Keynes – one of the last – or indeed those of any other new town, you will find examples of the best in modern industrial layout and architecture; and needless to say the landscaping effort was carried in full measure into the industrial areas.

In most towns, bus timetables and the location of the bus stops were carefully planned in collaboration with the bus operators to encourage and maximise the use of public transport for the work journey. Lay-bys have generally been provided at the bus stops to avoid obstruction of the traffic flow and to serve as a waiting place for buses arriving a few minutes before knocking-off time. At Runcorn, the Busway track was looped into the centre of the main industrial areas in such a way that the person arriving at the bus stop would generally be closer to the factory than his workmate arriving in the car park. Some companies

140

have found it possible to introduce differential work times relative to neighbouring factories, or even flexi-time working, to reduce congestion on the journey to work. But many employers found that staggering the working hours led to other complications, for example when their employees customarily shared transport with workers from another factory. Moreover the bus companies could not always fit in with differential starting and finishing times.

Walking accounts for a good deal of industrial area movement, both at journey to work times and in the lunch break; so wide footways have generally been provided, with pedestrian subways or pelican crossings where distributors or busy industrial area roads had to be crossed. Separate provision for cyclists was not usually provided; cyclists normally used the carriageways. But a few towns had cycle tracks within their industrial areas, for example Stevenage, Harlow and Peterborough. The tracks were normally routed alongside the footways and taken through a common underpass.

There has always been a huge parking demand in the industrial areas, because of the custom in most one-car families for the breadwinner to commandeer the car to go to work. The subject of car parking is examined in chapter 13.

New town industry and commerce provide the majority of the job opportunities in the town; other principal places of employment being offices, service workshops and so on. In most towns there is a considerable number of workers commuting outwards, probably to London or other major employment areas, although this is generally balanced to a greater or lesser extent by people coming in daily from the region to work in the new town. Take for example East Kilbride. The published figures for 1981 showed:

Population	72,000
Total number in employment	32,600
Number working elsewhere	13,500
Number living and working in East Kilbride	19,100
Incoming commuters	7,200
Total employed in East Kilbride	26,300

The extent of commuting into and out of the towns is further discussed in chapter 10.

In the 1940s and early 1950s when housebuilding programmes in the Mark I towns were small, allocation of rented houses was very strictly selective; the majority went to skilled and semi-skilled workers because these were the categories most in demand by employers although the situation became progressively easier as housebuilding forged ahead. The need for office staff in the early years was small. Later on when so many offices were relocated in new towns, the balance changed greatly; fortuitously many of the new clerical vacancies were neatly filled by second generation new towners, the sons and daughters of the original pioneers. In the 1960s and early 1970s few were out of work and new towns in particular were boom towns.

It cannot be denied that the new towns have been exceptionally hard hit by the recent years of recession; unemployment has escalated in line with, and in some cases ahead of, the national average. The October 1982 unemployment figures for the English new towns made sad reading. The original 'London' towns came off best; they were mostly below the average of 10.4 per cent – only 6 per cent at Crawley, Hatfield and Welwyn. However, in the Midlands and north of England some of the towns were showing unemployment figures well above the national average. The Scottish towns also fared badly; details of the employment and unemployment situation in East Kilbride in 1981 are given in Table 9.1.

Table 9.1
East Kilbride: employment figures 1981

Estimated Economic Classification of Employed Inhabitants	Per cent
Skilled/semi-skilled manual	42.2
Unskilled manual	7.2
Clerical, retail and service	36.7
Managerial and professional	13.5
Others	0.4
	100.0
Categories of Jobs in East Kilbride	
Manufacturing	38.0
Non-manufacturing	19.0
Public administration	28.0
Retail	8.0
Others	7.0
	100.0
Unemployment (October 1981)	Per cent total
Great Britain	12.2
Scotland	14.4
Strathclyde Region	17.1
East Kilbride (estimate)	14.2
Source: East Kilbride Development Corporation	

Corby was hard hit by the closure of the British Steel Corporation's huge steel-making plant, which had a calamitous effect on the

142

employment situation. In an effort to deal with this, the government designated the first of Britain's Enterprise Zones in Corby, to be operative for a ten year period from June 1981. The intention was to see how far industrial and commercial activity could be encouraged by the removal of certain tax burdens and the relaxation of controls. The Corby enterprise zone covered some 280 acres (113 hectares) available for development and already serviced with roads and utilities. A whole package of benefits was made available to both new and existing enterprises, and these were in addition to the regional development grant and to some capital assistance from E.E.C. funding. In the first eighteen months some fifty-two companies had set up in the enterprise zone and, together with other new arrivals in Corby, had employed over 2,000 people.

However improved road structure was vital. British Steel Corporation had in the past relied mainly on rail freight for supplies of new materials and dispatch of finished products whereas the new industries were depending almost entirely on road transport. The proposed M1/A1(M) link was seen as essential to sustain Corby's industrial growth.

Yet we should at our peril ignore the words of James Bellini:

> The developed world faces at least two decades of painful readjustment as it attempts to escape from its dying traditional industrial base into a data-dominated, automated, cybernetic micro-processed twenty-first century lifestyle. Not all countries in the Western world will make that transition successfully. . . . Thus while the developed world is going through a vast technological revival, Britain is being left behind. Despite an innate genius for invention, the country has consistently turned away from the practical possibilities of new ideas. . . . Thus Britain seems doomed to a bizarre fate in the super-industrial world of the next century. From being the workshop of the world, the country will become an archaeological site from the Western industrial past, full of entrancing and mysterious survivals. But there will be no industry. When the seeds of renewal were being planted by other industrial nations, during the 1960s and 1970s, Britain continued on its neglectful way.

(Bellini, 1981)

If James Bellini was correct in predicting the early demise of manufacturing industry in Britain and in asserting that future hope lies only with cybernetics and so forth then at least the new towns are on the right lines.

Yet not everyone agrees with Bellini. An alternative scenario shows an upturn in the economy, and the new towns with their advanced technology base and their encouragement of new small businesses may well be in the forefront of the revival. The modern factories, good living and working conditions and excellent communications are well adapted to the needs of the latter part of this century and hopefully of the next. Furthermore the construction industry, which has suffered much in the years of recession, is waiting for the opportunity to expand; it may well, as in the 1930s, play a leading part in the recovery. For if nearly everything in new towns is 'new', the opposite is true of nearly everywhere else. We need to replenish the country's housing stock. Older towns need new roads and bypasses and renewal of their ageing infrastructure; and, if Britain has fallen behind in the technology stakes there may yet be time to close the gap, for as Bellini admitted 'the policies currently being implemented in an effort to avoid disaster may, indeed, succeed'. His book was written on the assumption that they will fail.

10 Public transport

For new town residents, there are two basic types of public transport journeys: in and around the town and journeys to places outside the town.

Journeys out of town may be for business, recreational or social reasons. A particular example is that of the commuter who goes each day to work in some other place – in London perhaps or one of the other big cities. Originally in order to qualify as a tenant of a corporation house the applicant had to have a job in the new town; but this proved to be a short-term arrangement, gradually relaxed as housing programmes forged ahead. This lead to a great deal of outward commuting, balanced in many of the towns by people coming in daily from the surrounding region to work in the towns. Details of the numbers of commuters in both directions for some of the towns in 1974 are given in Table 10.1. Less regular trips out of the town are made for a variety of other reasons – visiting relatives and friends, going on holiday, business journeys and so forth.

Many of these trips may be made by car; but discussion in this chapter relates to situations where some form of public transport is involved, either solely, or for some part of the journey. Possible ways of travelling by public transport outside the town are: by air, by train, or by regional bus or coach service.

Proximity to a civil airport was not considered of major importance when selecting the site for a new town. Nevertheless easy access to an airport is now seen to be a considerable bonus. For example,

Table 10.1
Commuter journeys into and outward from some New Towns 1974

Town	Bracknell	Stevenage	Harlow	Basildon	Runcorn	Redditch	Milton Keynes
Population (1974)	40,000	73,000	81,000	80,000	43,700	44,700	58,000
Total no. of commuters out of designated area	2,600	6,000	9,000	12,400	9,000	5,900	2,000
Total no. of commuters into designated area	5,800	9,000	7,000	13,600	7,500	4,200	2,000

Source: A review of public transport in New Towns
(New Towns Technical Officers' Committee, 1974).

Warrington thinks itself advantageously situated about 21 km (13 miles) from Ringway (Manchester) airport and a similar distance from Speke (Liverpool). Gatwick, which before the Second World War was but a tiny flying field, is now the second London airport and, after Heathrow, the country's busiest; it is a mere 8 km (5 miles) from the centre of Crawley. So here the obvious benefits for industry and employment and for holiday and business travel are offset by being too close to the airport and suffering the disadvantage of aircraft noise.

Railway facilities on the other hand, were considered to be of great importance at the time of the early designations, both from the point of view of attracting industry to the town and as a means of personal long distance mobility. It had been an important feature of Howard's concept that Garden City should be satisfactorily linked to the outside world, with a well-sited passenger station and a loop line threaded through the industrial belt, with sidings as required by industry. His Social City thesis too depended greatly on an inter-municipal railway to link the Garden Cities with each other and with Central City. (Howard, 1965). The Reith Committee seems to have taken it for granted that sites selected would be on a railway line (see Appendix 1, para 27(8)) and it made some optimistic recommendations about the requirements of a railway station for a new town. (See Appendix 1, paragraph 116). The progressive decline of railways in Britain was not foreseen by the Committee.

Accordingly all save one of the Mark I designations included a length of railway line, in some cases an important main line, as at

Hatfield on the Kings Cross to Edinburgh line and at Hemel Hempstead on the Euston to Birmingham line. However, the presence of a railway line through the area could be a serious constraint in the planning of the town. Both Bracknell and Basildon were bisected by a main line railway running centrally across their areas. New railway bridges are very costly, so it was inevitable that crossings of the railway both by roads and footways were kept at a minimum. There was one advantage however – a new station could be sited actually within the town centre, as at Basildon, whereas in most cases, at Hemel Hempstead for example, the existing station was on the edge of the town. New passenger stations were also built at Harlow and Milton Keynes and these stations in new towns are among the very few to have been built in Britain since 1945. They were fine stations even if they fell short in some respects of the standards proposed by the Reith Committee.

By the time of the Mark II and Mark III designations, the likely overall pattern of movement was more clearly established; it was recognised that railways were of no great significance in the new town transportation system, although fortuitously, some of these later designations included towns which had long and historic connections with the railways – Peterborough, Runcorn and Warrington for example were important railway towns in their own right. At East Kilbride, Cumbernauld and Irvine the commuter lines to Glasgow and Edinburgh still survive probably only because new town commuter traffic is there, helping to make them viable. But at Washington the designation of the new town and the closure of the railway station were actually both announced in the same week. At Basildon, which now has three stations, a substantial number of both in-town work trips and in-town shopping trips are made by train.

The principal method of making public transport journeys outside the town was provided by the regional bus services. There were country buses running through all of the new town areas prior to designation, serving existing townships and villages. They utilised whatever road system existed to pass through the area. With progress on construction of the primary road system of the town, regional bus routeing changed to take advantage of the new road pattern. With the growth of the town, demand increased and the travel pattern changed. Some of the outward commuters went to work on the regional bus while people living in the surrounding district came in by bus to work in the employment areas or to shop in the town centre. At a later stage in the development, a bus station was provided in the centre of most of the towns, and this served as the focal point of regional as well as of the in-town bus services. Regional buses were routed mainly on the primary roads with occasional diversions, where justified, onto a local road – perhaps into an industrial area. It was desirable to arrange the bus stops at these points to avoid the situation where passengers were obliged to congregate on, and might have been tempted to jay-walk across, main traffic routes.

The most important element of new town public transport is the in-town service, concerning which the Reith Committee had this to say:

> In a town of the area contemplated a frequent internal bus service is indispensible. The local transport undertaking or public board should be encouraged to provide such a service, and, in default, the agency should itself provide it.

(See Appendix 1, para. 113)

This particular recommendation of the Committee was not however explicitly carried through to the New Towns Act 1946, which appeared to depart from it in two important respects:

- it gave no specific mandate for a development corporation itself to provide an internal bus service in the event of the local transport undertaking failing to do so; and
- on the other hand it provided for the development corporation to be authorised 'to operate trolley vehicle services for the purposes of a new town'.

This was widely interpreted to mean that a development corporation could itself provide a trolleybus system (they were obsolescent as it happened by the 1950s) but not a bus service. This interpretation was wrong. The authoritative view is that the general powers of the development corporation 'to do anything necessary or expedient for the development of a new town' was wide enough to cover running an internal bus service. The reason for the special provision about trolley vehicles was that otherwise a separate Act of Parliament would have been necessary to empower a development corporation to operate a trolleybus system.

No development corporation ever attempted to run a bus service. Yet it has to be said as a general statement that public transport has been one of the least successful of all new town services.

Commuting has, as we have seen, become a way of life for some new town residents; but by far the greater number both live and work within the new towns. In the late 1940s not many families had a car. Many could walk or bicycle to work, but most of the Mark I towns were spread about over a considerable area quite different from the 'small is beautiful' concept of Garden City or the compact planning that was later to be featured at Cumbernauld and Skelmersdale. Take Harlow for example; unless you happened to live in a neighbourhood close to your job, you were most likely to have a journey of about 3 km

(2 miles) to get to work. It was obvious that bus journeys were going to be of great importance. How surprising then to find so little attention paid to public transport facilities in the early master plans.

It seems certain that the development corporations did not see public transport as their special responsibility because in every case there were one or more bus companies operating in the locality. As far as they were concerned buses run on normal public roads and the development corporations were constructing a very good road system. With the infrastructure provided, the appropriate bus facilities were expected to appear automatically. But bus operation was a commercial venture attracting no subsidy, and the operators were understandably reluctant to embark upon new or improved services until potential patronage was sufficient to support a profitable outcome. Thus the new town presented a quite different situation from that of the established town, where a good bus service had evolved over a period of years to meet established local needs. It is remarkable that such an obvious fact was apparently not recognised, that the need for, and financial provision for, public transport in the towns were inadequately followed through in the planning process.

In the event, a local bus service emerged in all the Mark I towns – not as early in the development as might have been desired, or as frequent or reliable a service. But it was an economical means of travel and the bus was there to serve many people – factory or town centre workers, schoolchildren, the disabled – everyone in fact who for a particular journey did not have the use of a car.

Until 1969 many of the bus operating companies were still private companies and, naturally, they were in business to make a profit. When nationalised under the Transport Act 1968, virtually all the companies operating in the English and Welsh new town areas were absorbed into the National Bus Company (NBC) – generally under their existing names and retaining a fair degree of autonomy. In Scotland the companies were merged into the Scottish Transport Group (STG). (A list of the towns and their relevant county councils and bus operating companies appears in Table 10.2.) Up to a point, nationalisation improved the situation: forward investment in new town services could to some extent be off set against profitable operations elsewhere; but it was to a limited extent. The problems of the individual NBC subsidiary companies varied in each case, but they all had to face the same basic financial constraint, because the Government had never relaxed NBC's overall duty to break even. The development corporations were generally able to assist in the provision of lay-bys, special bus tracks and bus stations, but it seems to have been on an *ad hoc* basis, and of course always subject to Ministry approval. On the reorganisation of local government in 1974, county councils were given prescribed responsibilities for public transport, including powers to grant subsidies in aid of local bus services. This change was helpful, but of course it was not likely that new towns (generally unloved in county council circles) would be singled out for preferential treatment. At that time also some of the development corporations were authorised to make capital and revenue grants to bus operators and some corporations have contributed greatly as will be shown.

The situation might have been considerably improved if the respective financial responsibilities of central government, develop-

Table 10.2
The new towns with relevant Bus Companies and County Authorities

New Town	NBC or STG subsidiary	County Council
England		
Stevenage	London Country	Hertfordshire
Crawley	London Country	West Sussex
Hemel Hempstead	London Country	Hertfordshire
Harlow	London Country	Essex
Aycliffe	United Auto	Durham
Peterlee	United Auto	Durham
Hatfield	London Country	Hertfordshire
Welwyn	London Country	Hertfordshire
Basildon	Eastern National	Essex
Bracknell	Alder Valley	Berkshire
Corby	United Counties	Northamptonshire
Skelmersdale	Ribble	Lancashire
Redditch	Midland Red West	Worcestershire
Runcorn	Crosville and Ribble	Cheshire
Washington	Northern General	Tyne & Wear
Milton Keynes	United Counties	Buckinghamshire
Peterborough	Eastern Counties	Cambridgeshire
Telford	Midland Red North	Shropshire
Northampton	United Counties	Northamptonshire
Warrington	Crosville	Cheshire
Central Lancashire	Ribble	Lancashire
Wales		
Cwmbran	National Welsh	Gwent
Newtown	Crosville	Powys
Scotland		
East Kilbride	Central SMT	Strathclyde Region
Glenrothes	W. Alexander & Sons (Fife)	Fife Region
Cumbernauld	W. Alexander & Sons (Midland)	Strathclyde Region
Livingston	Scottish Omnibuses	Lothian Region
Irvine	Western SMT	Strathclyde Region

ment corporations, county and district councils and the operating companies had been hammered out centrally in regard to development cost of the service network, including special busway tracks, bus stations, depots and rights of way.

Details of bus routes were one of the many details discussed between the development corporations and the bus companies. In general, the required routeings were:

- to connect each residential area with each industrial area;
- to connect each residential area with the town centre; and
- to link each residential area with the other residential areas.

Guidelines established for the local services included: buses to be routed as far as possible only on the local distributor roads; all bus stops to be located on these roads; buses not to be allowed to penetrate onto the access roads, which were not designed for them; passengers should never have to board or alight on primary roads.

Arising out of his consultations with the Alder Valley Company, the chief engineer at Bracknell noted the following factors as important to a satisfactory bus service. They are typical of the findings in all towns:

- journey times to be minimised in order to reduce operational costs and increase competitiveness with the car. (Passengers probably judge the value of the bus service to them in terms of frequency, speed and reliability, with cost and comfort at a secondary level.);
- the generative capacity of bus stops to be maximised by their being located at the centre of, or adjacent to, housing groups, work places, railway station and shopping areas;
- major points of generation and attraction to be directly linked; and
- routes through congested areas to be avoided at peak times.

(New Towns Technical Officers' Committee, 1974)

With the level of car ownership escalating through the late 1950s and early 1960s, the difficulties of bus operators increased in new towns, as elsewhere throughout the country. With more and more people having the use of a car, bus patronage dropped, and to the profit-orientated bus company this meant either a reduced service or increased fares – or both. The point was approaching when it would be almost as cheap to use the car as to travel by bus; but this bore heavily on the many who did not have the use of a car and had to rely on a seemingly ever-reducing service for their in-town mobility. Sir Colin Buchanan summed up the dilemma: 'The public's perception of public transport is one of deteriorating services and rising fares; managements see declining demand and ever rising costs.' (Buchanan, 1981). It seems likely that the shortcomings of public transport at the time were a contributory cause of the much publicised 'new town blues'.

In the heady days of the mid 1960s, when it seemed as though full employment was a permanent state of affairs, the standard of living on an ever-rising curve with car ownership increasing year by year, engineers were embarking on the country's biggest road-building programme since the Romans, and planners were thinking up fresh ways to keep the traffic moving. In this climate Cumbernauld and Skelmersdale were planned for full motorisation; though scant provision was made for public transport.

But in towns up and down the country, the pressures of increasing traffic were being felt, not least in those Mark I towns where enlarged population targets had been set. It was clear that there was a limit to what town road systems and central parking arrangements could stand.

Bracknell provides an example of how the difficulties were compounded in the Mark I towns by the large increases of planned population decreed in the wake of the *South-East Study* (Ministry of Housing and Local Government, 1964). The road system was designed for the original target population of 25,000. When the ultimate population was suddenly 'upped' to 60,000 it made nonsense of all the careful planning that had been done. After the master plan had been revised, Bracknell town centre became a mainly pedestrian area situated inside a ring-road – a one-way, three-lane road with clockwise circulation, having four connections – three dual and one single carriageway. This road provision gave access to car parks and service yards inside the ring but no access for buses. With traffic at a much greater level than originally planned, bus passengers came off badly. There were bus stops with laybys on the outer side of the ring road, each provided with a bridge or underpass crossing of this busy road although, human nature being what it is, passengers did not always make use of them. Returning, laden with shopping, the ring road had to be crossed again.

Several of the Mark I towns found themselves saddled with problems, particularly in the central area, and forced to consider costly major roadbuilding in the shape of elevated roads and perhaps demolition of nearly new buildings. What was to be done?

As mentioned in Chapter 6 somebody had come up with what seemed a quite revolutionary alternative strategy. If public transport could be greatly improved so as to present a really attractive service charging very low fares, would not people be content to leave the car in the garage and go to work by bus, to go shopping by bus? Would not the problem then disappear?

This idea was seized upon with enthusiasm by politicians, planners, development corporation members, everybody in fact – yet, generally, it must be added, on the implicit assumption: 'a car for me and an excellent bus service for everybody else.'

Some of the Mark I towns were not in the peak hour affording the free flow traffic conditions for which they were designed, even though their situation was not as serious as that of many an older town. So the idea that a greatly improved public transport system might bring relief was of great and general interest. It was the new towns that led the way, and it is illuminating to examine the different approaches they made towards the objective of providing a more attractive and efficient bus service. Consider then the situation as it appeared in the early 1970s in the New Towns of Bracknell, Stevenage, Harlow, Basildon, Runcorn, Redditch, Peterborough and Milton Keynes.

Bracknell

It was only to be expected that Bracknell would find itself with particular problems. With its mammoth 140 per cent increase in planned ultimate population, with the railway line running across the middle of the town and fast moving traffic circulating around the one-way inner ring, planning for improvement of the central road system was a formidable task. Improvement of the bus service too presented considerable difficulties. With the two main industrial areas both adjacent to the railway but on opposite sides of it and with no direct link between them, it proved difficult to plan the timetable – one bus could not, for example, suit similar factory starting and finishing times in both areas. In the Radburn layouts, bus routes were necessarily circuitous whereas the footpath system was comprehensive and direct. The distance to be travelled by bus could be as much as two and a half times the straight line walking distance. It was often quicker to walk. To contemplate a bus service so much upgraded as to persuade people to leave the car at home seemed out of the question. Nevertheless some improvements were made both to the road system and to the bus service in Bracknell:

- the east-west route (A329) was realigned;
- the layout of later neighbourhoods was changed to give a more direct road pattern;
- provision of a bus/rail interchange was initiated; and
- several bus-only links were introduced.

Several other bus-only links proposed by a joint study group were not built. These would have connected culs-de-sac on opposite sides of neighbourhood centres, allowing buses to traverse the residential areas on a direct route between distributor roads. The proposals were abandoned following public consultation but, inevitably, the absence of these links in the bus network has resulted in a bus service less frequent and less direct than might have been achieved.

This kind of experience was not unique to Bracknell, or indeed to Mark I towns. At Skelmersdale bus-only links were not provided and sometimes, so it is said, it is quicker to walk than take the circuitous bus journey. At Telford, green strips designated as bus-only links were left through certain residential areas. Some of the links have been built but elsewhere the buses still use the perimeter routes, which upsets some of the planning logic, if for example old people instead of living close to the bus route find themselves with the longest walk of all the residents to reach the bus stop.

Stevenage

Of the Mark I towns it was Stevenage that made the most significant move towards improving the standard of public transport. The 1966 master plan revision, catering for an ultimate population of 105,000, had detailed the probable traffic situation at the turn of the century on the assumption of unrestricted use of the motor car with the bus service continuing at about the existing standard. The report had concluded that the road system already completed in the older parts of the town would be satisfactory only until the late 1970s, after which elevated roads, and in particular grade separated junctions, would be needed if traffic congestion at peak times was to be avoided.

In the 1960s, the bus service at Stevenage was inadequate, and so the development corporation resolved to seek ways of providing a bus service designed for passenger attraction rather than mere economy of operation. The definitive objective was to reduce car usage in the journey to work and at main shopping times, with the further objective of disarming public criticism by providing better bus facilities throughout the whole day.

Nathaniel Lichfield and Associates were commissioned to collaborate with the development corporation's staff under Eric Claxton, the Chief Engineer, and with the bus operators, to report on the alternative strategies available and to analyse the costs, including 'social' costs, and the benefit, defined as 'the greatest net benefit to the community'. Of the different options studied, only two need be considered here:

- the private transport scheme, which contemplated the building of grade separated, elevated sections of road, multi-storey car parks and additional surface car parks; coupled with only a 'residual' bus service; and
- the Stevenage Development Corporation public transport scheme, which comprised an express bus service routed along the primary roads from fourteen terminal points in the residential areas,

serving the industrial area with a five-minute frequency at peak times, and terminating at the town centre. In addition the scheme visualised a public charter bus service between the residential areas and the factories, operating, airline-style, with booked seats, a strict timetable and with a hostess on board the bus.

Expressed simply the analysis showed that, at 1967 prices, the highway improvements would cost £51 million whereas the public transport proposals could be carried out for about £42 million. Thus the public transport scheme won hands down on cost/benefit analysis, and it could also be expected to show quicker results and better social and environmental conditions for the whole community. But would it work? Unless it resulted in much greater bus patronage the concept would fail. Clearly it was necessary to put it to the test. The co-operation of the bus operators, London Country Buses Limited, was sought and was readily forthcoming. A working party was formed on which all the organisations concerned were represented and plans were made for experimental operations. Initial financial support was to be given by the Department of the Environment and Stevenage Development Corporation.

The first experiment was Blue Arrow, on a route between Chells, a large neighbourhood of about 13,000 people on the eastern side of the town, and the industrial area situated on the extreme western side. Started in 1969, this was a special peak-period service superimposed on the existing timetable; seats had to be pre-booked and each bus was timed to provide a specified arrival time at the factory.

The next stage of the experiment was the upgrading of the general service to the level recommended by Lichfield. This was again between Chells neighbourhood and the industrial area, serving also the town centre on the way. The service began in 1971 and improvements were introduced in five phases to enable the effect to be monitored at each stage. This then was 'Superbus 1'. Its success may be judged from the increase in bus ridership on this route between May 1971 and April 1974 from 20,000 to 50,000 passengers per week (Figure 10.1). Most of the increase was caused by change to bus from car travel, rather than from other modes; but the reduction in fares introduced in phase 5 did not have much effect on peak-period travel. On the other hand off-peak patronage went up enormously when fares were lowered; with the ability to get conveniently and cheaply from home to the centre, many people were making additional trips which, without the cheaper fare coupled with the more attractive service, would probably have never been made.

In 1972 'Superbus 2' was inaugurated. This further experiment was mainly for the purpose of checking whether the Chells results were

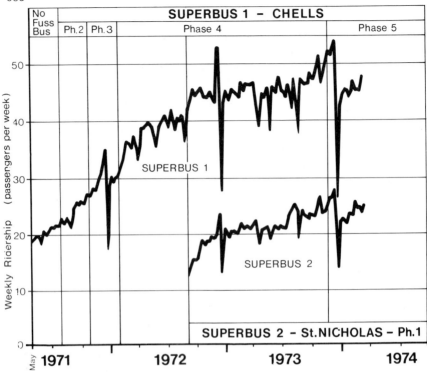

Figure 10.1 Stevenage: the development of Superbus.

typical. The new service, on similar lines to 'Superbus 1', was routed from St Nicholas, a neighbourhood of 10,000 people at the north-east corner of the town, to the town centre and then on to the industrial area. It resulted in an increase in bus ridership parallel to that at Chells. Not surprisingly a clamour arose for a full town-wide service.

Following the early experimental work, responsibility for financial support was taken over by the district council and by Hertfordshire County Council. The arrangement of a working party on which all the authorities concerned were represented together with the bus company had turned out to be a very satisfactory control mechanism. The results from the experiments were incorporated into the *West Hertfordshire transportation study*, completed in 1974 and were intended for use in planning an upgraded local bus service for Hemel Hempstead, on lines similar to Superbus, but the Hemel Hempstead service was never launched and, even in Stevenage, the Superbus service has now been somewhat watered down from its original form.

Harlow was less troubled than Stevenage by the threat of congested roads, so the idea of attracting motorists back to the buses to relieve rush hour congestion was not pursued. Nevertheless the local bus service, in Sir Frederick Gibberd's words: 'had to go on record as one of the development corporation's least satisfactory attempts to achieve a good service for Harlow residents'. (Gibberd et al, 1980). This was mainly due to the familiar effects of increased private car ownership and the need to make the bus service pay its way.

An experimental service on very different lines from Stevenage Superbus was introduced in 1974. This, the Harlow Dial-a-Bus service, was part of a research programme intended to reproduce the characteristics of a full-scale dial-a-bus system. The experiment was sponsored and supported financially by the development corporation, Harlow District Council, Essex County Council, the Department of the Environment and Ford (GB) Limited, while London Country Bus Services Limited agreed to operate the service and to carry out certain maintenance and operational services without charge. Representatives of all these organisations together with officers of the Transport and Road Research Laboratory, Cranfield Institute of Technology and all the affected trade unions were brought together in a working party to plan the service.

Dial-a-bus is defined as a demand-activated, road-based public transport that operates in the gap between conventional bus and taxi services. The Harlow service was to link the Old Harlow neighbourhood with the town centre, the Stow (a neighbourhood shopping centre), Harlow Town railway station and Harlow Hospital. It provided small buses to carry passengers from origin to destination on demand. To utilise the service from your home in Old Harlow to the town centre you would have telephoned the control centre giving your address, the required destination and time for collection. Control was able to instruct the bus driver by short-wave radio to enable your journey to take place. Unlike the conventional bus service, this system had no fixed routes, no set timetable and few fixed bus stops.

The working party's proposals laid down that:

> during the day, buses will leave the stand in Old Harlow at roughly 20 minute intervals to start a collection tour to pick up passengers at their doorstep who have booked calls by telephone, or otherwise made arrangements for a call. The buses will not follow a fixed collection route, but they will always pass three specified bus stops to pick up any waiting passengers. 'Hailstop' passengers may stop the bus anywhere in Old Harlow. The route of the buses into the town centre after the collection tour will be flexible, depending on

whether any passengers wish to go to the Stow, Harlow Town station, the hospital, or all three.

(New Towns Technical Officers' Committee, 1974)

Not every household had a telephone and it was decided to install twelve free telephones at strategic points with direct lines to the control. The vehicles used were sixteen-seat Ford buses; three buses operated throughout the day from 0700 hours to 1950 hours and a single bus between 1950 and 2330 hours. It was necessary to maintain a fleet of five buses to ensure that three were always operational.

A programme of data collection and surveys was conducted for the Transport and Road Research Laboratory (TRRL) by Cranfield Institute of Technology to ensure that as much as possible was learned from the experiment. It comprised household surveys, on-vehicle surveys, analysis of the dispatcher's log sheet and specific measurements. From the start of the experiment passenger figures exceeded that assumed in the design. A TRRL report of 1976 drew these (amongst other) conclusions:

1. The Old Harlow dial-a-bus service has increased the use of public transport by residents of Old Harlow by between 30 and 40 per cent. Passenger journeys had reached a daily average of 690 by February 1975.
2. By November 1974 7 per cent of dial-a-bus passengers had transferred from cars and 3 per cent from taxis. Some 11 per cent of passengers would not have travelled by any other mode and 15 per cent would have walked or cycled. 62 per cent would have used a conventional bus.
3. The experimental service is recovering about one-third of its total cost from revenue. A non-experimental service could be expected to recover 60-70 per cent of total costs from revenue.

(Transport and Road Research Laboratory, 1976a. Reproduced with permission of the Controller of Her Majesty's Stationery Office).

The experiment was discontinued after two years. Once again, it was a question of cost. If such a system could be expected to recover only 60-70 per cent of total costs from revenue, neither the government nor any of the interested authorities was prepared to pick up the bill for the shortfall. Yet only a quite heavily subsidised public transport system is likely to persuade a significant number of people to utilise it instead of the car; for 'public transport cannot do everything that cars can do', Sir Colin Buchanan wrote in 1981, 'but cars can do just about everything that public transport can do provided there is enough road space.' (Buchanan, 1981). People have developed a new way of life in the motor car age.

The ownership of the car and its mobility often determines where [the residents] live, where they work, where and when they shop. It is not just a case that journeys which were once made by public transport are now made by car; if that were so, it would be easier to reverse the process. The fact is that the majority of journeys now made by car could not be made by public transport; the car has allowed the worker to take a new job or buy a new house untied by a fixed public transport route. The car has enabled the shopper to fill the car with large volumes of goods once a week from the supermarket, which it would not be possible to carry on public transport without a new form of bus design.

(Basildon Development Corporation, n.d.).

The situation at Basildon was analogous to that of Bracknell. It had:

- a railway line bisecting the designated area and acting as a constraint on cross town movement;
- a population target swollen to 160 per cent of the original intention;
- a heavily loaded junction of primary and local roads adjacent to the town centre; and
- industrial areas confined mainly to one side of the town.

By the mid 1970s traffic congestion, severe by new town standards, was becoming evident during the work journey peak and to a lesser extent at peak shopping times. The difficulties at Roundacre, the worst trouble spot, were described in chapter 6; the elevated road proposals had come in for criticism by the district council and others and were rejected by the development corporation, who instead agreed to examine whether a much improved bus system could be devised with the objective of inducing people to use public transport for internal town journeys in preference to the private car. Bus ridership meanwhile had taken a knock in 1974 when the new central railway station was opened. People commuting out of the town to London, who previously used the bus to get to Laindon station, found it much more convenient to catch their train at the new Basildon station, and housewives from the Pitsea or Laindon areas found it an easy journey by train into the main shopping centre of the town.

It was clear that a solution for Basildon was going to be very hard to find. One difficulty was the large amount of commuting into the town. It was found that about 50 per cent of the cars parked at employment centres came in daily from outside the town and similarly about half the shoppers using the car parks in the town centre and the two sub-centres had come from the surrounding region. So it was obvious that improvement of the town services alone would not suffice; the improvements would also have to extend to much of the regional bus system, thus greatly enlarging the requirements.

One idea was to make a charge for worker parking, but, unless this were to be done regionally, how, in those days of full employment, could Basildon employers have retained their key workers? Similarly a suggestion of heavy charges for car parking in the town centre would inevitably have influenced shoppers to make for other nearby towns. Consultations with Basildon industrialists produced a favourable reaction to the idea of an improved bus service but they expressed doubts about any great increase of patronage by their workers.

The idea of a segregated bus track, such as was included in the master plan for Runcorn (see p. 162) was considered. Yet, short of facing up to huge expenditure and to the demolition of recently completed buildings, this seemed out of the question. A segregated bus track needs to be planned from the start and built along with, or in advance of, the development. The Stevenage Superbus experiment was examined to see if it could be applied in Basildon, but with four principal industrial areas and a primary road system having its most heavily trafficked node at the town centre, it could not be made to fit. None of this was very encouraging.

A public transport working group was constituted in 1975 consisting of representatives of the development corporation, Basildon District Council, Eastern National Omnibus Company, Essex County Council, the police and other co-opted parties. Establishing a working relationship between the members of the group and 'selling' their ideas to the bus operators turned out to be a slow process. Areas in which the group felt that it could have some influence were identified as:

● unreliability of the existing service;
● indirect routeing;
● neighbourhoods on the periphery of the town being poorly served;
● complex fare structures;
● lack of information about services; and
● need for some traffic management.

From these headings stemmed the first phase of a restructuring of the town's public transport system of which the main items were:

● provision of an adequate service between each neighbourhood and the town centre;
● introduction of a travel card covering the new town;
● house-to-house distribution of promotional material as part of a large scale public information exercise; and
● numbering and naming of each bus stop to facilitate cross-

160

referencing between map or timetable and for identification on the ground.

The first item involved new routes, and for these it was necessary to construct lay-bys and bus turn-arounds at the ends of some of the routes. A road, closed some years previously, was re-opened as a bus-and cycle-only track. The district council supported all these proposals, the Traffic Commissioners approved the necessary new licences and the county council provided a grant for the new services.

Six new services were introduced in 1978, all operating to regular frequencies and giving a close headway along the main routes to and from the town centre. The result was an increase in bus ridership within eight months of 15 per cent overall; in one area where the service level increased from four to six buses an hour, patronage went up by 30 per cent.

Great attention had been paid by the working group to the distribution of promotional material so that everyone was aware of the extent of the improvements; for again and again it had been shown that people did not consider using the bus simply because they did not realise it would serve the journey they wished to make. A paper describing the improvements concluded:

> There were of course many problems in implementing the new services, and some failures. The most obvious of these was that the worsening staff situation meant that many of the new services had to be temporarily curtailed. But determination by the company and help where possible from the other authorities in the group and the trade union led to improvements in recruitment and training.
>
> (Brown and Mackenzie, 1980)

The experience of Basildon illustrates what, from an unpromising starting base, can be achieved by collaboration and a determined effort by all the organisations involved in public transport. The results may not be sufficient to obviate for all time the need for elevated road building but, at least, they have postponed the need and at the same time increased the general mobility of a great many inhabitants.

Of the Mark II towns, Cumbernauld and Skelmersdale stand out as representatives of the era of expansion when full motorisation appeared to be within reach, the era of compact planning when job, school and shops were generally within walking distance; 'and if it's too far to walk get the car out'. Yet 'full motorisation', whatever it may mean, certainly does not mean that every member of every family will have a car available on every occasion. However many cars are owned per family, some members will be too young to drive, others too infirm; there will always be those who cannot pass the driving test and the transgressor who has lost his licence. Some people will always need the bus. Yet the master plan for Cumbernauld was silent on the matter of public transport and that for Skelmersdale seems to have relied on the regional bus service to satisfy also the intra-town needs.

So what a contrast when, only a few years later, the master plans for Runcorn and Redditch were unveiled – both dedicated to the promotion of public transport.

Runcorn

The boldest innovation in new town public transport strategy was at Runcorn. 'It is considered', said the master plan report, prepared in 1966 by Professor Arthur Ling 'that the contribution of public transport to a new town is of such importance that it is essential to plan for it as an integral part of the town structure and not to provide it as

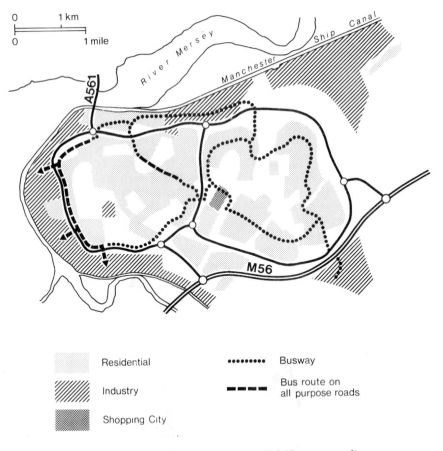

Figure 10.2 Runcorn: the Busway system (1968 proposal).

162

an afterthought', (Runcorn Development Corporation, 1967). These were no empty words; Ling set out with the conscious objective of achieving a balance between public and private transport, and the whole town was designed around its two transport systems with not a little bias towards public transport.

First of all, alternative forms of public transport were investigated. Monorail, tramways and computer controlled automatic systems on rails were all examined, but it was demonstrated conclusively that the conventional single deck bus, operating on a reserved track, was by far the cheapest and most flexible system available. This was the basis of Runcorn's Busway. The track reserved for the public service vehicles took the form of a figure of eight across the town with the crossover at Shopping City. It threaded its way through the centre of each residential area connecting them with one another and with the industrial estates, shopping areas, railway station, schools and playing fields (Figure 10.2). The routeing was much more direct than travelling by the expressway system, and there was said to be as much as a 50 per cent saving of distance when Runcorn was compared with towns of similar size in which the buses used the general road system. This planned infrastructure appeared to present a unique opportunity for an operator to provide an economical and efficient public transport service, and the operators, Crosville Motor Services Limited, were quick to seize the opportunity, responding with keen interest and full support.

The main details of the Busway are given in Table 10.3. The track was fenced throughout its entire length, the only pedestrian access to it being at bus stops. Where ground levels permitted the track crossed either over or under other roads, but elsewhere the crossings were at grade, controlled by traffic light signals, programmed to give automa-

Table 10.3
Runcorn: design criteria for the Busway

Length of Busway track	19 km (13 miles)
Width of reservation	12.2 m (40 feet)
Width of track	6.7 m (22 feet)
Maximum gradient	4 per cent
Standard camber	1 in 40
Maximum superelevation	1 in 24
Minimum headroom at overbridges	3.7 m (12 feet)
Design speed	64 km (40 miles) per hour
Average journey speed	32 km (20 miles) per hour
Source: Runcorn Development Corporation	

tic priority to approaching buses. The generous grass verges alongside the track provided the utility services authorities with an enviable route for their underground service distribution mains.

In the industrial areas, care was taken to route the Busway so as to ensure that the bus traveller was at no disadvantage compared with the car user. Thus the track was looped into the heart of each industrial estate with bus stops as close as possible to the factory entrances. At the multi-level Shopping City the Busway entered at high level and there were stairways, ramps or escalators down to the shopping centre one deck below. In the residential areas, bus stops were normally located at the local shopping centre, the focal point for the pedestrian system of the area, and the layouts were such that over 90 per cent of the dwellings were no more than 500 metres (one third of a mile) or only about five mintues' walk from a Busway stop.

As in several of the other towns, the planning and implementation of the public transport scheme was carried through by a joint working party consisting essentially of members from the development corporation and from Crosvilles but with representation also of the other organisations affected. This working party handled every facet of the Busway concept from initial route planning through to the appearance design of the bus stops; for this was not a scheme conceived by theoretical planning but by a practical and painstaking progression on the part of the working party and bus operators. All the time they were steering through uncharted waters.

A survey was made in 1973 by the Transport and Road Research Laboratory to determine the travel behaviour of residents in the new estates and to observe the operation of buses on the then partially completed Busway. The following were amongst the conclusions:

- Average journey speed including all stops and delays was 31 km/h (19 mph) compared with 19 km/h (12 mph), typical of conventional bus services;
- a modal split between Busway use and private car trips of 53:47, slightly ahead of the master plan assumption of a 50:50 split was established. This was at a time when 51 per cent of households had the use of one or more cars; and
- a simple cost/benefit analysis showed that the construction and land costs for the Busway of approximately £6m were justified by reduced expenditure on other transport infrastructure and by benefits to the bus company and bus users. The analysis related to conditions applying when Runcorn was being planned.

(Transport and Road Research Laboratory, 1976b. Reproduced with the permission of the Controller of Her Majesty's Stationery Office).

No more up-to-date appraisal is available; the recession, unemploy-

23. *Runcorn: the Busway at Shopping City.*

ment and the high cost of private travel, as well as of bus fares, may well have changed the economic balance. Responsibility for maintenance of the track remains with the development corporation at present, but it is anticipated that Cheshire County Council will shortly take this over.

Redditch

A somewhat similar, although much less exclusive, system was developed as the bus route for Redditch. It also basically comprised a figure of eight, but the framework made considerable use of existing roads. The route entered each of the residential and industrial areas, threaded its way through and then passed on into the next area. This concept was likened by the planners to a necklace, the beads being represented by the various districts and the string represented by the public transport route.

Unlike the exclusive fenced Busway at Runcorn, the road by which the buses entered each area was the all-purpose local distributor from its perimeter as far as the area centre, where ample parking and turning space was provided. Other vehicles could penetrate no further, but the buses continued through a short length of buses-only route to reach a corresponding local distributor leading to the other side of the area and thence through another short buses-only link on to the next

165

area (Figure 10.3). While not giving a segregated bus route as at Runcorn, the short lengths of reserved bus route were found to be remarkably effective; for private vehicles had no chance of using the convenient figure-of-eight route for their cross-town journeys. This was far more direct than the all-purpose route and, of course, with only very limited use by other vehicles, buses were able to operate efficiently and without delays. There was grade separation wherever a primary route was crossed by the public transport route, so no traffic light signals were involved and, where footways crossed the bus route, a pedestrian underpass or bridge was invariably provided.

The layouts were designed so that most homes were within eight minutes' walk of the bus stop, which meant that each area extended no more than about 0.8 km (half a mile) from the public transport route. For the distinctive Reddibus service, single-deck one-man operated buses were used by the operators, Birmingham and Midland Motor Omnibus Company Limited (Midland Red) but in a further development, an experimental fleet of articulated buses, known as Bendibuses has been used.

There was a variation on the same theme at Irvine, where existing

24. *A community route at Irvine.*

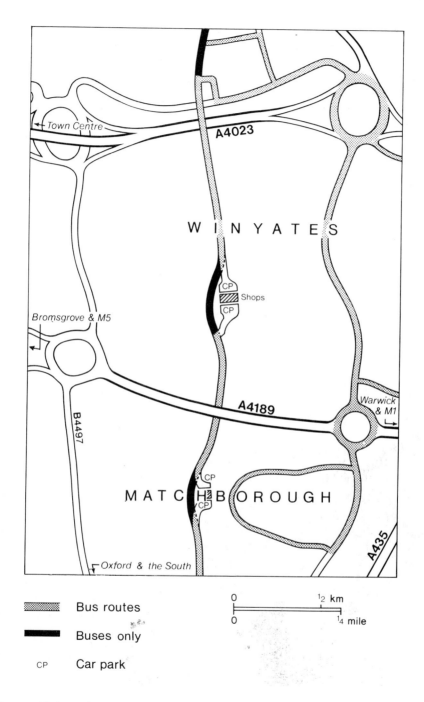

Figure 10.3 Redditch: bus route system.

roads which did not have a role in the road hierarchy were designated as "community routes" – primarily for public transport – while continuing to give access to existing development which could not economically be served by the new road system. The new community facilities were located close to the community route so that a high proportion of the population would be within walking distance of the bus route. The development corporation recognised that the community routes needed to be introduced in phase with development so as to encourage the use of public transport from the outset.

Peterborough

Peterborough was another town where public transport facilities were firmly built into the master plan with particular regard to the journey to work made by people working in the city centre.

> The better the public transport service, the larger the proportion of potential car commuters that can be induced to use it; and the higher the demand for it, the more frequent, convenient and comfortable it can profitably be made. Clearly, it will be easier to get this process started before rather than after the rate of car ownership has risen much higher.
>
> (Peterborough Development Corporation, n.d.)

The Peterborough system owes something to Runcorn and something to Redditch but certain features are unique. The linked system of operation preferred by the Eastern Counties Omnibus Company provided each of the townships with a direct link to the city centre via the shortest possible route. It made use of certain lengths of all-purpose road within the residential areas linked by sections of bus-only track. Where a secondary distributor was crossed, a bridge was provided wherever levels were suitable; otherwise it was an at-grade crossing controlled by signals, programmed to give priority to the buses. Most dwellings were within 400 m (¼ mile) of a bus stop; all were within 800 m (½ mile).

Milton Keynes

Provision of a good quality public transport service was central to the transport goals of the master plan for Milton Keynes. The 20 per cent of people expected to use public transport in the journey to work peak hour represented those workers who would not have a car (or a lift in a car) for the journey. Moreover, as at Runcorn and the other towns featured above, it was believed that a high quality public transport service, quick and economical, might persuade people to leave the car at home. It was felt that, if only the time differential could be eliminated, then 50 per cent of those able to drive or get a lift to work might choose instead to use public transport. This would swing the balance 60:40 in favour of public transport.

The transportation consultants researched the alternative possibilities: fixed track systems; a segregated bus track; and a conventional bus service, with alternatives for different sizes of buses from 14 to some 80 passengers. The consultants' assessment was pragmatic in its conclusions and costings. A monorail system was rejected as it proved the most costly solution of all. A proposal that buses should run on a segregated track was examined, then discarded as also too expensive. Dial-a-bus was tried out in the Woughton area on a similar basis to the Harlow experiment, using a fleet of six 15-seat buses and charging standard bus fares. Ridership fell short of that assumed in the design and the revenue/cost relationship was only about 25 per cent. So a system comprising conventional buses running on the grid roads was ultimately adopted. A report on the first two stages of the transport studies put it this way:

> A public transport service based on buses or minibuses will provide for a maximum of flexibility to accommodate changes in trip patterns. It also allows for easy adaptation to the city's growth, because route and vehicle size adjustments to meet changing requirements can be accomplished relatively easily and at low cost.
>
> (Milton Keynes Development Corporation, 1969)

However in the final report it was admitted:

> Thus, in the context of the remainder of the goals established for Milton Keynes and in the light of the selected land use plan, the provision of a competitive form of public transport does not make practical sense. This consideration of maximisation of freedom of choice has therefore been discounted. Because of the high standards of convenience implicit in providing good accessibility and complete freedom to use the car, no public transport system is likely to attract significant numbers of choice riders, except at excessively high cost.
>
> (Milton Keynes Development Corporation, 1969)

Both the development corporation and the United Counties Omnibus Company came in for heavy criticism.

So, in the fashion of the 1970s, a public transport committee was formed with representatives from all the interested authorities, which set out to make the best arrangements possible in the circumstances. The idea of relying on natural evolution to produce an efficient service was abandoned in favour of a planned strategy to provide:

● a service at 15 minute intervals throughout the day from each developed area to the town centre;

- this service to be available from the date of first occupation of houses or factories in the area;
- no house to be more than 400 m (¼ mile) from the nearest stop; and
- a covered bus shelter at every stop.

This strategy has been implemented with the result that there is now a bus service along virtually every grid road with a stop at about the middle of each side of every 'square'. The village footpath system connects to these four bus stops, and in many cases there is a pedestrian underpass leading to the corresponding stop on the other side of the grid road. Journey times are good on the relatively lightly trafficked grid roads and there are only a few diversions on the bus routes into housing or industrial areas.

It may be wondered how this considerable upgrading of the bus service could be achieved within the bus company's financial constraints. In addition to the subsidy paid by the Buckinghamshire County Council, the Milton Keynes Development Corporation contributes over half a million pounds each year to United Counties in revenue support. The Corporation has also provided:

- a bus lay-by, bus shelter and connecting footpath at every stop;
- a temporary bus servicing depot and, more recently, an elaborate permanent servicing depot; and
- a large bus station, sited close to the railway station.

The service with its comparatively low fares is widely used for travel to the town centre, for both shopping and for the journey to work. However it is not much use to workers in the industrial areas, due to the difficulty of servicing so many individual areas.

In all the towns, most local and regional bus routes were arranged to terminate at, or pass through, the centre, preferably at a common point to facilitate passenger interchange. Initially the provisions consisted of no more than a series of lay-bys with a small waiting room and office, but, by the late 1960s, much better facilities were provided. In Livingston for example the covered bus station has well planned circulation, good passenger accommodation and covered connections to the shopping areas. The building has pleasing elevational treatment and the plans allow for phased extension when required.

In some of the towns it has been possible to provide a complete integral transport interchange. Redditch, for example, is not now on a main railway line although the service to Birmingham is an important commuter facility. The bus station was built in the town centre adjacent to the railway station – to serve as the terminal for both the

Plate 9 Public transport

(a) Stevenage Superbus.

(b) and (c) Runcorn: the Busway in residential areas and . . .

(d) and (e) . . . at Shopping City.

(f) The bus station at Livingston.

(g) Northampton's bus and coach station.

Plate 10 Footpaths and cycleways

(a) ....me from school at Milton Keynes.

(b) ....rom the day's work at Stevenage.

(c) Cyclew... and footpath at Stevenage.

(d) Ske'... ... footpaths.

(e) Cycling ... ...the Redways at Milton Keynes.

(f) Pedestrian/cycle ... ...pass at Bracknell.

(g) Stevenage; pede... ... ...ng in the town centre.

(h) Warrington: an e... ... graphed prior to la...

Plate 11 Parking the car in the residential areas

a) Kerbside parking: an early housing development
   at Harlow and . . .

b) . . . the same at Hemel Hempstead.

c) Residential parking provision at Bracknell.

d) A Radburn layout at Basildon: back access and
   car park.

e) Washington: parking provision in one of the
   villages.

f) Bracknell: car park at an early neighbourhood
   centre.

g) A village centre car park at Washington.

Plate 12 Parking the car at work and at the town centre

(a) A factory car park at Basildon.

(b) Surface car park: Stevenage town centre.

(c) A car park in central Milton Keynes.

(d) Stevenage: a multi-storey car park.

(e) Multi-storey at Bracknell town centre.

(f) Well landscaped car park access at Redditch.

(g) Redditch: exit from another of the multi-storey car parks.

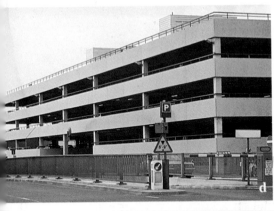

local and regional services. A staircase, ramps and subway connect the rail and bus stations; lifts and escalators join the bus station to the covered shopping area. There is a taxi rank, a 'park and ride' parking area and a 'kiss and ride' turning and waiting area. Thus, there are opportunities to interchange between:

- rail and bus;
- local bus and regional bus;
- rail/bus and taxi;
- rail/bus and private car; and
- rail/bus/taxi and town centre facilities.

At Northampton the bus and coach station was designed and financed by the borough council and it is neatly integrated with the Grosvenor shopping centre. The contours are such that buses enter at ground level at the rear of the building and underneath are two decks of shops, the lower deck being at the level of Market Square at the front of the building.

In summary, the main conclusions relative to public transport in new towns are these:

- public transport has an essential and continuing role to play in new towns in offering a reasonable measure of mobility to the many people who do not, for whatever reason, have the use of a car. Their numbers are likely to decrease somewhat, over time, but will always be significant;
- people who do have the use of a car may perhaps be persuaded to leave it at home if the public transport service is made very attractive and cheap;
- if more people use public transport for the journey to work, it relieves pressure on overcrowded roads, and may obviate or postpone the need for roadbuilding. Particularly in town centres, it relieves the long-term usage of precious car parking space;
- improvement of the local bus service of an established town can be achieved, as at Stevenage and Basildon;
- a segregated busway system as at Runcorn, although costly, is an immense boon to the bus user. A good result can be achieved more economically as was done at Redditch and to a large extent the principles can be applied in an expanding town as at Peterborough; and
- the absence of a clear cut and adequate financial structure for public transport has been an unsatisfactory feature of new town development, particularly during the early years. It was naive to suppose that a fully efficient bus service would come into being without a considerable measure of financial support.

None of the new towns was able to establish a fixed rail rapid transit even on an experimental basis. This might have been useful in complementing the findings of the Tyne and Wear Metro and might have helped to point the way to possible urban transport systems of the twenty-first century.

One other form of in-town public transport is the taxi service. This has flourished particularly in the Mark 1 Towns, where residential areas were well dispersed. Often the housing built and occupied first was the most remote from the town centre or work places. Bus services, in the early years especially, were very poor, so considerable use was made of taxis – alone or shared – by housewives for their weekly shopping trips. The disabled, too, were sometimes able to utilise taxis. The prototype of a new design of taxi for the severely disabled is now plying in Peterborough. Based on the landrover, it has a boarding facility and space for a wheelchair and occupant alongside the driver.

11 Walking

Earlier chapters have touched upon the provision made for pedestrians in the residential areas, the town centres and elsewhere in the towns; this chapter will draw together the threads, trace the overall walkway patterns of the towns and discuss the changes in thinking that have occurred over time. Walking – the simplest form of personal mobility – was not until fairly recently looked upon as contributing to the transport system of a town. A new footpath was generally provided only as an adjunct to a new street. The Buchanan report recognised pedestrians' needs:

> The simple act of walking plays an indispensable part in the transport system of any town. . . . It does not seem to be far from the truth that the freedom with which a person can walk about and look around is a very useful guide to the civilised quality of an urban area.

> (Buchanan et al, 1963)

Yet all through the 1960s and early 1970s official thinking seems to have focused on and been obsessed by the disturbing findings of the current transportation studies and with the central problem of how to keep the traffic flowing. Walkers were regarded mainly in terms of the hindrance they caused to traffic flow.

Government official comprehensive national travel surveys were carried out in 1972/3 and in 1975/6; but, in the published findings, all journeys on foot of less than 1 mile (1.6 km) were excluded. An

173

independent and detailed analysis of the data obtained in these surveys was made by Dr Mayer Hillman and Anne Whalley; who, commenting on the exclusion of walk journeys less than 1 mile, said:

> This misleadingly deflates the proportion of walk journeys by a factor of 3 and thereby inflates that of all other travel methods. Indeed, this distorting procedure results in the exclusion of 25 per cent of all personal travel. It is made all the more illogical because journeys under one mile by other methods are included.
>
> A further effect of this exclusion is that a not insignificant proportion of people are wrongly deemed as having made no journeys at all during the week of the survey.
>
> (Hillman and Whalley, 1979)

Hillman and Whalley's comparison of the modal split excluding and including walk journeys of under 1 mile is given in Table 11.1. They continued:

> The reason for the extent of this distortion is that almost three-quarters of walk journeys are less than 1 mile long. . . . Journeys under one mile by all travel methods account for about one-third of *all* journeys and almost 90 per cent of them are made on foot. . . . The distorting effect . . . results in only half the school journeys and only two-thirds of the shopping journeys being recorded.
>
> (Hillman and Whalley, 1979)

Hillman and Whalley concluded that nationwide there had been official neglect of walking as a travel method although, as they convincingly demonstrated, that is what it is. Did these strictures apply to the new towns?

Table 11.1
Comparison of modal split excluding and including walk journeys of under one mile

	Walk	Car	Bus/ train	Other	N/a	All journeys
	%	%	%	%	%	%
Modal split *excluding* walks of less than 1 mile*	12.4	59.9	19.6	6.1	2.0	100
Modal split *including* walks of less than 1 mile*	35.2	39.5	11.3	4.4	9.6	100
Source: Mayer Hillman and Anne Whalley, op. cit.						

Early layouts for development in the Mark I towns had complied with the byelaws of the relevant ' authority. This meant that, in general, footways had to be provided either side of the carriageway on every new town road, from the heavily trafficked primary road down to the smallest cul-de-sac. It was a general requirement throughout the towns of Britain if the roads were intended to be handed over to the local authority. Irrespective of what new town architects and planners might have wished, there was little hope in those days of any relaxation of the requirements. In fact there was not much wrong with the arrangement at that time because of the relatively low level of motor traffic. The roads were generally routed directly between points of attraction, which meant that there was no better route available for the footways to follow. Of course there was potential danger through pedestrian/vehicle conflict but no more, probably less, than was accepted as inevitable in towns in Britain at that time. Traditionally also, the underground services – water, gas, electricity and telephone mains – always followed the road pattern; it was customary to lay these services beneath the footways, which could be taken up and relaid if necessary for access to the mains.

It is therefore not surprising that in taking the first tentative steps in New Town development neither the development corporation nor its chief engineer was anxious to risk confrontation over byelaw requirements or the routeing of services; in that uncertain climate the development might never have got off the ground! Few realised that, in a few years time, residential streets would be lined with cars each night or that crossing the road would be hazardous. All the Mark I towns were planned on the neighbourhood system, so that local shops, the pub, community hall and the primary school could all be reached on foot without crossing a major road. No one yet contemplated the expense of building pedestrian subways, and such was the effect – social as well as physical – of the neighbourhood structure that friends, and particularly a child's school friends, were likely to be living in the same community. The majority of walk journeys tended to be within the neighbourhood without involving the crossing of a primary or secondary road. (It was this 'insularity' which was later to be used as an argument against the neighbourhood principle.)

In addition to footways alongside the roads, there were some independent cross-town footpaths provided where a shorter route was possible, say to the primary school or the town centre. Of course the walker invariably sought out the shortest or most advantageous route and 'it is no bad idea', suggested one corporation member, 'to wait until the worn tracks appear across the landscaped areas and then step in and pave them to form the official footpath'. It is not known whether the suggestion was ever adopted but clearly there was a case for using the empirical in preference to theoretical pedestrian desire lines.

Most if not all the designated areas were already criss-crossed by a network of public footpaths and bridleways which had to be taken into account in the planning. Footpaths and bridleways can of course be extinguished using the powers of the New Towns Act 1946 or other legal procedure, but the disappearance of a footpath could be upsetting to existing residents in the area. As a rule development corporations tried to avoid this, preferring to perpetuate a footpath or bridleway route, even though in the developing urban environment it had in places to be diverted on to a new alignment. Where existing narrow lanes were superseded by the town road system, these were often retained as cross-town footpaths – perhaps serving as cycleways and bridleways as well. This was done very effectively at Harlow where, in the words of Lord Esher: 'In June, vast lawns spread in all directions and scented footpaths wind secretly through the may and alder.' (Esher, 1981).

The first real indication of how the walker was identified and his safety defended in new towns was the adoption of the Radburn principle at Basildon and elsewhere in the 1950s. The aim was, as we have seen, complete segregation of pedestrians from motor transport – footpath access at the front of the house, cars and garages at the back. It was one of the first attempts at a local level to do something positive to combat the alarming road accident figures; it was also a complete break with normal byelaw requirements and a calculated risk on the part of development corporations who could not be certain that these independent footpaths would be adopted by the local authority in due course. The Radburn layouts seemed like a pedestrian's charter: a tranquil lawn and shrubbery in front of the house, where the children could play in safety; a paved area not far away with all the paraphernalia of an adventure playground; the primary school and the neighbourhood centre within a few minutes walk – all without crossing a traffic road. These were young towns for young people with young children, and the designers kept this in mind. The footways were well paved with easy gradients and there were few if any steps, which made pram pushing easy. Now, thirty years on, the age structure is more akin to that of any other town, but the same footpaths well serve the partially disabled and those in wheelchairs. The Radburn layout, sometimes in considerably modified form, was taken up by many of the Mark I towns, and for a dozen or so years it held unquestioned sway.

Meanwhile the great debate on town centre design had been raging in the Mark I towns – the architects and planners going all out for pedestrianisation while the estates people and the Ministry, together with the traders generally opposed it. The result? As we have already seen, uneasy compromise in most of the towns. And then the

Stevenage breakthrough. Walking around the Stevenage centre today one might be excused for asking what all the fuss had been about. It all seems so logical – even old fashioned when compared with later developments in Runcorn, Northampton and the rest. Yet, to have excluded the motor vehicle entirely from a large shopping centre, giving it over completely to this one mode of movement was arguably the boldest, the most innovative move ever made in any of the twenty eight new towns.

It was then necessary to provide footpath connections from the town centre through to the Radburn footpath systems – at least in the neighbourhoods nearest to the centre. This could not be done without crossing a primary or secondary distributor and so, to avoid vehicle/pedestrian points of conflict, the prototypes of the many hundreds of pedestrian subways were built in most of the towns. In the other direction, the footway system extended from the Radburn residential areas to the principal industrial estates and then on to the perimeter of the town and to the open country beyond, and where these footpaths crossed the main town roads, a pedestrian subway or footbridge was generally provided – perhaps not initially, but later on when the need was established and money became available. Cumbernauld's *Preliminary planning proposals* will serve as a general description of what was being aimed at in all the towns in the 1960s.

> Within the housing areas designed so far, the most direct routes possible have been selected to give pedestrians access to the major and minor foci – the central area and major playing fields, for instance on the one hand, and the local shops, pubs, primary schools and toddlers' play areas on the other. Such routes have tended to define the sizes of development groups of buildings and, consequently, have led to the location of underpasses and pedestrian bridges. The channelling of pedestrians to such crossings begins at a point distant from the road so that the opportunity for conflict with vehicles is minimised. These main footpaths have determined the location en route of a variety of social facilities provided within housing areas.
>
> This system has now been extended into the peripheral areas of the town to give the pedestrian the opportunity of reaching a variety of out-of-town environments quickly, easily and in safety. Reaching out from the central area where the maximum freedom of movement is provided for the pedestrian, routes pass through the housing areas to the country beyond.
>
> (Cumbernauld Development Corporation, 1962)

In the development of the new towns it is noticeable how suddenly quite fundamental changes occurred in one town and then spread quickly to others. This was so with the adoption of Radburn housing layouts and with the all-pedestrian town centre. In its turn the Radburn concept gave way to new ideas. It had always had its critics. Its shortcomings, which on balance were not serious ones, are discussed on pp 108 and 109.

It is hard to imagine a more complete reversal than occurred in Runcorn when the Halton Brook site, a high density Radburn-type layout, was followed by The Brow. The former layout with virtually complete pedestrian/vehicle segregation, followed by one where the pedestrians and vehicles often actually shared the same track. The trick was to manufacture an appearance of domesticity, such that the driver could not fail to be aware that he had entered a different ambiance, that he was only there on sufferance. Trick or not, it seemed to work. There had been no outcry concerning danger to pedestrians or to children at play; no reports of accidents. The Brow was designed in 1966. It was followed by the design guides from Essex and Cheshire County Councils, and finally the whole idea was made respectable by the Department of the Environment/Department of Transport joint *Design Bulletin 32* (Department of the Environment, 1977).

If it be thought that the pedestrian had lost out by this change in residential area design, this could certainly not be said about the cross-town footpaths. Their planning was receiving very careful attention to secure the most direct routeing, improved landscaping and pedestrian subways in numbers hitherto unimagined – of the order of a hundred or so in many of the towns. Great care was taken to avoid steep descents or steps leading down to the subways.

Walking had certainly not gone unrecognised as a mode of transport in new towns. At Milton Keynes, for example, each village (grid square) was reticulated with footways giving access to the local centre, schools, employment centres, the bus stops situated on the grid roads and, through subways under these roads, to adjacent villages. These paths are known as Redways and serve as combined pedestrian and cycle routes. Yet there was no certainty that walkers would use the subways. Observations made in 1976/7 at three of these road crossing points indicated that some 42 per cent of pedestrian cross-road trips at these locations were made on the road surface. As Dr Stephen Potter commented: 'It is clear that in this area of Milton Keynes, pedestrian/vehicle segregation is failing by a large margin to resolve the safety conflict between the two modes'. (Potter, 1978).

However the Milton Keynes 1976/7 findings were not necessarily typical of experience in all the new towns – indeed pedestrian behaviour in Milton Keynes itself may have improved with greater familiarity with the system. The need was to change people's perceptions of the working of the system – easing the slopes down to the subway, eliminating steps, and increasing the barricading of the distributor roads. But as well as careful planning and attractive design, there is a need too for high standards of maintenance and of cleansing.

Also significant in the context of walking are the shopping facilities in the neighbourhoods, new districts or villages; easily reached on foot they demonstrate that the village life of earlier times has an up-to-date equivalent in the friendly neighbourliness of these modern centres. Among the most attractive are those former village main streets where buildings have been carefully preserved and the space between the shops tastefully pedestrianised. But let Lord Esher have the last word:

> To hear footfalls, laughter, bird-song in the very heart of cities is a real recapture of territory lost to civilisation, and the fact that the surrounding architecture is generally mediocre and sometimes absurd does not seem to matter and confirms once again the truth, often proclaimed by architects, that urban design is about the creation of spaces and not about the particular decor of the facades that wall them in.
>
> (Esher, 1981).

12 Cycling

People with long memories who were teenagers between the First and Second World Wars often look back with affection to the acquisition of their first bike, that first wonderful taste of personal mobility. Limited only by your own physical capacity, the bicycle would take you absolutely anywhere on well surfaced roads, as yet uncluttered by a surfeit of motor traffic. Earlier on, at the turn of the century, before the introduction of tarred road surfaces, cycling had not been so satisfactory and it is of interest that the first call for better road surfaces was made not on behalf of motorists, but of cyclists, by William Rees Jeffreys, then honorary secretary of the Roads Improvement Association.

But where, in the latter half of the twentieth century, does the cyclist fit into the complicated movement pattern of towns? The twenty-eight British new towns provide no single answer for, more than any other facet of transport provision, cycling has been evaluated quite differently between one new town and the next.

Some parts of Britain have of course a stronger tradition of cycling than others, depending on factors such as the nature of the terrain and climatic conditions and the relative prosperity of the populace. Thus there is not much demand for cycling facilities on the windswept hillside of Cumbernauld, but much more in the flatter country and low rainfall areas of Essex and East Anglia. While the idea of trying to segregate the pedestrian from the motor vehicle was accepted more or less universally in the 1950s, there was no clear-cut policy for dealing with the cyclist. In normal town streets, there was never any question of excluding him from the carriageway – indeed it was the only part of the street he was allowed to use. Yet, with his inherent wobble and in some cases indifferent road sense, he was perhaps more in conflict with the motorist than even the pedestrian. In the new towns one might have expected a strong case to be made for cycle tracks. However this solution was by no means universally accepted when the master plans for the Mark I towns were prepared. Separate tracks for cycles would cost a good deal of money – none too plentiful in those days. At that time, too, it seemed inconceivable that car ownership would ever rise to a level that would cause congestion of a new town's liberal road system. There was a theory too, based on inter-war experience, that cyclists tended to ignore the tracks when provided, opting instead for the better surfaces and more even gradients of the main road system.

Such doubts were not entertained at Stevenage. In the early years of development with petrol rationing still in force and relatively few cars still on the road, use of the bicycle for the journey to work and to school was taken for granted; and it says much for the development corporation's judgement and the persuasive powers of its officers (Eric Claxton is a doughty protagonist of cycling) that they foresaw that the carriageways of the town roads would not for ever be capable of accommodating the cyclists with any degree of comfort or safety. A comprehensive cycle track network was devised (Figure 12.1).

In general the primary roads of Stevenage followed direct routes between the residential areas and the main employment and shopping areas; the corridors reserved for these roads were made wide enough to incorporate a single two-way cycle track. At road junctions, the cycle track and also the footway were taken through a subway beneath the joining road, and subways were also provided at intervals to enable cyclists using the track to reach the neighbourhood on the opposite side of the primary road. This segregation extended right into the heart of the industrial area with cycle tracks on either side of the road, and right into the town centre. In addition, various lengths of independent cycleway were constructed alongside the footpaths to provide short-cut links to schools and other destinations. Routes were provided through parks and woodlands and some of the existing country lanes were closed to motor traffic and utilised as cycleways and footpaths.

The length of the cycle tracks and cycleways at Stevenage is about 40 km (25 miles). Some design criteria are given in Table 12.1. The underpasses are visually pleasing while being economical in cost and serve pedestrians as well as cyclists. The motorist of course benefits too through the absence of cyclists on the carriageway and more particularly at the junctions.

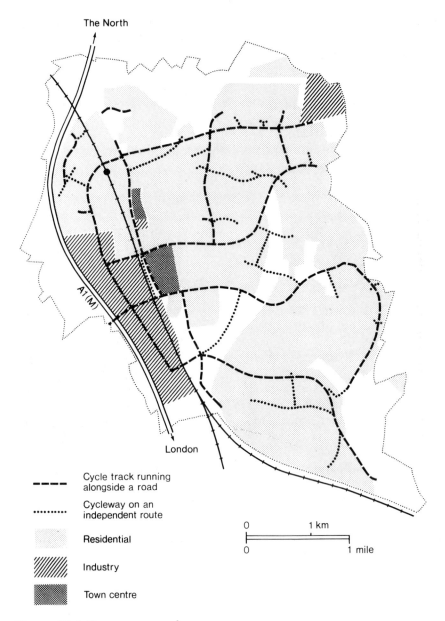

The North

A1(M)

London

	Cycle track running alongside a road
	Cycleway on an independent route
	Residential
	Industry
	Town centre

0   1 km

0   1 mile

Figure 12.1 Stevenage: cycleways.

Lighting of the cycle tracks was adequately provided by overspill light from the road lighting system and at roundabout junctions the ramps, and indeed the whole area, were brilliantly illuminated from 35 m (114 feet) high columns, giving a feeling of security to all. The interior of the subways was also generously lit but with relatively cheap fittings that could readily be renewed if vandalised. The independent cycleways were themselves appropriately lit.

25. All transport modes well catered for at a Stevenage junction.

Table 12.1
Stevenage: cycleway design criteria

Two-way cycleway width	3.56 m
One-way cycleway width	2.7 m
Ruling gradient	4 per cent
Maximum gradient	5 per cent
Ruling embankment slope	30 per cent
Maximum embankment slope	50 per cent
Minimum verge width (between cycleway and footway)	0.6 m
Minimum kerb radius at cycleway junctions	3.0 m
Minimum headroom through underpass	2.25 m
Source: Stevenage Development Corporation	

183

The aim of Stevenage's pioneering was to maximise the attraction and safety of the system for cyclists. In fact it did more – many people (some already car owners) bought a bike to secure the benefits of this quick, safe and healthy mode of transport at negligible cost to themselves, and there were some, too timid to venture on to the carriageways, who were quite at ease on the segregated tracks. Approximately 8 per cent of journey to work trips at Stevenage in 1973 were by bicycle, i.e. some 10,000 trips each week and 5,000 journey to school trips (and in the years of recession, probably many more). Accidents to cyclists were averaging 50 a year of which only 15 occurred on cycleways.

Without detracting from the Stevenage achievement, it seems certain that cycle tracks in new developments would never again be routed along main roads but would penetrate the residential and other areas, the 'no-go' territory for motor vehicles[1]. Sir Frederick Gibberd puts it thus:

judging from the practice of running cycle tracks along the main town roads, it cannot be so obvious that the two systems are, in theory, diametrically opposed. The motorist will find it easiest to follow the smooth flow of the main roads between the built-up areas, but the cyclist and pedestrian always take short cuts along the local roads because the comparatively narrow tracks and right angle bends present no difficulties to them and, above all, they are saved physical energy. It would seem logical therefore that cycle tracks and pedestrian ways should run through the heart of the housing areas and should connect their centres to the industrial areas and the town centre.

(Gibberd, 1953)

As was to be expected, Gibberd took these observations on board in the planning of Harlow – the only other Mark I town to make serious initial provision for cyclists. The length of cycleway provided was about 16 km (10 miles) – much less than at Stevenage. But the outstanding feature was that none of these tracks followed the town's roads; they were all on independent routes offering the cyclist, in nearly all cases, a shorter journey than he could make by road.

By no means all the Harlow cycleways were newly constructed tracks. Several old country lanes within the designated area had been closed to vehicular traffic and were now reserved for cyclists and pedestrians only. Consider for example the 3 km (2 miles) long cycle route from the north-east corner of the town linking Old Harlow and other residential areas through beautiful parkland to the town centre. Not much of this route was new construction and it enabled the old lanes with their trees and hedgerows to be preserved and enjoyed by cyclist and pedestrian alike, while offering an excellent direct route to the town centre. Eastwards this cycleway extended to the boundary of the designated area and to the open country beyond.

Equally useful and almost as direct was the north-south cycleway between Potter Street neighbourhood in the south-east corner of the town and the principal industrial area. This route was extensively used by workers cycling to the industrial area and also by housewives, usually pushing a pram, making for The Stow neighbourhood centre. Complaints received from walkers on this route caused the planners to think again about the compatibility of cycle traffic and pedestrians, with the result that later developments endeavoured to keep cyclists and pedestrians apart.

As at Stevenage there were underpasses at every crossing of a primary or secondary road, but the number of these was relatively small. This, coupled with the incorporation of existing lanes into the system, made the Harlow cycleways provision very economical.

As car numbers increased, cycle numbers dropped – many cyclists becoming motorists – and this trend persisted through the 1950s and 1960s. The Mark II new towns, cradled in years of prosperity, practically ignored the cyclist, although, to be fair, any ideas there may have been of providing cycleways would at that time have been hard to justify. Nevertheless the wind of change that blew so many things off course in the mid-seventies brought a change in people's attitudes to cycles and cycling. Contributory factors were:

- big increases in the price of petrol;
- ever-rising fares on public transport;
- reduction of the general level of prosperity; and
- in some towns, a measure of congestion on the primary roads particularly in the work journey period.

While some people were turning to use of the cycle, it is likely that many more were deterred from doing so by the difficulties and inherent danger of cycling on congested roads and negotiating the surface roundabouts and other junction layouts. Parents dissuaded their children from cycling to school, preferring to get the car out, so adding to the congestion. The demand for cycleways was strong and, with a turnaround in official thinking, cycleways became respectable again. In 1978 the Department of Transport issued *Local Transport Note 1/78* 'Ways of helping cyclists in built-up areas', to encourage 'more consideration for cycling and to provide better facilities for cyclists where possible'. Meanwhile current layouts were being scrutinised in all the towns to see where cycleways could be fitted in, aiming at something on the lines of the Harlow pattern – not easy to achieve in a substantially developed town.

26.   *Journey from school at Bracknell.*

The situation in Basildon was described in a joint planning and engineering report of 1981. At that time the town had 4 miles (7 km) of independent cycleways linking the industrial areas with adjacent neighbourhoods, and further facilities had been planned to extend the system into current development areas in the south-west of the town. Another proposal was for a cycle/pedestrian bridge across the A127 (Southend Arterial Road) to link Noak Bridge housing scheme with the industrial areas. Yet these additions would still not link together into a comprehensive network to enable cyclists to travel on a safe and convenient route. The system would continue to be of a piecemeal character.

To examine the problem further a Cycle Group was formed, comprising representatives of the development corporation, district council and county council, and a scheme was prepared for a comprehensive network covering the whole town and intended significantly to improve the mobility of the population in which, at that time: 34 per cent of households were without a car, and 75 per cent of individuals were without personal access to a car of their own. The scheme was designed on a low-cost basis, cutting new construction to a minimum through the introduction of the following measures:

- *advisory routes* Lightly trafficked roads requiring no special facilities, apart from signs indicating 'Recommended cycling route'. Many housing area roads were in this category. It was sometimes possible to link sections of advisory route by allowing cyclists to use buses-only routes;
- *shared cycle/pedestrian paths* Many existing footways, such as those along the town's primary roads where pedestrian flows were light were changed to shared cycle/pedestrian paths by Traffic Regulation Order. Where there was potential conflict it was dealt with by some device such as white line separation; and
- *cycle pelican crossings* Existing pedestrian subways or bridges could sometimes be safely adapted for shared use. Failing this, cycle-activated, signals-controlled 'pelican' crossings were installed in some locations.

Yet compared with Stevenage or Harlow the system was clearly rather makeshift.

At Redditch, Runcorn and elsewhere the question arose as to the potential danger of allowing pedestrians and cyclists to mix on joint paths. Where no separate provision had been made for them, cyclists were in fact using the pedestrian paths, so the real question was whether to accept and legalise the arrangement. Clearly before doing so, each case had to be carefully examined by the development corporation with the local authority and police, but, on the whole, it seemed better to recognise and legalise the situation, to clarify the position for both pedestrians and cyclists. Certainly it was less dangerous to mix cyclists and pedestrians than to mix cyclists with heavy motor traffic, usually the only other option.

Amongst the Mark IIs and Mark IIIs, it was Peterborough alone that adopted a policy for cycleways from the outset. Cycling has always been popular in this city as the site is generally flat; in 1966 cycling accounted for about a third of all journey to work trips. Although the master plan recognised that this proportion was bound to reduce as the town expansion increased the distance most workers would have to travel, it advocated a system of cycleways from the neighbourhoods to secondary schools, township centres and industrial estates. This was developed into a firm policy in 1974 in a report which made the case for expenditure on a cycleway system (Peterborough Development Corporation, 1974). The system comprised four different forms of cycle path defined as:

- *Cycle track* parallel to existing road or buses-only route or on a completely independent alignment;
- *Cycle lane* in the older parts of the town, a clearly marked lane in the carriageway, separated from other traffic by a painted line;
- *Cycle route* a lightly trafficked road where cyclists were given priority over all other road users except pedestrians; and
- *Cycle trail* through parks, woodland and countryside; following the route of bridlepaths, unused railway tracks of the Nene Valley railway etc.

Since the bus routes were deliberately planned to follow the most direct path to the Peterborough industrial areas and township centres, it was logical for the main cycle tracks to follow the same route. Thus in the residential areas it was quite usual to see bus route, cycle track and main footpath side by side, though with physical separation between. Where the bus track made an at-grade crossing with a secondary or local distributor road, the cycle track and footway descended to an underpass crossing. Some 50 miles (80 km) of cycleway had been provided by 1983 out of the planned total of 72 miles (115 km).

In 1974, the Transport and Road Research Laboratory undertook a study of ways of improving conditions for cyclists in urban areas to determine whether the provision of special facilities would reduce the travel difficulties of cyclists and their accident rate; also whether this would encourage non-cyclists to take up cycling and cyclists to cycle more. In collaboration with the Peterborough development corporation, the Laboratory planned a comprehensive experiment incorporating a great variety of facilities. Whereas the corporation's cycleway proposals had provided direct access from the neighbourhoods to the township centre and the industrial estates, the TRRL experimental route linked the cycleway system within the Bretton township by an uninterrupted route, through the old built-up areas, right into the city centre. As far as possible the whole route was segregated from motor traffic and, because it was planned to pass through areas already developed, it was necessary to use a variety of different facilities to achieve this uninterrupted passage. The experiment is described in a TRRL report and the particular facilities provided were:

- with-flow cycle lanes;
- contra-flow cycle lanes;
- cycle track/pedestrian path (segregated);
- cycle track/pedestrian path (unsegregated);
- cycle track in subway;
- cycle track/pedestrian path (unsegregated) in subway;
- traffic signal controlled cycle crossing; and
- cycle junction (separate phase for cyclists in traffic signal controlled junction).

(Transport and Road Research Laboratory, 1981. Reproduced with the permission of the Controller of Her Majesty's Stationery Office.)

The experimental cycle route was opened in July 1977 and monitored by TRRL through the next 15 months. The experiment terminated in October 1978 and the Laboratory's general conclusions, in brief, were as follows:

- there was an increase in flows along the roads served by the experimental route relative to a general decline in cycling elsewhere in the city;
- almost everyone (cyclists, motorists, pedestrians, residents and traders) was in favour of retaining the cycle route, and
- there were insufficient data on accidents involving cyclists to enable any conclusions to be drawn on the effect the experimental cycle route had on cyclists' safety.

(Transport and Road Research Laboratory, 1981. Reproduced with the permission of the Controller of Her Majesty's Stationery Office).

The cycle route was retained after the experiment as a permanent part of the traffic system in Peterborough.

Amongst all the new towns only Stevenage, Harlow and Peterborough sustained a coherent and comprehensive network of cycleways throughout their development, although nearly all incorporated some lengths of cycleway into their later planning. In Milton Keynes there was time to introduce the comprehensive network of Redways referred to in the previous chapter (Figure 12.2). The system is well used by cyclists for the journey to school, to work in the widely dispersed industrial areas, to the central area and as the most direct route to the villages in neighbouring grid squares. The quality of

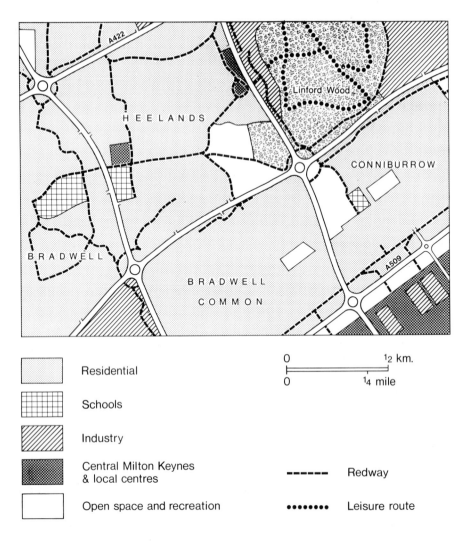

Residential	
Schools	
Industry	
Central Milton Keynes & local centres	
Open space and recreation	

0 ———————— ¹₂ km.
0 ———————— ¹₄ mile

------ Redway

•••••••• Leisure route

Figure 12.2 Milton Keynes: the Redways system and leisure routes.

materials used at Milton Keynes was very high – red asphalt paving throughout, polished granite facings on some of the subways and excellent landscaping. The design criteria were similar to those at Stevenage. Mingling of cyclists and walkers on the same track does not appear to have caused any particular difficulty; but where there was heavy cycle traffic, for example at the approaches to secondary schools, the Redways were increased in width from the standard 3 m (10 feet) to 5 m (16 feet) and separate paths for cyclists and walkers were demarcated. In practice, the great distances involved at Milton

190

Keynes dictated that much of the system became principally a cycleway, providing a very satisfactory linkage for the whole city, quite separate from the roads.

Far from proving an anachronism, cycleways in the new towns are well used and, in the light of the present cult for cycling and the increasing costs of motoring, it is possible they may attract much greater usage in the future. And if oil supplies dry up in the foreseeable future as some, though by no means all, the experts predict, the bicycle and the horse might again become the principal vehicles of personal mobility, in which case it could be the direct route cycleways which became congested; for relaxed travel it would be back to the spacious new town roads system.

But for the present it is salutory to restate the case for capital expenditure on providing facilities for cyclists in any major new development – as clearly summarised by the Peterborough officers in their 1974 report:

- *Environmental* The cycle needs no fuel, gives off no fumes and makes almost no noise;

- *Convenience* Much of the time involved in walking to and waiting at bus stops and hunting for car parking spaces is avoided by the cyclist. The cycle offers door-to-door travel;

- *Time* The cycle competes favourably with other forms of transport on congested urban roads;

- *Cost* The cycle is an economic form of transport. It is cheap to buy and maintain and has very low running costs;

- *Car parking* About sixteen cycles can be parked in the area required for one car and significant land saving would be made, particularly at local centres if cycleways were developed and their use encouraged;

- *Safety* The provision of cycleways will mean a considerable reduction in accidents involving cyclists by reducing conflict with motor vehicles; and

- *Transportation conditions* A cycleway system encourages the use of an alternative transport form. It offers increased mobility, particularly to children and housewives. The displacement of cyclists from roads on to cycleways will increase road capacity and efficiency.

(Peterborough Development Corporation, 1974).

An additional benefit to the individual must surely be the relaxing, health-giving attributes of this mode of transport when relieved of conflict with the motor vehicle.

Note

1 However, when cycleways were routed along classified, or potential classified, roads, they formed part of the highway and therefore
qualified for a contribution by the county council as highway
authority. The county council in turn received a government grant
towards such contribution. These arrangements no longer obtained
after local government reorganisation in 1974.

13 Parking

Much has already been said about providing for the safe and efficient movement of motor vehicles in the new towns; yet for 95 per cent of its life the motor vehicle is not in a state of motion but in a state of rest. The average private car measures about 4 metres by 1.5 metres (13 feet 4 in by 5 feet 2 in) but, allowing room for opening the doors, for movement around the car and for the fact that some cars are much bigger than average, it is usual to allow 5 metres by 2.5 metres (16 feet by 8 feet) that is about 12 square metres (128 square feet) as the space needed to accommodate each car.

The trouble is that this provision is required not just in one location but in several: at home; at the place of work; and at the town centre. In general the peak times of need in each location are about the same for all, or most of, the cars. There are, of course, other locations where space for cars is needed – the local centre, churches, cinemas, playing fields, leisure centres and so forth – but these are generally easier to cater for and can sometimes be combined with each other, or with town centre parking at off-peak times. Thus car parking comprises an important spatial commitment; additionally it poses a difficult aesthetic problem.

Garaging or parking the car at home

The scale of provision of garages in the residential areas was never very closely related to anticipated demand. Whereas most requirements connected with the transportation side of new town design were determined either by previous experience, or research, garage provision appears always to have been linked to the number of houses in a given layout and thence to the cost controls and yardsticks in vogue when the particular housing layout was designed. This was because garages, car ports and parking spaces were financed in the same way as the dwellings and attracted housing subsidy. The number of garages to be provided was not determined by the designers but laid down from time to time by the Ministry as a percentage of the number of dwellings on the site.

Accordingly, in the 1940s, garage provision was only 8 per cent, one garage to every twelve houses. With low car ownership and petrol strictly rationed this was fair enough. Today, with car ownership up to one car per household, the streets of those early housing schemes are lined with parked cars, nose to tail each night and the carefully landscaped areas are constantly at risk to 'fly-parking'. Aesthetically the carefully designed street scene has been ruined. Yet the average householder is not greatly worried; the private car is rated so high in his book that he accepts it without limitation as a part of the scenery. Having the car at his front door saves the walk to the garage – not to mention the expense of its rental.

Not until 1956 did the Ministry agree any increased provision, when corporations were authorised to build one garage to every eight houses and to leave space to build another one to eight houses later on.

Then, in the boom years of the 1960s, the scene changed. It became permissible at last to provide adequately for the dramatically increasing numbers of vehicles. So the Mark II towns were designed on more expansive lines. Take Washington as a typical example, the early housing layouts provided parking initially at the rate of 130 per cent, with space allocated for expansion to 200 per cent. About half of the initial provision was as garages or car ports, the rest as paved parking space.

When, in 1976, the government set out to make economies in housing construction costs, it seemed inevitable that parking provision would be cut back. New limits were set for local authority and new town housing and, quoting Washington again, the numbers of places were reduced to 80 per cent initial provision, with space available for increase to 100 per cent ultimate provision. The building of garages or car ports for rented houses was banned except for disabled people. Washington's car ownership figures at that time were about 56 per cent of families owning one car and 3 per cent owning more than one, so that, in theory, the provision seemed adequate. In practice it was not. For it was found that the more affluent tenants tended to live in the newer 'villages' so that high levels of car ownership were matched with low levels of car-standing provision; and, without any garages, the overspill parking that is often available on garage drives and forecourts was non-existent.

As with other transport-related provisions in the new towns, garaging and parking in residential areas seemed to swing from one extreme to the other, then back again.

Central area car parking

It is in the town centre, where land values are at their highest, that the car parking demand is most concentrated and it is there also that its environmental impact can be most damaging. For the truth is that, while an individual car may well be a thing of beauty, a triumph of ergonomic and appearance design as well as of mechanical engineering excellence, yet, where several hundreds of these paragons are herded together, cheek by jowl, the effect can be very disagreeable, unless attenuated by skilfully handled landscaping.

In a town centre surface car park, although the net size of a car space was the same, 12 square metres (128 square feet), allowance had also to be made for circulation lanes, and for such soft landscaping areas as the development corporation decided upon. Thus the actual area needed usually crept up to 20 to 25 square metres (about 240 square feet) for each car space, which allowed around 450 car spaces per hectare (180 per acre). Some designers took the view that, to achieve a satisfactory aesthetic result, no less than one half of the area should be given over to tree and shrub planting, screening, sound barriers and other landscaping features and, if the landscape architect had been given his head, the number of cars accommodated might have been further reduced; but in central areas, with land values at their highest, this treatment was seldom affordable. This was the dilemma.

In Hemel Hempstead, it would have been very easy to culvert the River Gade, turning over the whole area of 3.7 hectares (9 acres) west of the town centre to surface car park. Instead the development corporation laid out just about half the area as car park, approached from the town centre by footbridges across the delightful water gardens. This treatment provided spaces for 470 cars and, because more accommodation was needed, a multi-storey block for 270 cars, of unusual and pleasing design, was erected at the south end of the gardens. Not many development corporations felt able to handle town centre parking on such a generous scale. It is only fair to add that the remainder of the Hemel Hempstead town centre car parks, with about

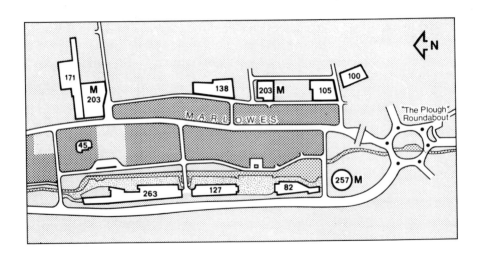

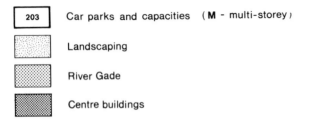

203	Car parks and capacities (**M** - multi-storey)
	Landscaping
	River Gade
	Centre buildings

Figure 13.1 Hemel Hempstead: town centre car parks

1,000 car spaces, on the east side of the centre, are run-of-the-mill surface or multi-storey car parks and, being rather nearer the shops, these are probably the ones that get filled up first; so much for the aesthetics of car parks. The location and capacities of the Hemel Hempstead town centre car parks are shown in Figure 13.1. No charge is made at any of these car parks.

The future car parking demand at Telford central area was estimated first of all on the assumptions previously used in studies for Dawley town centre. The master plan proposals also gave details of two other prediction methods which were used by the traffic consultants (Freeman, Fox and Associates). The results indicated that by 1991 some 8,000 car spaces would be needed, increasing to about 10,500 spaces by 2006. (Telford Development Corporation, 1969). If ground level parking only was intended, this meant that 50 to 60 acres (20 to 24 hectares) would eventually be required for car parks. These very large numbers were in keeping with the bullish spirit in which Mark II and Mark III development proposals were framed. In 1983 the factual situation concerning central area car parking at Telford was:

shopping	3,116 spaces
offices	464
overspill area	350
total	3,930 spaces

The location and capacities of the car parks are shown in Figure 13.2. All existing car parking is at surface level and the current policy is to continue in this way; there are several further sites available but it may be that multi-deck parking will have to be considered at some stage.

Landscaping treatment in Telford's first constructed car parks was fairly minimal, probably occupying only about 10 per cent of the area; but the more recently constructed car parks have been more heavily planted – nearly 30 per cent of the area being devoted to soft landscaping. Electronic equipment has been installed at the four main car parks to enable parking demand to be monitored and to motivate fibre optic signs indicating when car parks are full. No charge is made for car parking in the town centre, and this seems likely to remain the development corporation's policy into the foreseeable future.

The chief engineer's 1982 update of car parking requirements at Telford is given in Table 13.1. The total figures are not related to any specific year but rather to the eventual ultimate capacity for development in the central area.

Table 13.1
Telford: central area: 1982 update
of peak car parking demand

Purpose	Predicted peak demand			
	Low		High	
	Fri.	Sat.	Fri.	Sat.
Shop	3,809	4,761	4,156	5,194
Office	2,534	281	2,798	292
Leisure	755	880	755	880
Other	380	255	380	255
Total	7,478	6,177	8,088	6,621
Source: Report by Telford Development Corporation Chief Engineer 1982.				

Not all of the development corporations elected to risk their necks at the master plan stage as Telford did by publishing their estimated

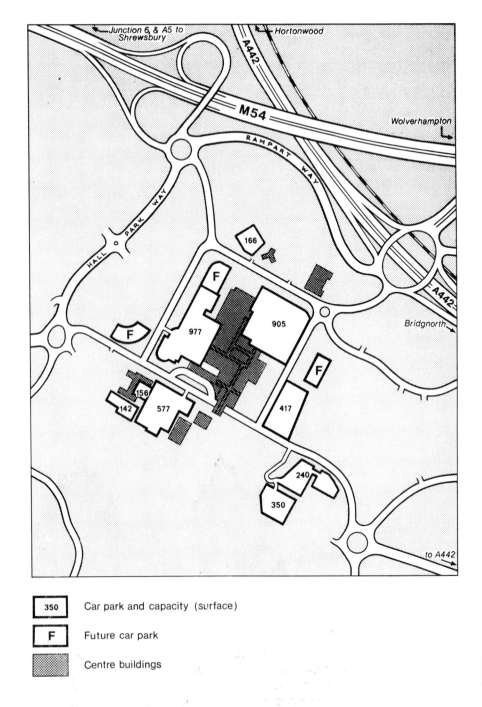

Figure 13.2 Telford: town centre car parks

198

central area car park requirements. The Warrington outline plan merely stated:

> If all the requirements were to be accommodated in surface parking areas the spaces would occupy an area larger than the Commercial Core itself and would displace many of the facilities that they were intended to serve: their very size would prevent convenient access to the remaining facilities and would seriously impede the efficient functioning of the Centre. On economic and operational grounds the required spaces must therefore be accommodated in multi-storey car parks.

> (Warrington Development Corporation, 1972).

Multi-storey car parks have become necessary in many of the Mark I town central areas, for example in Welwyn, Hemel Hempstead and Harlow, simply to keep pace with current needs, while some of the Mark II and Mark III centres, those at Redditch, Warrington and Peterborough for instance, were designed on the basis that most of the parking provision would need to be in multi-storey blocks.

As new town design has in general encouraged the use of the private car for the journey to work by providing ample free parking in the industrial areas, it was natural perhaps that office worker and shop assistant car owners should look for equal facilities in the town centre. This was a more difficult matter. In the early years of the Mark I towns, there was plenty of room for everybody, but, as each town progressed, pressures on the available parking space increased and so did land values; car parking charges were introduced in some of the towns and central area workers were obliged to rely more and more on public transport. The master plan for Peterborough faced the situation squarely:

> Every white-collar worker who pre-empts a city-centre parking space from nine to five because his car is his only acceptable means of getting to and from the office will be depriving these businesses of potential sales to 'out of town' customers, for most of whom the alternative to parking in the city centre will not be to use public transport but to take their custom elsewhere.

> (Peterborough Development Corporation, n.d.)

The Runcorn master plan, Busway-conscious as always, reckoned that some 3,100 car spaces in the town centre would be adequate, based on an overall 50-50 modal split between those arriving by car and those coming in by bus. (Runcorn Development Corporation, 1967).

In some of the towns there was a conscious effort to 'populate' the central area, so as to encourage it to stay alive in the evenings and at weekends, residents did not generally find it satisfactory to rely on a public car park which might be full when they needed it. The Skelmersdale master plan proposals gave full recognition to this with an estimated requirement of some 4,000 garages or parking spaces for residents living within the centre and their visitors; however, owing to design changes within the town centre this scheme was not carried out.

The Redditch master plan gave forecasts of town centre parking needs for design years 1980 and 2010 as detailed in Table 13.2. Clearly the planning proposals forecasts were too high – owing to over-estimating future traffic levels, in the prevailing style of the 1960s, and over-estimating the office and business needs of the town. By 1983 some 3,000 car parking spaces had been provided and the likely total future requirement was seen as 5,000 spaces. These figures did not cater for residents living within the centre for whom there were separate parking areas, nor for commercial vehicles for which an area had been set aside. Parking for shoppers was mainly in four multi-storey car parks where the level of charges for all-day parking was high enough to discourage their use by town centre workers. A fifth multi-storey block caters for the long-stay parker.

Table 13.2
Redditch: planning proposals (1966):
forecast of parking in the town centre (Friday afternoon)

	1980	2010
Employees' parking	2,710	3,280
Shopper parking	2,232	3,500
Residents' parking	680	880
Visitors' parking	340	440
Commercial vehicle parking	824	1,072
'Recreational' parking	1,610	3,360
College parking (students)	40	100
	8,436	12,632

Source: Hugh Wilson and Lewis Womersley; (Redditch plan-ing proposals, Redditch development corporation, 1966).

The most convenient and comprehensive parking arrangements of all are probably those at central Milton Keynes. Using the great planning advantage of a vast, level virgin site, the extensive linear buildings containing the shopping malls were provided with surface car parks immediately adjacent and running parallel for their whole length. The car parks were laid out to a very generous module, with larger than normal car spaces, clearly marked, and with wide aisles –

27. Stevenage town centre: a multi-storey car park.

all making for very easy manoeuvring. The high quality materials used, such as granite kerbs and block paving, were chosen for an attractive environment and easy maintenance. These linear car parks were designed to lie in a slight declivity, so the parked cars are little seen, except perhaps from the tops of the double deck buses waiting at the stops on the grid road close at hand. As always in Milton Keynes, a prodigious tree-planting programme was carried out and the screen will become increasingly effective as the years go by. Some 8,000 parking spaces have been provided and further provision when required will present no problem. At the present time all car parking is free.

Reference has been made to the difficulty of screening from view the large open car parks in town centres. Yet the alternative in the form of multi-storey car parks can also be visually unattractive. New town architects and engineers have endeavoured, and not without some success, to produce pleasing designs. The ingenious example, built quite early on in Hemel Hempstead, has already been mentioned.

There are numerous more recent and far larger examples of well designed multi-storey car parks; four blocks at Redditch built in the 1970s have a total capacity of 2,600 cars; they are well sited and of pleasing elevation. There are good examples also at Northampton, Peterborough, Harlow and in many of the other towns. Yet not much can be done to improve the inside of multi-storey car parks, whether in new towns or anywhere else. Many people find them tedious when driving in and out; gloomy and unattractive when the car has been parked. Perhaps the Milton Keynes designers should be congratulated on their solution and on their good fortune in having the conditions which made it possible.

Car parking in the industrial areas

Having established the increasing extent to which private cars have come to be used for the journey to work, it is now necessary to examine the nature of the parking demand this has caused at every industrial area.

The larger industrial companies were generally reckoned to be self-supporting in respect of parking accommodation and were encouraged by the development corporations to provide surface parking within their curtilage on a scale that was expected to be adequate although, particularly in the case of the Mark I towns, this has sometimes not worked out and resort to multi-storey parking has been necessary. At Redditch the corporation's current *Development Brief for Industry,* (Redditch Development Corporation, 1979), requires the developer to provide car parking within the site to the schedule at Table 13.3.

Table 13.3
Redditch: general development brief for
industry: car parking provision

Offices	1 space per 30 m^2 of office floor area
Production and storage areas	
Up to 99 m^2	1 space per 30 m^2 of floor area
100 to 999 m^2	1 space per 60 m^2 of floor area
1000+ m^2	1 space per 90 m^2 of floor area

These requirements are typical of those laid down in most of the towns – Washington, for instance, required one car space per 45 square metres of factory floor space. The smaller companies, in particular those occupying unit factories, have not in general provided for worker parking, mostly relying on communal car parks provided by the development corporations.

At Runcorn the provision of car parks within the factory sites was discouraged, the development corporation themselves providing public car parks for everybody. This was not of course the munificent gesture it might have seemed, for development corporations' estates

202

Plate 13 Townscape

(a) Tree and shrub planting on a primary distributor at Washington.

(b) A well landscaped road at Skelmersdale.

(c) Beautifying the Busway at Runcorn.

(d) Skelmersdale: road bridge and footbridge across the River Tawd.

(e) Shrubs and hard landscaping in a Washington residential area.

(f) Established planting at Runcorn.

(g) Washington: man-made lake alongside the River

Plate 14 Townscape: road bridges

(a) Runcorn: a district road passing over the Ex-
    ...sway.

(b) ...l bridge over British Rail main line at
    ...rington.

(c) ...ln...dale: bridge carrying primary road over
    ...tric...ad.

(d) ...thampton: viaduct carrying primary road
    ...British Rail main line.

a

b

Plate 15 Townscape: footbridges and underpasses

(a) A footbridge at Warrington and . . .

(b) . . . a Skelmersdale design.

(c) Another footbridge at Skelmersdale.

(d) Northampton: footbridge across the River Nene.

(e) Telford: a cable-stayed footbridge leading directly to the town centre.

(f) Colourful retaining wall at Telford.

(g) Underpass at Skelmersdale.

(h) Milton Keynes: Redways underpassing a grid road.

c

d

f

Plate 16 Some other features of townscape

(a) Architect's anathema?

(b) and (c) Lighting units: some Milton Keynes designs.

(d) High mast lighting at Warrington.

(e) Skelmersdale: night scene.

(f) Stevenage: street name plate.

(g) A water feature at Milton Keynes.

(h) Hemel Hempstead: water gardens.

(i) 'Mother and Child' at Stevenage.

officers always took this sort of situation into account when negotiating industrial rents or purchase prices. Ever mindful of the interests of the Runcorn Busway, the idea was to ensure that people arriving by bus had no greater distance to walk from the bus stop than those who travelled by car.

In some of the towns the location of car parks within the industrial areas and the starting and stopping times of work in the factories were factors that had to be carefully considered, to try to avoid congestion and its attendant frustrations when too concentrated a movement took place over too short a period.

Accommodating workers' cars was not the only parking requirement in an industrial area; provision had also to be made for goods delivery vehicles. The permitted weight of laden vehicles has been raised progressively over the years and, following the Armitage Report[1] to the Secretary of State for Transport in 1982, a Ministry of Transport White Paper[2] increased the maximum permitted gross weight of a heavy goods vehicle and its load to 40 tonnes (39.4 tons) on five axles – a large increase on the gross weight of the largest lorries that were around in 1945. Car parking areas have been provided for

28. *Factory car park at Bracknell.*

these large and heavy vehicles and, as with the industrial roads and distributor town roads, the geometry and specificaton of the car parks has had to be adapted to suit.

Although a less sensitive issue than in town centres, car parking in the industrial estates presented a considerable environmental problem; comparable standards of screening and landscaping were adopted in most of the towns.

The years of recession in the early 1980s have naturally caused a lull in the rate of increase of cars used for the journey to work, due to reduced work forces and generally lowered prosperity. Some people have tended to change to other forms of transport – to catch the bus, to buy a bicycle or to walk to work, and most of all to share their car journey with other drivers. This has given a respite to some industrial estates where car parking demand was becoming a pressing problem; but, given any reasonable and sustained economic recovery, there is little doubt but that the upward trend will quickly be resumed.

Notes

1　An inquiry into freight transport matters, chaired by Sir William Armitage, reported to the Minister of Transport in 1980.
2　'Lorries, People and the Environment' Ministry of Transport, 1981, Cmnd 8439, HMSO.

14 Townscape

Until comparatively recent years, 'landscaping' was thought of mainly in connection with Britain's stately homes or the Royal parks where large-scale earthmoving and planting had been undertaken to achieve the beautifully contoured parks, lakes and tree-lined avenues that give so much pleasure to visitors today. In the private development and council estate roads of the 1920s and 1930s there was seldom more than a nod in the direction of landscaping – the planting of a tree (probably flowering cherry or something of the kind) just behind the kerb line every 30 m (100 feet) or so. These estates would have seemed like a treeless desert but for enthusiastic effort on the part of their inhabitants in individual gardens. In only a few developments, such as the Garden Cities, was any real attempt made to beautify the roads themselves by extensive planting of trees and shrubs. Postwar the situation has been quite different – at least in the new towns; if the motor car was seeking to dominate the towns with a vast infrastructure of roads, interchanges and car parks, quite evidently landscaping was the best hope of containing the onslaught.

Compared with the problems in existing towns and cities the designers of the new towns were at a great advantage. Hugh Wilson looked forward with confidence to the challenge:

> The landscape or townscape in the town must receive special care, not as something added to a building layout but as an integral part of the total design. It is not just a matter of planting but of the

comprehensive approach to the relationship of surfaces and elements – pavings and steps, walls and fences, garages and transformer stations, car parks and playgrounds, street lighting, telephone boxes, seats, all the impedimenta of town life.

(Skelmersdale Development Corporation, 1964).

On the other hand Lord Esher referring to Milton Keynes pointed out:

The fact is that the roads dwarf the city, as the car does the house, for perfectly respectable reasons. The sort of buildings that would have put such roads in their place would have been the sort that none or few would have chosen to live in. The policy of putting known contemporary desires ahead of architectural preconceptions and protecting people from traffic noise produces Milton Keynes as naturally as Victorian society produced Kensington and Camden Town. If the private car disappears the way the servants did, similar adaptation to the unpredictable will have to be made.

(Esher, 1981)

Rather than thinking of 'landscaping' the roads or the pedestrian ways as an independent function, the principle in new towns has been to design in terms of 'townscape' – the overall visual appearance of the town. This term is particularly apt as it neatly covers its three complementary but interdependent elements:

- earthmoving – as required for 'ground sculpture';
- planting of trees and shrubs; conservation of existing growth; also 'hard landscaping' – the provision of pavings, walls, flower boxes and the like; and
- the built environment.

Earthworks

As a by-product of the large-scale earthmoving needed for roadworks and building operations in the New Towns, there were sometimes opportunities to carry out imaginative or profitable schemes, such as:

- improvement of the landform;
- extraction of sand and gravel for incorporation in the works;
- extraction of coal for sale to the National Coal Board;
- creation of water features; and
- reclamation of derelict areas.

While some towns started with a reclamation problem, the lucky ones had a built-in advantage, such as sand and gravel deposits within the designated area which could be exploited with economic benefit. At

206

Welwyn, gravel had already been extracted and the resulting pit was turned into a first-class stadium; former clay workings at Cwmbran had also left a hole in which a sports stadium for that town was built.

Large-scale earthmoving was involved for road cuttings, especially at the large and numerous grade-separated interchanges of the Mark II towns. It has been facilitated by the remarkable change in the size and sophistication of earthmoving plant which has taken place over the forty years overall construction period of the new towns. Excavated material was, when suitable, incorporated as fill material to form the embankments. If unsuitable, it was available for disposal in other ways. One obvious use was to construct earth bunds as sound barriers between main traffic routes and the residential areas but, in the early years, no one foresaw the necessity for these so no space was provided for the bunds and the surplus spoil was taken to a tip and thrown away.

To avoid this wasteful procedure, in the northern part of Basildon, for example, where the generally flat terrain, heavy clay sub-soil and lack of water tended towards a featureless landscape, surplus clay was put to good use forming artificial hills, screening from view the sewage works and certain industrial developments, while in the town park another hill 12 m (40 feet) or so high was formed – almost alpine by contrast with the generally flat terrain. Close by, in this parkland setting, the surface water drainage design for the town decreed that a washland area was needed to balance the flow of surface water passing through existing culverts under the A127 (Southend Arterial Road) and thence to a watercourse of modest size. By lowering the ground level of the washland area slightly a permanent lake was formed, a rare and pleasant feature in 'waterless' Essex and a great attraction for model sailing enthusiasts and juvenile anglers.

On a much bigger scale, three large lakes totalling 53 hectares (130 acres) form the graceful centrepiece of Nene Park, Peterborough. These resulted from the extraction of gravel used in the building of the town. Fed by the river Nene, they are linked together and perform an important function balancing the flow in the river and the rainfall run-off from the new developments, as well as providing incomparable facilities for sailing, windsurfing and boating. The gravel extraction was done by private enterprise and, under the arrangements for reinstatement, this fine water feature was secured at relatively little cost to the development corporation.

Special problems arose in designated areas where mining operations had taken place. For example, at Skelmersdale, on the edge of the South Lancashire coalfield, the mines had already been worked and, because of the risk of subsidence and the presence of mines special precautions had to be taken in designing the foundatio buildings and infrastructure. Peterlee on the Durham coalfi serious subsidence problems, the precautions taken in some cases proved inadequate and remedial work has been necessary to a number of buildings. Corby was on the Northamptonshire ironfields and at Telford there was a quite remarkable history of mineral extraction which left a legacy of dereliction and ugliness in the Shropshire countryside.

Coalbrookdale colliery within the designated area of Telford was one of the oldest in the country. The environmental effect of mining in this area 'cradle of the industrial revolution' (as on hundreds of other areas) was disastrous. Some 2,000 hectares (5,000 acres) within the designated area consisted of derelict land, most of it comprising deposits of spoil and waste from coal and ironstone workings. There were thousands of old mineshafts, some shallow and others as much as 400 m (1,300 feet) deep and adits driven horizontally into the hillsides to intercept the coal seams. As each mine had been exhausted, the shafts and adits had been abandoned and the activity moved on to the next area. Not until 1872 was there any legal obligation on a mine owner to record the location and details of the shafts at his mine nor, until 1911, was he required to take any precautions or safety measures when a mine was abandoned. So the vast majority of the early mineworkings were uncharted and there were no records of the shafts and adits from which they were worked. Moreover, few of the thousands of shafts in the area had been given any form of safety treatment at the time of their abandonment. Such was the inhospitable environment confronting the Telford engineers and planners.

At the time the area was designated, there was still a certain amount of mining activity by the National Coal Board – extracting coal by the opencast method. The development corporation set up meetings with the Board to phase the work into their construction programme and ensure that areas disturbed by the Board would be fully restored and landscaped.

Over the years natural vegetation had become established on the waste tips and efforts were made to retain the best of such areas, incorporating them into landscape schemes; but where waste tips stood on land needed for roads and bridges, or for buildings, extensive works were necessary before construction could begin, to remove debris and unsuitable or contaminated fill material, and to remodel the ground to fresh contours. The old mineshafts were generally grouted with pulverised fuel ash and capped at rock level. It was a long and painstaking task.

Basildon was another designated area that had to be 'cleaned up' in a rather different way. The majority of the small shacks, railway cars and so forth, in which people lived or kept for occasional use, had to be acquired and demolished before construction could go ahead. Acquisition was in some cases a sensitive task, as always when dealing with people's homes.

Trees and shrubs and hard landscaping

It is impracticable to think of landscaping only in terms of roads, footpaths, and cycle tracks. The planting of trees and shrubs was required not only for beautification of the new roads and for screening purposes, but also for the embellishment of the whole urban scene; trees can be seen from a considerable distance, and it is the total effect that matters.

Nearly all development corporations appointed a consultant landscape architect to confirm and augment the advice of their own staff. This advice sometimes ran counter to the most cherished principles of highway engineering – traffic routes, for example, could never be allowed to follow a circuitous course around existing trees. The landscape architect's ideal that, on clay sub-soil, no road or structure may trespass upon the ground beneath the spread (or likely future spread) of a tree was impossible to apply on a housing site at a density of thirty dwellings to the hectare (12 to the acre). Nor could planting (other than low shrubs) be permitted within the prescribed sight lines at road junctions. Nevertheless any differences of opinion on such matters were resolved through inter-disciplinary discussion and compromise and, as far as is known, no blood was spilled.

Most primary roads followed completely new routes, but, in cases where they followed existing roads, great care had to be taken to preserve as far as possible the roadside trees and hedges. (Some new town designated areas were well endowed with existing trees; Crawley, Harlow and Bracknell amongst others were exceptionally fortunate in this respect.) Sometimes when it was possible to utilise the old road to serve as one carriageway of a dual-carriageway distributor, trees and hedgerows on one side were retained in the central reservation and on the other side a footway was constructed behind the hedge. This treatment was not always possible, since alignment, width and gradient of the old road were so often sub-standard and had to be improved, so occasionally trees or hedges were sacrificed. However this only happened after hard-headed thought and discussion with the landscape architect and it seems unlikely that even one established tree was felled in a new town unless absolutely necess~~e Many of the smaller old country lanes have survived inta out independent walkways and cycleways. 1afts,

In preparing a tree planting scheme the caprices of the ons of climate had to be taken into account. The basic aim was vis eld had than botanical and the general rule seems to have been to 'play safe' by using indigenous species almost exclusively; this tended to give a high success rate and a happier integration with the existing growth. At Cumbernauld, and similarly in most of the other towns, the development corporation found it worthwhile to set up its own tree nursery as more than a million plantings were required there. At Redditch more than three million trees and shrubs are said to have been used and even higher figures are quoted in some of the towns. Indeed at Milton Keynes it was claimed, with characteristic aplomb, that, up to the end of 1983, 7,553,143 trees and shrubs had been planted.

It was always recognised that the speed and density of traffic on the distributor roads was out of sympathy with the domestic scale of the residential areas; so special attention was given to the planting of trees and shrubs alongside these roads with the two objectives of providing visual and other benefits for the driver and his passengers and of insulating the residential areas and other amenities from the fast traffic – from its sight, sound, smell and hazards. One town in which this has been noticeably effective is Cumbernauld. Now that the trees and shrubs have reached maturity it is rightly said that 'the town has turned its back upon the roads'. This is but one example; the principle applies in all the towns.

If the primary roads were concealed from the environmental areas, they remained in full view of the motorist and his passengers. The buses also used the primary roads in many towns and the bus passenger had more opportunity to cast a critical eye upon the passing scene even than the driver or passenger in the faster moving private car. The Mark I towns had ample grass verges without much planting and generally with large roundabouts at the principal junctions; some of the roundabouts had pedestrian subways and there was scope for 'land sculpture' and planting. At Basildon for example, where the landscaping of Roundacre was carried out with the advice of Sylvia Crowe[1] bright mosaic fascias were provided at the subway entrances to make the pedestrian route across this busy junction more attractive. The River Gade flows through the island of The Plough roundabout at Hemel Hempstead at the downstream end of the town's water gardens.

Collaboration of landscape architects with the engineers has produced some of the finest new urban road prospects in Britain; take Queensway, the 8 km (5 mile) length of the A442 in Telford. This dual two-lane expressway, with numerous grade-separated junctions, is generously and most effectively planted throughout its whole length; or the 48 km (30 miles) of wide and impressive new parkways at Peterborough, of which some 35 km (22 miles) had been constructed by the end of 1983. Nearly all the primary roads constructed in the

1960s and early 1970s, and notably the urban expressways of the Mark IIs, had grade separation at the principal junctions, presenting a considerable challenge to the engineer and landscape architect. The cutting slopes were generally planted with gorse, or whatever seemed an easy indigenous species, rather than being left as grass, which would have involved heavy maintenance on such large slopes. An example from amongst countless numbers is the large Hollinswood interchange on the A442 at Telford.

Most of the main roads in the earlier towns have now been handed over to the highway authority – normally the county council – together with responsibility for the upkeep of all landscaped areas within the highway boundaries.

In the earlier Radburn schemes, the houses had fronted on to extensive open lawns, beautifully maintained in the earlier years by the development corporations' estates departments. However, in the harsher economic climate of more recent years, this treatment was difficult to sustain. To save money the maintenance of grassed areas became more relaxed with fewer grass cuttings in the year, which did however give a visual bonus – wild flowers reappearing by natural propagation augmented by new sowing and planting. When, on the demise of a development corporation, the local authority took over the housing, it generally also took over the landscape maintenance team and was in fact the agent for the New Towns Commission in maintaining those landscaped areas for which the Commission was still responsible.

In the Radburn layout planting and hard landscaping was of great importance so that the pedestrian route to the primary school, the local shopping centre and the nearest industrial area was seen to be direct and attractive to users. The trouble with the higher densities was that too much of the site had to be given over to the motor car; there was no hope of providing the generous landscaped areas that were a feature of the original Radburn concept.

When the 'shared access' layout in residential areas was adopted in the wake of The Brow at Runcorn, the nature and function of the landscaping had to be re-assessed. Design of the paving of the culs-de-sac and footpaths was crucial. Vehicles had only to be able to move at very low speeds and this was to be achieved, not with traffic signs and road paint, but by the subtle regulation of 'way' width and alignment and paving types and by judicious planting of shrubs. The driver had to be convinced that this was pedestrian territory and that he might only creep in a-tiptoe. The narrow, winding car route may have been mainly of tarmacadam or concrete, but there were no kerbs; other paving forms such as granite setts, paving bricks or concrete blocks, shallow steps, rockeries and shrubberies were carefully integrated to give the impression of being in a private curtilage. It was a remarkable change of concept.

The design of children's play areas has been progressively developed, with emphasis on vandal-resistant equipment. However, vandalism has not been particularly serious in the New Towns – less it seems than elsewhere – an important consideration where so much careful and costly planting of trees and shrubs has been carried out. The pride and satisfaction that residents feel in their houses and their town seems to be shared also by many of their children.

Landscaping the town centres with trees and shrubs was initially given low priority, and some of the Mark I town centres looked bare and treeless at the start before the new planting was significantly established. The practice of transplanting mature trees was introduced in the 1950s and some development corporations, Basildon for one, were among the early developers to try out the process. Twenty-five years later in the sophisticated covered and heated shopping centres, tropical planting was introduced, such as the fine show of full-sized date palms in the Kingfisher shopping centre at Redditch.

It was in the town centres, notably the open pedestrian ways of the Mark I towns, that ideas for hard landscaping were most fully developed. Precast slabs for paving these walkways were available in a variety of sizes, shapes and colours, but most towns enhanced the scene further by judicious use of natural stone slabs, paving bricks, cobbles or granite setts. Concrete block paving, introduced in the 1960s, provided another variant; obtainable in various shapes and colours, the blocks made a neat clean-looking pavement which was found to be relatively inexpensive and served not only for footways but, with a stronger base, for car parks and carriageways as well. Great care was lavished on the design of such other 'hard' features as walls – whether retaining, boundary or just ornamental – and on items of outdoor 'furniture' such as seats, flower pots, litter bins, bus shelters and so forth.

It seemed that every town centre had to have its water feature; normally in the main square and in the style of a pool with perhaps a piece of sculpture. Some towns, Harlow for one, managed something a little less formal and more extensive. One of the most attractive is at Hemel Hempstead where an area of 2 hectares (5 acres) or so on the west side of the town centre was beautifully laid out as water gardens. The River Gade had meandered 'naturally but somewhat forlornly' through this space and the design by G. A. Jellicoe[2] allowed, by excavation and the forming of two weirs, an enormous increase in the width and significance of the river. Spoil arising from the excavation was used to form banks screening the car parks from view. 'Everyone' wrote Jellicoe in 1957 in an emotive report to the Development

Corporation, 'is drawn to water, whether for contemplation or exhilaration, and here is an asset enjoyed by few other towns.'

Hemel Hempstead Development Corporation wisely accepted this advice and these well-tended gardens with their mature trees and shrubs now form the visual link between the town centre and the hillside to the west with the car parks and busy Leighton Buzzard road concealed from view. Dominating the whole scene is the water with its charming bridges, fountains, islands and waterfowl. At the southern end, between the two weirs, the river widens to form an extensive lake where can be seen Hubert Yencesse's sensitive sculpture 'Rock 'n' Roll', reminder of the swinging sixties, a boy and a girl dancing on the water.

Landscaping of surface car parks was a difficult task and the larger the car park the greater the problem – not of course a technical problem but a spatial one. The suggestion sometimes made that half the car park site should be devoted to landscaping is rarely achieved, although this is what was done at Hemel Hempstead. The alternative solution was to tuck the cars away in multi-storey parks as was done at Redditch (and is happening to some extent in most of the towns) or underneath the shops as at Cumbernauld and Runcorn.

The built environment

The third important component of townscape was of course the buildings themselves in their relationship to the roads, footpaths and cycleways. On this wide subject discussion will be confined here to those structures that are transport related, such as bridges, subways and multi-storey car parks and to items of street equipment, such as traffic signs and street lights.

Overbridges and underbridges are of equal importance in the townscape; both must be aesthetically satisfactory when motoring or walking and, most important of all, when viewed from a distance. In the early years of the Mark I towns the opportunity to build bridges seemed as remote to development corporation engineers as did the building of multi-storey flats to the architects. Only when a new road under the railway was needed in a hurry, and the railway engineers were unable to take on the design work or where a new road crossed a major watercourse, did the opportunity arise. By the 1960s the rules of the game had changed: grade separation at the intersection of primary roads was the norm, and bridgebuilding programmes, which collectively were the equivalent of those in a major motorway project, were put in hand.

Now in new towns there seem to be examples of just about every

29. *Viaducts carry the diverted A13 road at Basildon.*

30. *Primary distributor bridge spanning the River Wear at Washington.*

214

type of bridge construction, with prestressed concrete designs predominating. In general they are clean, unfussy, contemporary structures doing the job quietly and efficiently. New town houses may run the whole gamut from the brutalist to the bizarre, from the formal to the folksy, but the bridges are reassuringly normal. They were mostly designed in the chief engineers' departments of the respective development corporations and only occasionally has the designer produced something especially striking, such as, for example, the eyecatching footbridges at Telford, Basildon and Skelmersdale.

A notable design in structural steel is the Almond bridge at Livingston,[3] which carries Livingston Road, the north-south primary distributor road, across the valley of the river Almond. It is a structure of ten continuous 30 m (100 feet) spans of width varying between 30 m (100 feet) and 35 m (114 feet) to accommodate the dual three-lane urban motorway and slip roads at a height of 18 m (60 feet) above the river. The deck is composite of welded plate girders and reinforced concrete slab. The design concept was translated into practice by the use of structural steel to limit the weight of the large movable elements

31. *Footbridge in East Kilbride which won a Civic Trust commendation award.*

215

which constitute the intermediate supports; the deck system had to be immediately self-supporting on erection and be capable of stabilising the portals.

One of the Structural Steel Design Awards for 1972 was given for Almond bridge. The judging panel, consisting of well-known members of the professions made these comments on the design:

> A pleasing unobtrusive over-bridge of simple lines – one of the essential requirements of a modern motorway complex. The apparent simplicity belies the thought given to the basic requirements of standardisation, site conditions, erection economy and ease of maintenance, all of which are so essential in a bridge of this length.
>
> (from the report by the Constrado panel of judges)

Pedestrian subways are inclined to be unattractive, forbidding features, liable to be potential danger spots where loiterers might lurk. Consequently in the new towns special care was taken in their design. The aim was to make them look inviting and safe with the access as wide as possible and straight approach ramps at an easy gradient. Thus enabling people approaching to see right through the tunnel while still a fair way off. Decorative treatment of the wing walls was often undertaken and surfaces made as resistant as possible to defacement by graffiti.

The solution adopted for a standard subway by the Redditch Development Corporation met all these considerations. Their chief engineer rejected the idea of an *in situ* concrete box structure in favour of a 'mini bridge', to provide an underpass which was light and airy, and gave good visibility through to the approach ramp beyond. The structure was simple, reducing the amount of specialist design and specialist labour to a minimum. A simple computer programme supplied finished levels and dimensions for all stages of construction upon the insertion of the finished carriageway level and width. The only fair face concrete occurred at the edge beams as brickwork was used extensively within and outside the subway. The lamp fittings were inset within the ceiling and well protected. There was no mousehole effect about the Redditch subways. The pathway through was 3 m (10 feet) wide increasing to 7 m (23 feet) at ceiling level and the headroom was 2.5 m (8' 2"). Fifty of the standard subways have been built in Redditch and the chief engineer considers them cheap and easy to construct, attractive and virtually maintenance free.

In new towns there was seldom need for retained cuttings or retained embankments, such as are so often featured where an urban motorway is constructed through an established town. This was because sufficient land was normally available for adequate side slopes

– with consequent saving in cost and more pleasing visual effect. At Telford there is a reinforced concrete wall 330 m (1082 feet) long and 10.4 m (34 feet) at the highest point retaining the bank on the east side of the expressway. Its appearance has been greatly enlivened by tile facing in strong colours to a design which portrays the varied and much-faulted geological strata of the area.

Multi-storey car parks are seldom (if ever) intrinsically beautiful, but care has generally been taken in the new towns to blend their design with that of other central area buildings, and to soften their stark outlines with appropriate planting. Take Redditch, for example. The multi-storey car parks sit happily in the ambience of the town centre, helped by skilful landscaping. Garages and petrol stations are notoriously garish and untidy, but discussions which took place with the petroleum companies seem in many cases to have achieved quieter designs in new towns and to have restrained the advertising excesses.

A subject which in the early years, led to controversy between new town architects and engineers was a simple one – the humble lamp post; indeed the discussions seemed to generate a great deal more heat than light. The debate was clear cut; the engineers were trying to achieve efficient night-time illumination for the town; the architects objected to the daytime appearance of the 'forest of poles' supporting the light sources and they disliked most of the contemporary lantern designs as well. Every view of their houses and other cherished designs appeared chopped into vertical slices by these monsters; half a dozen or so dominated every street scene. Other people have a knack of cutting out unwanted detail in the visual image (from your seat in the dress circle you hardly notice that the heads of people in front cut out small corners of the stage). Not so the architects, apparently; and their views gained support from the vitriolic protests of Ian Nairn in his *Architectural Review* articles entitled 'Outrage'.

Just about every possible lamp post design was tried out in new towns: concrete columns, steel columns, glass reinforced plastic, even a wooden column; tungsten lighting, mercury vapour, sodium discharge and fluorescent lanterns. They tried placing the columns back in the hedgerow instead of on the kerbline and fixing lanterns to the buildings instead of columns. It lowered the lighting efficiency a little, but it also lowered the inter-departmental temperature. Manufacturers too were very willing to co-operate, and some development corporations designed their own lighting units. Ironically, the most generally liked lighting columns, used in the culs-de-sac of one new town, were some obsolete gas lamps bought second-hand from the Gas Board and wired up for tungsten lighting. The illumination was terrible, but the peace was wonderful. *Vivat Victoriana.*

Yet it would have been wrong to dismiss the objections as

architectural whimsy. There was a genuine problem and it received official recognition when CP 1004, *Code of practice for road lighting,* was published. (HMSO, 1974). This did not insist upon rigid interpretaton but, subject to compliance with safety standards, allowed scope for individual design. In some development corporations, architects and engineers were able to introduce and develop their ideas in collaboration with the manufacturers of columns, brackets and lanterns, and with the agreement of their respective lighting authorities.

The need for good lighting increased with greater traffic weight and higher speeds on the main traffic roads, and with the advancing trend of lawlessness in residential areas. As the years went by the efficiency of street lighting improved. Lighting installed on primary distributors during the 1970s was to the latest Group A standards and high mast lighting was often installed at the interchanges. Interesting designs were developed for some central areas and simple domestic scale units for the residential areas. At Milton Keynes, for example, the designers decided upon square, rather than round, section columns and upon white, rather than yellow, light in central Milton Keynes and in most of the residential areas. Some details of the Milton Keynes provisions are scheduled in Table 14.1 and similar details of Peterborough's street lighting provision are given in Table 14.2.

Table 14.1
Milton Keynes: lighting details

Location	Column	Light source	Average spacing
Grid road	10 m	135W sox	38 m
Secondary distributor	5 m	80W MBF/U or 35W sox	30 m
Central Milton Keynes			
Boulevards	6 m	150W SON	22 m
Amenity	4 m	80W MBF/U	16 m
Industrial roads	8 m	90W sox	36 m
Residential areas	5 m	80W MBF/U	
and		or 35W sox	30 m
Redways		ditto	50 m
Source: Milton Keynes Development Corporation			

The appearance of traffic signs in the urban environment also gives displeasure to many. The rules are all laid down in the *Traffic Signs Manual* (Ministry of Transport, 1965) which details the informatory signs, mandatory signs, directional signs and so on. Size, shape and colours are all spelled out, symbols and lettering are detailed and instructions given about the siting of the signs. There is not much

Table 14.2
Peterborough: lighting details

Location	Column	Light source	Light output
Parkway (motorway standard)	12 m	135W sox	20,000 lumens
Primary distributor	10 m	135W sox	12,000 lumens
City centre	5 m	70W SON	6,000 lumens
Residential areas	5 m	35W sox	2,000 lumens
Footpaths and cycleways	5 m	35W sox	2,000 lumens
Source: Peterborough Development Corporation			

flexibility, and highway engineers tend to interpret the instructions very rigidly. In the new towns the worst excesses have generally been avoided. Yet direction signing could perhaps have been done better. In some of the towns it has become far too parochial. There's plenty of information about the whereabouts of neighbourhoods or districts, but too little help for the visiting stranger who wants to make for another town or village – or even those who just want to get out of the new town.

The engineers at Warrington came up with some improved designs for the signs themselves and for their illumination. They first identified a number of shortcomings on traditional assemblies, such as:

● unsightly root boxes, often with flimsy doors;
● rotation and misalignment of lanterns;
● plates of varying lengths; and
● proliferation of plates, conduit, brackets, and so on, which often varied on different signs at the same junction.

The Warrington improved standard design featured rectangular section hollow steel posts, plastic coated, with the sign board housed at either end in slots in the posts, and secured by bolts hidden inside the posts. The lighting units were designed in the form of trays, secured to a rectangular horizontal frame, also of rectangular section. The terminal block and fuse unit were contained in one of the posts, behind a flush door. The signs complied with the Highway Authority's requirements and they have been described as 'extremely well-mannered'. Adaptation to every situation has been achieved by careful design, and the construction and materials chosen appear to be vandal-resistant and low in maintenance costs.

Gantry signs can also be unattractive, but they are required at the approach to a major intersection on the primary distributors where drivers need to move into the correct lane. It is reassuring to visit Redditch, for example, to see what was done to produce an aesthetic

32. A Warrington-designed road sign.

design of both gantry and signs.

Street name plates needed to be clear but unobtrusive, and it was probably the architects' insistence that ensured something distinctive in the design in new towns. The royal blue plates, for example, with

Kindersley alphabet, designed for the first housing site in Basildon, are still being used thirty years later.

One of the most important landscape features in any new town is the town park and each of them has its own particular landscape character. The parks were mostly located close to the centre and often, in association with playing fields or golf course, provided an open, traffic-free corridor stretching from the town centre out to the open country. At Skelmersdale such a linear park follows the course of the River Tawd right across the middle of the town. Footpaths, cycleways and bridleway are routed through the parks and plenty of seats, shelters and other facilities were provided. Among the attractions of Nene Park in Peterborough are the steam trains of Nene Valley railway – an unexpected transport mode in a New Town. Several towns have established nature reserves, and, at Washington, an unique development is the Waterfowl Park on the north bank of the River Wear, with its collection of over 1,200 birds of some one hundred separate species – some very rare. It is one of the seven centres of the Wildfowl Trust.

All these things helped to make up the visual bread and butter related to the movement of people and vehicles in new towns. Was there never any visual jam? Well, there was indeed. For every town has its show pieces – quite apart from all the fine architecture – in the form of contemporary sculpture. Just look at Harlow, whose marvel-

Table 14.3
Harlow: sculptures

Sculpture	Sculptor	Situation
Chiron	Spencer Watson	The Stow neighbourhood centre
Family Group	Henry Moore	Civic Square
Contrapuntal Forms	Barbara Hepworth	Glebelands housing area
Meat Porters	Ralph Brown	Market Square
Portrait Figure	F. E. McWilliam	Market Square
Eve	A. Rodin	Water Gardens
Bronze Cross	Henry Moore	Water Gardens
Korr	Betty Rea	Old Harlow
Help	F. E. McWilliam	Town centre
Boar	Elizabeth Frink	Water Gardens
City	Gerda Rubinstein	Bishopsfield area centre
Echo	Antanas Brazdys	Great Parndon area
The Obelisk	Frederick Gibberd	Broadwalk, town centre
Pisces	Jesse Watkins	Town park
Sheep Shearer	Ralph Brown	Mark Hall South
Trigon	Lynn Chadwick	Broad Walk, town centre

Source: Harlow: the Story of a New Town: Publications for Companies: 1980

lous collection of sculpture includes pieces by Rodin, Moore and Hepworth (Table 14.3).

Notes

1   Dame Sylvia Crowe was consultant landscape architect to Basildon Development Corporation and a number of others.
2   Sir Geoffrey Jellicoe prepared the master plan for Hemel Hempstead and designed the water gardens there.
3   Almond bridge, Livingston, for Midlothian County Council. Structural engineers: Chief Engineer's department, Livingston Development Corporation (Chief Engineer: J. Munro).

15 The safety factor

Chapter 2 drew attention to the appalling number of casualties on the roads of Britain between the wars. By 1960 the total had leapt up to about 340,000 casualties – this in a year when the total number of vehicles was about 9 million. Within quite narrow limits this figure has remained as the annual casualty rate ever since, while the number of vehicles has escalated enormously; it was about 15 million in 1970 and over 18½ million in 1979 – the casualty rate remained the same while the number of vehicles on the roads doubled. Which is good news as far as it goes, but of little comfort to the victims of road accidents, their families and dependents. The cost of road accidents in monetary terms has been enormous. In terms of human suffering it has been incalculable.[1]

On what types of roads do these accidents mostly occur? Table 15.1 shows that, in terms of distance travelled, there are about two and a quarter times as many accidents in built-up areas as on rural roads and motorways.

A Transport and Road Research Laboratory Report of 1975, (No. 159 VC) showed that, overall, the average number of casualties in towns is equal to about 0.6 per cent of the resident urban population, that there are no large regional differences in accident types or rates for the different classes of road user, and that up to a quarter of all accidents in each of the towns studied occurred in its densely trafficked central area, covering only a few square kilometres. The report reviewed the prospects for reducing urban accidents and identified the

Table 15.1
Great Britain Accident rates by type of road
(Injury accidents per hundred million vehicle kilometres)

	1970	1975	1980	1981	1982
Roads in built-up areas	183	157	146	143	134
Roads in non built-up areas	64	48	46	48	46
Motorways	21	16	14	14	15
All roads	125	99	89	88	85

Source: Basic Road Statistics 1984; British Road Federation.

more promising courses of remedial action:

- large scale traffic management;
- pedestrianisation in central areas;
- improved junction control;
- improved parking control;
- pedestrian crossing facilities on arterial roads;
- exclusion of non-access traffic in residential areas;
- improved junctions in residential areas; and
- provision of children's play areas in residential areas.

These suggestions may have a familiar ring, for they are very much the stock in trade of the new town engineer and planner. The Reith Report had listed sixteen safety points 'to be borne in mind' (see Appendix 1, para. 110) and everyone recalled the advice of Alker Tripp and the example of Stein and Wright in their original Radburn development. There was a firm intention that maximum measures for road safety should be built into the new towns' transport systems.

Naturally some of the towns have been more successful with their safety measures than others, and it would be enlightening to make a pragmatic comparison between a number of the towns from this standpoint to see how they have performed *vis-à-vis* the overall national figure; to find out whether Stevenage with all its cycle tracks is in fact safer than, say, Crawley; whether Cumbernauld with so much segregation is safer than Stevenage; and whether a shared access residential layout, like The Brow, is in practice any more hazardous than a Radburn. Unfortunately, there seems to be very little hard information on which to base a meaningful comparison.

When records are kept, they are not always on a comparable basis. An accident often results in more than one casualty. The British Road Federation figures (Table 15.1) relate to 'injury accidents', that is, accidents which may have resulted in one, or more, fatalities and/or serious injuries and/or slight injuries. *Transport and Road Research Laboratory report no. 159 UC* suggests that the average number of casualties per injury accident is about 1.2. (Transport and Road Research Laboratory, 1975).

As we have seen the idea of pedestrian/vehicle segregation began to take off in the 1950s and much of the pioneer work was done in the new towns. It manifested itself in pedestrianised town centres and neighbourhood centres, in Radburn type housing layouts, by the provision of a footpath system quite separate from, and more direct than, the roads, and by bridges or underpasses where footpaths crossed the distributor roads. The provision of a cycle track system in some towns also made a contribution to safety.

Regrettably, however thoroughly the segregation principle is carried through, there is no certainty that people will use the walkways as intended. The worker getting a lift from the factory in his lunch hour may alight on the primary distributor at the point nearest his home. And if the 'country' bus stop is on the distributor passengers may be tempted to dash across the road on a bee-line for home. A couple of girls walking home at night may feel less threatened by the fast-moving traffic on the distributor road, with its brilliant illumination, than threading their way along the footway system, with its lower level of lighting, passing the trees and shrubs and their dark shadows, with fears of molestation preying on their minds.

Without doubt it was the elaborate cycleway system and the fully pedestrianised town centre which helped to make Stevenage the safest town in Hertfordshire and one of the safest in Britain. The development corporation's chief engineer kept an annual record of casualties in injury accidents in Stevenage between 1957 and 1979, relative to the town's population each year, and made a comparison over this twenty-two year period between the results for Stevenage and the national averages for towns in Britain. He identified the slight downward trend in the record for British towns as a whole from 6.7 to 6.5 casualties per 1,000 population, but a much stronger trend at Stevenage from 6.0 down to 3.9 casualties per 1,000 population by 1979.

At Runcorn and Cumbernauld also, the development corporations' chief engineers made a year-on-year study of the casualty figures in their respective towns. Runcorn went about it by making a comparison with the similar-sized town of Widnes on the opposite bank of the Mersey. Accident figures were analysed for the five-year period 1976-80 (Table 15.2) and the following indications were noted:

● Runcorn had half the number of fatal accidents as there were in Widnes;

- Runcorn had two-thirds as many personal injury accidents as Widnes; and
- the population of Runcorn averaged 8 per cent more than that of Widnes over the period.

Table 15.2
Widnes and Runcorn
Comparison of numbers of casualties

	Widnes				Runcorn			
	Population	Casualties			Population	Casualties		
		Fatal	Serious	Slight		Fatal	Serious	Slight
1976	56,100	4	37	241	55,700	6	26	151
1977	56,400	4	52	260	59,000	4	29	194
1978	56,600	3	41	210	61,400	3	50	170
1979	56,100	7	83	187	64,600	1	26	144
1980	56,850	10	51	192	65,658	1	39	167
5 year average	56,410	6	53	218	61,272	3	34	165
Source: Warrington and Runcorn Development Corporation.								

The principal features of the Runcorn layout thought to have contributed to lower accident figures were:

- segregation of vehicular and pedestrian traffic on the expressway;
- segregation of buses from other traffic on the Busway; and
- exclusion of vehicles from shopping areas in Shopping City.

Too much should not be concluded from the comparison between Runcorn and Widnes, since the traffic patterns of the two towns are significantly different. Cross-river traffic may have a comparable impact on both towns, but Widnes has also to contend with a substantial east-west traffic flow, some of it on much older-style roads than those of Runcorn.

Cumbernauld was safety conscious from the start. The essence of the master plan proposals was to minimise points of conflict between motor vehicles and pedestrians, and the plan was very successful in doing so. In contrast to what had been found possible in the Mark I towns, the distributor roads were treated solely as traffic routes which pedestrians had no reason to use. Within the residential areas the most direct routes possible were selected to give walkers access to the town centre and other places such as schools and playing fields – always with grade-separated crossings of the traffic roads. The theme of safety was always kept in view and the development corporation's chief engineer maintained a year-on-year record of road accident casualties which he analysed in order to compare one year with another and to make comparison with other towns and with the national average. Results were reported to the development corporation each year and used for identification of black spots and early remedial measures.

Casualties on Cumbernauld's roads between 1971 and 1975 and between 1978 and 1981 are summarised in Table 15.3. The totals, held to moderate levels until 1978, doubled in 1979 and stayed at this disappointingly higher level in 1981 and 1982. The figures relate to accidents on roads developed by the corporation and, while useful for comparing one year with another they would need to be adjusted by the addition of the accident figures for other roads within the built-up area if a meaningful comparison with other towns or with the national average were to be made.

Table 15.3
Cumbernauld: summary of casualties 1971-81
on Cumbernauld Development Corporation roads

| Year | Population | Number of casualties | | | Total |
		Fatal	Serious injury	Slight injury	
1971	31,500	2	8	27	37
1972	30,215	–	7	73	80
1973	32,350	2	13	33	48
1974	35,400	1	12	43	56
1975	41,625	1	16	43	60
1978	48,050	2	16	41	59
1979	49,700	3	22	92	117
1980	50,500	3	23	74	100
1981	50,700	3	30	75	108
1971-81		17	147	501	665

Source: Cumbernauld Development Corporation.
Note: No records available for 1976 or 1977.

The effect of adding the accident figures for the remaining roads in the designated area, apart from the trunk roads A73 and A80, for the years 1978 and 1979 is indicated in Table 15.4. This also gives an estimate of the casualties that might have been expected on the basis of the national average for built-up areas. The figures underline the very regrettable upturn in the numbers of casualties from only 26 per cent of the national average for built-up areas in 1978 to a peak figure

227

equivalent to 46 per cent of the national average in 1979. Yet on any basis of comparison Cumbernauld must be rated a safe town, with a casualty rate averaging 30 per cent of the national average for built-up areas.

Table 15.4
Cumbernauld: casualties on all road in the designated area
(excluding trunk) 1979 (and 1978)

comparison with national statistics

Type of casualty	Number occurring in Cumbernauld		Possible casualties based on national average for built-up areas		Cumbernauld casualties as a percentage of national average	
Fatal	3	(2)	4	(4)	75	(50)
Serious injury	25	(23)	61	(60)	43	(38)
Slight injury	113	(51)	222	(227)	51	(22)
Total	141	(76)	287	(291)	46	(26)

Source: Cumbernauld Development Corporation.
Note: 1978 figures in brackets.

If Cumbernauld is 'safe', and if safety is about vehicle/pedestrian segregation, why have ten pedestrians been killed and 142 injured in road accidents in nine years? Table 15.5 shows the location of all these

Table 15.5
Cumbernauld: location of pedestrian casualties

Year	Total number of casualties	Main radial roads			Distributor roads			Housing access roads		
		F	S	SI	F	S	SI	F	S	SI
1971	13	2	1	–	–	3	2	–	3	2
1972	19	–	–	1	–	2	7	–	–	9
1973	12	–	1	1	1	–	2	–	2	5
1974	16	–	–	2	1	4	6	–	–	3
1975	15	–	–	2	–	2	3	–	2	6
1978	11	–	1	–	1	1	5	–	1	2
1979	18	–	1	1	2	5	4	–	–	4
1980	26	–	2	1	2	3	8	1	3	6
1981	22	–	–	4	–	4	4	–	4	6
Totals	152	2	6	12	7	24	41	1	16	43

Source: Cumbernauld Development Corporation.
Notes: No statistics for 1976 and 1977.
F – Fatal injury; S – Serious injury; SI – Slight injury.

casualties, and it will be seen that ninety-two of them were caused on the radial and distributor roads which by design should be pedestrian free; this demonstrates the additional risk to a pedestrian 'illegally' using a road system when the motorist is not expecting to be confronted by pedestrians.

Another town with a good record of road safety is East Kilbride where, however, the figures have been analysed in yet another way (Tables 15.6, 15.7 and 15.8).

Table 15.6
East Kilbride: analysis of road casualties 1976-80

Class of casualty	1976	1977	1978	1979	1980
Driver or rider					
Pedal cycle	15	9	13	11	11
Moped/scooter	3	2	1	2	2
Motor cycle	23	26	39	28	26
Car or taxi	84	74	105	80	78
Public service vehicle	1	2	1	1	0
Goods	10	11	13	9	7
Other	1	1	2	5	3
Passenger					
Pillion passenger	8	5	9	6	4
Car or taxi	59	62	84	57	74
Public service vehicle	15	2	5	4	9
Goods	10	4	6	6	5
Other	0	0	0	10	5
Pedestrian	62	65	71	62	72
Total	291	263	349	281	296
Source: East Kilbride Development Corporation.					

Transport and Road Research Laboratory report no. 159 UC (1975) included seven Mark I new towns amongst a list of twenty-one towns for which it deduced the mean numbers of personal injury accidents per year, for the years 1969, 1970 and 1971, per 100,000 of each town's resident population. (Details reproduced here with the permission of the Controller of Her Majesty's Stationery Office.)

Of the new towns listed,[2] East Kilbride showed up the best with an average of 232 injury accidents per 100,000 of population per year. The report suggested that, on average, the frequency of injury accidents in the new towns was about 20 per cent less than in other

Table 15.7
East Kilbride: analysis of road surface conditions at the scenes of road accidents 1976-80

Road surface condition		1976		1977		1978		1979		1980	
Dry		127		99		133		106		120	
Wet	Rain falling	77	42	90	46	86	46	65	37	83	55
	Not raining		35		44		40		28		28
Snow or ice		16		17		28		36		21	
Total		220		206		247		207		224	
Ratio wet/dry		0.606		0.909		0.647		0.613		0.692	

Source: East Kilbride Development Corporation

Table 15.8
East Kilbride: analysis of light conditions at the scenes of road accidents 1976-80

Light condition		1976		1977		1978		1979		1980	
Daylight		143		141		159		137		132	
Dark with street lighting	Wet c'way	63	–	47	–	69	–	46	18	74	43
	other		–		–		–		28		31
Dark street lights unlit		0		0		0		1		1	
Dark/no lighting		14		18		20		23		17	
Total		220		206		248		207		224	
Ratio dark/daylight		0.538		0.461		0.560		0.511		0.697	

Source: East Kilbride Development Corporation

towns.

The relevance of population numbers to the study of injury accidents in urban areas is questionable. If, for example, there is a strong element of commuting into the towns, which is, in fact, the general case, this adds nothing to the population figure, yet contributes enormously to the work journey traffic and thus to the accident probability in the towns. Total number of vehicle miles travelled would obviously be a better yardstick. However it would also be far more difficult to establish. What can be concluded in general terms is that:

- new towns appear to have distinctly fewer road accident casualties per unit of population than other towns;
- the casualty rate seems to be static while the level of car ownership may be increasing year by year; and
- the disparate nature of traffic accident records makes meaningful comparison difficult, if not impossible.

Note

1 Since 1982 however, there has been a significant reduction in the numbers of casualties due to traffic accidents in Britain.
2 Stevenage, Welwyn, Basildon, Harlow, Crawley, Cwmbran and East Kilbride.

16 Concluding appraisal

In a time span of nearly forty years, the new town enterprise has reflected all the changing moods in Britain – political, economic, social and technological. The Mark I towns, courageously started as an experiment in social development in the austerity of the immediate post-war years, emerged with solid government support, and within a dozen years, they had developed into thriving and successful enterprises. Confidence abounded. The Mark IIs, cradled in the Swinging Sixties, a period of great expansion and optimism, were able to incorporate such features as free-flow primary roads and multi-storey shopping centres in their planning. And the ambitious third generation of new towns was launched just in time to catch this flood tide before the decline began. Along with the Green Belts, the towns are among the few generally acknowledged successes of planning in this era.

New towns have been the trendsetters for many of the transport-related innovatory ideas of the mid-twentieth century. It is often difficult to establish who did what first, but it is likely that Radburn's first appearance in Britain was at Basildon; the shared accessway principle was introduced at Runcorn. Both ideas were immediately emulated in other new towns and ultimately adopted in housing schemes right across the country. Stevenage, defying alike the diehards and the fainthearts, pressed on to introduce the first all-pedestrian town centre; shortly followed to a greater or lesser extent by the other Mark I towns. Cumbernauld was first with a multi-storey centre, setting a pattern which was followed, with even greater splendour, by the other Mark IIs and Mark IIIs, and gradually raising the standard and sophistication of new shopping developments countrywide. The segregated Busway track at Runcorn was another important innovation.

It was the same too with the introduction of new construction techniques. New town architects did not escape the pressures to go in for system building and, as in the rest of the country, some of the systems used have given considerable trouble in recent years. Happily the 'white heat of the technological revolution' did not extend much to the materials used for roads and bridges, where sound engineering principles and, in the main, traditional materials continued to apply. This is not to say that new town engineers were reactionary, indeed a vast amount of experimental and innovative work was undertaken in the towns. One of the first ever pre-stressed concrete carriageways was laid in the Crawley industrial area and the Transport and Road Research Laboratory has always regarded the towns as seed beds for new ideas. Experiments for the Laboratory were put in hand at Basildon to determine the appropriate thickness of sub-base beneath carriageways on clay sub-soil and numerous experiments were conducted on behalf of the Laboratory in other towns. It was not a one-sided arrangement because the Laboratory was always ready to advise and assist on new town projects as, for instance, the redesign of the Plough roundabout at Hemel Hempstead, the dial-a-bus experiment at Harlow and the monitoring of Busway operation at Runcorn.

However, not all transportation problems in new towns were easily resolved and some of the solutions were less than successful. There are still lessons which must be learned for the benefit of future projects.

A difficulty that bedevilled the Mark I towns in their early years was caused by lack of acceptance of their standing – sometimes amounting to hostility on the part of local authorities. The development corporations were seen as upstart organisations with disproportionate muscle and resources and were accordingly treated with suspicion, if not open hostility. This was unfortunate in the transportation context, as from other aspects, because local authorities were also the highway authorities and the byelaw authorities; their standards had been set in days before the Second World War – some even before the First World War and could only be relaxed to accommodate new and progressive ideas with a great deal of goodwill and agreement, which were not always forthcoming. This was why the early new town residential layouts were stereotyped and dull, not geared to appropriate vehicular movement or pedestrian safety. It was why the Mark I primary road system was less imaginative and less forward-looking than might have been the case, why bitter arguments developed about how the cost of the main roads should be shared. These troubles and torments were healed with time and largely avoided in the Mark IIs. Could it have been done better from the start? Perhaps it could with clearer terms of reference and better communication. The lesson seemed to have been learned when Peterborough and the other Mark III expansion towns were designated, and Richard Crossman, then Secretary of State for the Environment was careful to set up a viable partnership between the elected authorities and the development corporations.

Although a great deal of flexibility was built into the early master plans, the idea of enormously increasing the planned populations proved a strain and, in transportation terms at least, caused difficulties and less than perfect conditions of mobility and access. Basildon and Bracknell are obvious examples. The lesson to be learned is that flexibility must always be in the forefront of the planner's mind and he must remember too that the population target figure can move downwards as well as upwards. Thus the Mark II towns with their generous primary road layouts and numerous grade separations had a built-in capability for future expansion. Yet, overtaken by an era of population cutbacks and recession, the roads are under-utilised and some of the towns are now stigmatised as being 'over-roaded', for example Washington, Livingston and Skelmersdale. You simply cannot win.

High density developments were tried in some of the towns, notably Cumbernauld, and generally found to be a mistake. They usually resulted in a large proportion of flats and in most towns these were unpopular. From the point of view of movement, high density meant too much traffic on the residential roads and more parked cars to be accommodated in less space.

Most of the Mark I towns went wrong when locating their industry. The usual pattern was to concentrate the main industrial development into one large estate, or perhaps two estates, located on the same side of the town. With the enormously increased use of private cars for the journey to work, this arrangement led to heavy tidal traffic and in some cases to congestion during the morning and evening rush hours. Once this situation was recognised care was taken to ensure that any additional industry was located on the far side of the town; in the Mark IIs the industries were distributed over four, or in some cases many more, industrial areas, well spread about the town.

One or two of the earlier towns made the mistake (for so it proved to be) of starting to base their town centre on a traditional 'High Street'; it was soon realised that this was not the best arrangement of a large shopping centre for a motorised society and in most cases pedestrian shopping was substituted.

Nowhere was the need for flexible planning greater than in the central area; ideally the centre should have been designed and built incrementally in step with the growth of the town, to a plan capable of adjustment from time to time in the light of changing requirements. Some centres were constrained on all sides by other development or by a ring road. Basildon, for example, is getting to the point where, to meet the shopping and traffic needs of an enlarged town, there is nowhere to expand except skywards. The fine multi-storey shopping centres of the Mark II and Mark III towns are lacking in flexibility due to the structural design and internal services provision, which cannot be altered, except at great expense. Perhaps they got it right at Milton Keynes where the imposing and highly sophisticated centre is generally no more than two or three storeys high and the linear arrangement lends itself to extension as required. Against this, it seems a very long walk (albeit a pleasant one) from one end of the shopping centre to the other – longer in fact than the pedestrian way at, say, Stevenage, but mercifully fully protected from the weather.

Where an inner ring road was drawn too tightly around the centre this tended to cause overloading at peak traffic times, as well as constraining any enlargement of the centre.

Some of the surface roundabout junctions of the Mark I towns have proved inadequate for the requirements of rush hour traffic. This situation was not necessarily unforeseen; there was at least one case of a development corporation proposing a grade separated junction which was then turned down on account of the cost. This parsimony was no doubt justified at the time but, luckily for the Mark IIs, a more liberal outlook, born perhaps of fresh confidence in the new towns, ensued.

Regrettably, at about the same time, the idea of providing a system of cycleways was abandoned in most of the towns. Although with the swing of the pendulum cycleways came back into fashion in the 1970s, interpolation of a makeshift pattern in some of the towns' plans could not achieve such good results as those of Stevenage or Peterborough. Cycling should have been recognised in the initial planning, along with the provisions for the motor car, public transport and the pedestrian system. In fact few of the towns have fully catered for all four transport modes, even though to do so may have been featured among the transport goals of their master plans. Stevenage and Peterborough were perhaps the most successful in catering for all four modes, but other towns, Milton Keynes for example, have achieved satisfactory results, by suitable adaptation.

The new towns generally have had a good record of road safety, although not perhaps as good as was hoped in view of their inherent planning advantages. It is a pity that accident records have not been kept more systematically in all the towns. A co-ordinated method would have facilitated the making of useful comparisons between one new town and another, as well as with established towns and with national averages.

If there was one facet of transportation for which provision in the new towns seemed inadequate it was the internal bus service. This headed the list of complaints when social surveys were made by development corporations and was featured again and again in annual reports to the Minister. The past thirty years have been difficult ones for the operating companies; the huge rise in car ownership meant a loss of patronage; inflation and high wages greatly increased operating costs; so fares escalated resulting in still further reduction of ridership, which led to still higher fares or a reduction of services (or both) – the law of diminishing returns.

The same sort of complaint was probably heard in most towns in Britain, but the predicament bore most heavily on the new towns, particularly in their early years. People who had moved out of London or other cities were accustomed to all the facilities of city life – which included a good bus service. It was the sort of thing which was said to cause 'new town blues'. Yet what could the bus companies do? They were expected to make a profit, or at least break even. There was goodwill and cooperation between the bus operators on the one hand and the individual development corporation, county council and district council on the other, but this does not in most of the towns seem to have been matched by the level of financial assistance. What was needed was a clearer overall policy and more adequate funding.

The curtailment of new town developments in 1976 clearly stemmed from political decisions. Amongst other effects it greatly disturbed many of the corporations' development programmes, it may well have resulted in the disposal of valuable assets on disadvantageous terms and it led to disillusionment, and the departure from the new town scene of highly trained and dedicated professionals.

There were no shameful mistakes. Even the Mark I towns, with so little precedent to follow, got it more or less right – except in the important respect of anticipating the growth of car ownership. So what of the future? Will Britain fail to survive in the twenty-first century world as suggested by Bellini's thesis (Bellini, 1981) returning to mediaeval standards and social relationships, or, will the recovery now clearly discernible in the mid 1980s, really take off and restore to health our industry and employment situation? What will be the transportation requirements of the twenty-first century? Perhaps oil supplies will last longer than some of the pundits suggest, or perhaps that elusive alternative power source will be found. Otherwise it may be back to the horse, the cart and the bicycle.

As for the new towns and the men and women who created them, they had their shaky start, their hour of glory and their fall from

236

political grace. Yet they have provided the best, most up-to-date environment for urban movement that exists in Britain today; and they may yet, in Sir Henry Wells'[1] phrase, prove to be 'the gold mines of the future'.

Note

1 Sir Henry Wells was successively Deputy Chairman of Bracknell Development Corporation 1949-50, Chairman of Hemel Hempstead Development Corporation 1950-62 and Chairman for the New Towns 1964-70.

Appendix 1 Extracts from the final report of the New Towns Committee. July 1946.

(These extracts embody the main recommendations of the Committee in respect to roads and other transport-related matters. Crown copyright. Reproduced with the permission of the Controller of Her Majesty's Stationery Office.)

TERMS OF REFERENCE

To consider the general questions of the establishment, development, organisation and administration that will arise in the promotion of New Towns in furtherance of a policy of planned decentralisation from congested urban areas; and in accordance therewith to suggest guiding principles on which such Towns should be established and developed as self-contained and balanced communities for work and living.

B. PRINCIPLES IN PLANNING

IV. Selection of Site

PHYSICAL FEATURES

27. (4) While a very hilly site may make development expensive and involve inconvenient road gradients, a reasonable degree of undulation is to be welcomed, since it may add greatly to the beauty and interest of a town. For residential areas a general southerly slope is preferable but not essential.

(8) It is better for a town to be on a through railway line than at the end of a branch; and in view of the importance of the rail traffic generated by a new town, or a group of such towns, the possibility of adding to and extending existing railways should not be ruled out.

(9) Access to an existing or proposed arterial road is important, and it must be possible easily to connect the site to the main road network of the region. Though an arterial road should not pass through the built-up area, it is an advantage if it skirts

238

the town through its green belt.

(10) River and canal communications are important only to very few industries, and can be disregarded in siting new towns. But there is considerable amenity value in the presence of a river or other water features.

DISTANCE FROM EXISTING TOWNS

28. Consideration of this problem has usually been limited to an attempt to prescribe a minimum distance, and we suggest that new towns in the Greater London area should be at least twenty-five miles from the centre; from other great towns a distance of ten to fifteen miles might be enough. The optimum distance is more difficult to determine. To locate new towns far away from existing great cities, in regions with a relatively sparse population but with good communications and other facilities available, might be very advantageous both in providing a new centre of cultural life and a more substantial economic foundation for local government services in the area selected. Whether it would be possible to induce industrialists and workers to move far from the centres to which they are accustomed we cannot be sure. Many firms are more or less limited as to areas of relocation because of close connection with other firms remaining in the conurbation, involving daily contacts between executives and frequent interchanges of goods and information, or because of their dependence on local ancillary services; and many must be at no great distance from the main centres which constitute their consumer market. These might, given good road communications not obstructed by traffic delays, move up to distances of thirty or forty miles. There are others whose range of relocation is quite elastic, and who could move to a new town without limit of distance. As to workers, there are many who will readily move to a considerable distance if employment and modern houses and good living conditions are there offered; to them the new towns wherever sited will be a strong attraction. Others, however, will be reluctant to move far afield because of attachments based on friendships or other associations in their present localities. We suggest that, before sites for all the new towns are chosen, a careful survey should be made to ensure that some are located in areas where they will confer benefit not only on those who are to live and work there but also on those who live in the surrounding towns and villages.

V. Importance of flexibility

30. Indefinite planning is not planning at all, and whenever and wherever construction has to proceed, lines and limits have to be laid down, so that the designers of individual works and buildings can conform to them. Precise planning should, however, never be too far ahead of actual construction. A growing town is a living entity, and its final shape in detail cannot be exactly predicted or prescribed. Moreover, changes in technique, in taste, in standards of living, and in habits and ideas, continually produce new requirements and put others out of date. There must be a master plan for the whole town based on the knowledge and expectations of the planning team, and in particular on careful estimates of the areas likely to be required for all foreseeable purposes. But this master plan, though its major principles must not be lightly changed, should be under constant detailed revision as knowledge grows and requirements change. And each section of development within the lines laid down in the master plan should be planned in detail before, but not long before, its construction is authorised.

33. The industrial zones and the central business zone should be convenient of

access from all parts of the town. They should, if practicable, be near each other and near the main railway and bus stations. The general urban zones should be grouped in relation to the industrial zones and civic centre so as to form a reasonably compact town, without road ribbons or scattered buildings on the outskirts.

VII. Layout, design and constructional standards

LAYOUT AND GROUPING

43. The principal roads within the town, especially where they are kept free of frontage building, as well as other topographical features, tend to group the residential areas of the town into more or less clearly defined parts or neighbourhoods. Convenient placing of primary schools, minor groups of shops, churches, refreshment houses, meeting places, and other public buildings, may also, as nuclei, have the same effect. The neighbourhood is therefore a natural and useful conception; but it should not be thought of as a self-contained community of which the inhabitants are more conscious than they are of the town as a whole. For many educational, cultural and social purposes people will look to the main centre of the town, and the primary civic unity will be that of the town. Neither an ideal size for a neighbourhood nor a general pattern of neighbourhood development can be prescribed. For the support of a good minor shopping centre, and for primary education, something of the order of 10,000 is considered convenient, but there can be wide variations.

BYELAWS AND BUILDING REGULATIONS

50. Existing byelaws for buildings and streets contain redundancies and anachronisms and they overlap clauses under town planning schemes. Their original purpose was to protect the public from the worst consequences of bad practice by enforcing observance of certain minimum standards. But because they were usually conceived in a period when there was little research and experiment in this field and standards of living were low, many have outworn their usefulness. They are indispensable where development is undertaken in the same area by a variety of private owners. Where, however, a whole town is developed under unified landownership with public responsibility, and all development is approved by one agency, the necessary control can be applied by building regulations under the leases.

51. We recommend, accordingly, that in the special circumstances of a new town the local byelaws should be revoked and the building regulations in the leases relied on. There are various enactments under which byelaws may be suspended or revoked and the New Towns Bill, now before Parliament, would give the Minister (or the Secretary of State for Scotland) power to suspend byelaws in the areas designated as sites of new towns.

VIII. Landscape treatment

59. The beauty of a town depends not only on its buildings but also on its relation to the surrounding landscape and on the disposition and treatment of the natural features, existing or introduced, within the boundaries. To fit happily in the regional scene it must either have harmony or considered contrast therewith. The contours and vegetation of the surrounding land form its permanent setting, and the flow of the land with its distant views may often suggest the direction of roads and placing of buildings within the town. The layout should therefore take full account of topography, and

240

beauty should be a constant consideration as well as convenience of building plots and easy road gradients. As examples, planting on higher ground can accentuate contours; and ribs of high ground and woods, or alternatively parkways in valleys, may be used to define boundaries between neighbourhoods or to separate industrial from residential zones.

60. There can be no single and generally accepted principle of landscape treatment. In one case it may be desirable to merge the town quietly into the surrounding landscape, by planting ecologically related to what exists already, with green wedges penetrating from outside into the town area. In another way it may be better that the town should stand out sharply from its rural setting, a clearly defined boundary accentuating the distinction between country and town. The planning team must have skilled advice in landscape design throughout.

61. Town planting is a study in itself, and in the choice of species and in the placing of trees, flower beds, lawns and green verges, far more variety is possible than is commonly used. Experience gained in the extensive planting at Letchworth and Welwyn and other large town estates and holiday towns could be more widely drawn upon. It must of course be remembered that town trees have to contend with such unnatural features as roads and underground services that obstruct or injure their roots, pedestrians, buses and overhead wires that restrict their growth, and children who mutilate them. These troubles can be met by the right choice of varieties, skilled siting, assiduous pruning and staking, and the creation of a preservative public opinion; but they must not be ignored.

62. Forest trees as well as smaller kinds should have a place. Existing fine trees, centuries old and with centuries of life before them, often justify modification of the layout of roads and buildings. Where there are few large trees, some forest species should be planted singly or in groups; they must of course have ample space below and above ground. Smaller trees can never attain the same splendour and dignity; but their enormous variety, coupled with skill in siting (in which the gardens of the houses should be regarded as part of the street landscape) will produce an infinite range of effects. For quick results, short-lived varieties may be used. Deliberate overplanting at the start is sound policy, provided thinning takes place in due time. Some evergreens should be planted for their winter value.

63. On some sites planting for shelter from cold or prevailing winds will be desirable; it is this that has given many old towns and villages the appearance of being natural growths in the landscape. Studied in conjunction with the orientation of streets, and with the contours of the site, windbreak planting can prevent the unpleasant funnelling of wind noticeable in some towns.

C. FACTORS AFFECTING THE PREPARATION OF THE PLAN

II. Services

STREET LIGHTING

94. Well-designed street lighting not only serves the convenience and safety of road users and acts as a deterrent to crime, but increases the attractions of a shopping area and the importance of a civic centre. There have been many significant advances in the technology of street lighting in recent years, and the recommendations of the Ministry

241

of Transport Departmental Committee on Street Lighting should be studied. The services or advice of an engineer experienced in street lighting should be available, but the design of standards should be approved by the chief architect. Trees in roads should be so planted that they do not interfere with the lighting.

III. Communications

ROADS

100. On road planning generally, useful advice is obtainable from the Report on Design and Layout of Roads in Built-up Areas by a committee set up by the Ministry of Transport with the concurrence of the Ministry of Town and Country Planning and the Secretary of State for Scotland.

101. The road scheme of a new town will depend so much on the situation and contours that it is impossible to lay down a general pattern. The town will fall within a network of existing roads, and the continuity of their routes must of course be maintained. The external traffic of the town will be distributed to other places by connections with these existing roads. The connections are likely therefore to radiate from the town outwards, the lines being influenced by topography; and these radial roads will often form natural boundaries for neighbourhoods within reach of which will be a network of streets, so spaced as to provide building plots of convenient shape and of depths suited to the intended types of layout, and so aligned as to give easy gradients for traffic.

102. The radial roads should not, as in so many existing towns, converge at a single central point, but should connect with an inner ring road, not necessarily symmetrical, around the main shopping and civic centre by means of which traffic may pass from one radial to another. This would keep the centre free of through or cross traffic. A further ring road, or series of connecting roads, should be provided between the inner ring and the green belt to enable traffic having its origin or destination within the town to find its way to or from the surrounding main roads without passing through the centre or residential neighbourhoods.

103. The main radial roads and the outer and inner rings should be designed as free-flow traffic channels, buildings on their frontages not having individual access to them. The areas bounded by the radial and ring roads should be so laid out as not, by providing shorter routes; to attract any through traffic, and the roads within these precincts should connect with the main roads only at a limited number of points. Subject to this necessary discouragement of the movement of through traffic across the precincts, the internal layout should be such as to provide for easy vehicular access between all parts of the town. It is not good planning to force needless detours on motorists and pedestrians, or to introduce twists and turns that make it difficult to find the way about.

104. If the conception of the plan included a wedge or wedges of open space connecting with the green belt, or a parkway in a valley, it would be advantageous, if practicable, to site a radial road or part of the outer ring road therein. Such a road may also run through or alongside a park or woodland reserve. But a radial or ring road should not directly adjoin playing fields or children's playgrounds.

105. Specimen cross-sections of the layout and width of such internal main roads are given in Part V of the Report referred to above. In a planned new town it will be possible to provide space for standing and waiting vehicles where there are buildings on the frontages, which, though an undesirable form of development, may not be

wholly avoidable. A secondary parallel road, giving access to the frontage buildings, will be necessary in some cases.

106. Radial and ring roads which may be expected to carry heavy traffic should be planned to accommodate dual carriageways. Where there is no frontage access, two traffic lanes in each direction should suffice, the carriageways being widened by embayments at picking-up and setting-down points of public transport vehicles only. Ample width of verges and of the central strip dividing the dual carriageways will make it possible to develop the road attractively and to provide space for any necessary underground trunk services and for road equipment, such as street lighting standards and traffic signs, which should not be put on footways.

107. Unless entirely separate routes are provided for cyclists and pedestrians, main radial and ring roads should have one-way cycle tracks nine feet wide, and footpaths not less than six feet wide on each side. Near the town centre wider footpaths are needed. The planning of separate pedestrian and cycle ways along independent routes, which makes for maximum safety, is dealt with in paragraphs 206-208 of the Report above referred to.

108. The same Report also recommends that the major intersections on the radial-ring system should be laid out with single level roundabouts; where, however, there will be a large volume of pedestrians and pedal cyclists, as at the junction of the main radials with the inner ring road, these classes of road users should be able to pass into the central area at a different level from that of the carriageways of the ring road. Where positive control of traffic is required at intersections within the central area, traffic light signals are to be preferred to roundabouts.

109. Residential roads carrying two-way traffic should be not less than 40 ft. wide between fences, and should have two footways. Carriageways in such roads should preferably be not less than 20 ft. wide, but exceptions can be made for roads developed on one side only. In short minor roads, cul-de-sacs; and squares the carriageway may, in particular circumstances, be reduced to 16 ft. or 13ft.; one footway is essential. The paved footway and the verge together should be not less than 10 ft. 6 ins. wide. Cul-de-sacs should have adequate turning space. Grass verges add much to the amenity of a residential road and are usually best placed between the footpaths and the carriageway. Frequent paths should be provided across the verges.

110. The road system should be planned for safety as well as freedom of movement and amenity. The points to be borne in mind, some of which are mentioned above, include:–
(1) Vehicles, cyclists and pedestrians on the main radial and ring roads to be segregated.
(2) No routes for heavy traffic to pass through the shopping or civic centre or residential precincts.
(3) Adequate width of roads where vehicles have to set down and take up passengers, as in shopping areas.
(4) Pedestrian crossings on traffic roads to be as few as possible.
(5) Side access roads into radial and ring roads to be limited in number, and not to be opposite each other.
(6) Buildings on frontages of busy streets to have access for loading at the back or within their own curtilages.
(7) Buildings attracting large numbers of vehicles, such as cinemas, hotels, and departmental stores, to have special parking spaces.
(8) Schools, playing fields and other places where many people gather not to adjoin heavy traffic roads.

(9) Footways to be of adequate width.

(10) Ample sight distance to be provided at intersections.

(11) Lamp standards, telephone and pillar boxes, litter bins, and traffic signs to be so placed as not to obstruct footways or the line of sight of drivers or cyclists.

(12) Road signs and street name plates to be easily seen, of standard and immediately recognisable types, and pleasing design.

(13) Street lighting on traffic routes to be adequate and uniform.

(14) Houses and other buildings to be numbered throughout the town on some easily understood system – as for example, outward from the centre, with odd numbers on left and even numbers on right, subsidiary roads being numbered from their junction with a major road nearest to the centre.

(15) Public conveniences, telephone and pillar boxes, bus shelters and other such facilities to be accessible from frequented footpaths and not to be on islands unless there is access by subway.

(16) Kerbs in busy streets to be so arranged as to make it easy for perambulators and invalid vehicles to get on and off footpaths.

111. An attractive sign giving the name of the town should be set up on all main approaches.

112. Methods of road construction are dealt with in Memorandum 575 (Roads) of the Ministry of Transport, and of bridge construction in Memorandum 577. A standard should be agreed with the local authority for all roads to be constructed in the town, whether by the agency or any other body.

BUS TRANSPORT

113. In a town of the area contemplated a frequent internal bus service is indispensable. The local transport undertaking or public board should be encouraged to provide such a service, and in default the agency should itself provide it. Connections with neighbouring places will also be required. Provision should be made for bus stations, including a central one near the shopping centre and, if possible, adjoining the railway station. The layout of roads and footpaths should take account of the need of convenient stopping places for internal and long-distance services, and where necessary for shelters for passengers. The development of bus traffic is such that for a town's main bus station there is now a need for a specially-designed building with waiting rooms, enquiry office and light refreshment service, and the site allocated should allow for this.

CAR PARKS AND GARAGES

114. When conditions become normal, heavy demands for space for parking cars will have to be met. When space is limited or land very expensive, there are advantages in an underground garage or in a garage with more than one storey, but the cost is high; such conditions should not arise in a new town. A number of well distributed small car parks are preferable to one or two large central ones, and if shoppers in cars are to be encouraged to use car parks they must be situated conveniently to the shops. Accommodation should also be provided for bicycles. Tree planting and careful siting will improve the appearance of car parks. Whereas about 200 sq. ft. per vehicle is a reasonable figure for open access system parks, there is no formula which indicates the total parking capacity likely to be required in any particular town.

115. The location of service garages should not interfere with the amenities of residential areas, or with the movement of traffic in commerical areas or on busy roads. Service garages should be available on the outskirts of the town as well as

centrally. Private garages will of course be required by many residents and space must be reserved. When separate garages are not provided for individual houses, small groups of lock-up garages are essential.

RAILWAYS

116. We suggest that the railway station should be very different from the vast majority of stations in this country, in which the facilities provided for travellers are certainly not in accordance with best modern practice. It should be an outstanding feature of the town, both externally and internally. Modern station planning segregates the arrival and departure areas, thus minimising noise and dirt and crowding. The setting, quality and service of refreshments should be such as is expected in a modern town. The siting and approaches will be part of the general scheme for the town, but the passenger station should be located as near as possible to the main shopping centre, and the railway and main bus station should be designed for easy interchange of traffic. There should be accommodation for motor cars adjacent to the station.

FACILITIES FOR FLYING

117. It is unlikely that new towns will, for a considerable time, generate enough traffic to warrant their service by regular air lines. New towns, however, should have facilities within a reasonable distance for private and club flying and for an air taxi service, and, where practicable, for gliding.

INLAND WATER TRANSPORT

118. If there is a canal system in the town site advantage should be taken of it for the location of works and factories which receive or despatch heavy and bulky goods not requiring speedy carriage.

VI. Shops policy

LAYOUT AND ARCHITECTURAL CONTROL

144. The importance of continuity in shopping frontages and the use of both sides of the street is stressed by retailers. Continuity can be facilitated by placing banks, post offices, and other businesses which do not require display windows, at the end rather than in the middle of a length of shops. Very wide shopping streets are deprecated by retailers, and a maximum width of about 96 ft. between building lines has been suggested in order to secure that friendly bustling atmosphere which many people are said to like. Squares seem to be unpopular with retailers. We feel, however, that the objections to wide streets and squares might not necessarily apply in a properly planned new town. The interests of amenity and the necessity for parking space for cars may make it desirable in particular cases to provide roads wider than the minimum required for traffic purposes, or to plan a square with shops round it. If not too long, shopping streets for pedestrians only, connecting the vehicular roads, are a possibility.

145. Another reason for wide streets in shopping centres, capable of taking four lines of traffic, is that they will enable cars to wait by the kerb for a limited time. Even with an ample number of car parks within reasonable distance there will be shoppers with only one call to make, and they will naturally wish to drive to the shop door and not to the car park; but parking of cars in the middle of streets could only be permitted

if the street is very wide.

146. To prevent vehicles waiting along the main road frontage to load or unload goods, rear-access roads should be provided. They should be of sufficient width to permit the passing of two vehicles. It may be advisable for some of them to be cul-de-sacs to prevent their being used as through roads, but in such cases adequate space for turning at the closed end is essential.

ARCADES

148. . . .A pedestrian arcade which furnishes a convenient through route from one main road to another might be commercially successful as well as pleasing architecturally, but it should not be less than 20 ft. wide.

BICYCLES AND PERAMBULATORS

150. A large number of cyclists must be expected in the shopping areas. To make it unnecessary for bicycles to be left against the kerb or shop window, cycle rests should be provided in the footway clear of the shop fronts. Provision should also be made for bicycles in the car parks. The solution of the perambulator problem lies in footways of adequate width and in suitable provision by the larger shops. The width of footways is dealt with in the section on communication.

D. EXECUTION OF PLAN

I. Organisation and administration

263. We now comment on the qualifications and duties of the executive staff:–

(4) Chief engineer. The chief engineer should be a civil engineer of recognised professional status, with adequate experience and the executive capacity to get things done. He should have such assistants as are required for the work to be carried out by the corporation itself in connection with the various services, in addition to the normal duties of a municipal or estate engineer. The extent to which he will call in consulting engineers will depend partly on his own expert knowledge and that of his staff; partly on the magnitude of the work involved; and partly on the advantage to be gained in avoiding delays and the difficulty of finding temporary staff by utilising the staffs of consulting firms.

II. Programme and method

266. The heavy civil engineering work, that is the main services – sewerage, water supply, levelling and earth works, surface water drainage, roads, railway connections – will take two to three years fully to establish and must be put in hand in advance of the general building development.

267. The programme should aim at the virtual completion, area by area, of these heavy civil engineering works before the main house building programme starts.

Appendix 2 Extracts from forecasts of numbers of vehicles in Great Britain 1970-2010

Source of forecasts	Millions of vehicles						
	1960	1965	1970	1980	1990	2000	2010
J. C. Tanner in a paper reprinted from *Roads and Road Construction*, 1965	–	–	17.9	26.5	32.1	36.2	39.6
A.H. Tulpule, *RRL Report No. 288*, 1969	–	–	16.0	24.6	30.1	34.2	37.9
A. H. Tulpule, *TRRL Report No. 543;* rev. 1972	–	–	–	21.5	26.8	30.2	33.0
J. C. Tanner, *TRRL Report No. 650;* rev. 1974	–	–	–	20.9*	25.8*	28.6*	30.4*
Basic Road Statistics 1984 British Road Federaton	–	–	–	–	21.3*	24.7*	27.2*
Actual numbers	9.4	12.9	15.0	19.2			

* *Middle forecasts, interpolated where necessary.*
Information in this table derived from T.R.R.L. reports is reproduced with the permission of the Transport and Road Research Laboratory. Information derived from *Basic Road Statistics* is reproduced with the permission of the British Road Federation.

Appendix 3 Extracts from forecasts of car ownership in Great Britain

Source of forecasts	Cars per head (middle forecasts)						
	1960	1965	1970	1980	1990	2000	2010
A. H. Tulpule, *TRRL Report No. 288, 1969*	–	–	0.23	0.35	0.40	0.42	0.43
A. H. Tulpule, *TRRL Report No. 543;* rev. 1972	–	–	–	0.31	0.38	0.41	0.42
J. C. Tanner, *TRRL Report No. 650;* rev. 1974	–	–	–	0.32	0.39	0.43	0.44
J. C. Tanner, *TRRL Report No. 799;* 1977	–	–	–	0.29	0.38	0.43	0.45
Actual levels	0.11	0.17	0.21	–	–	–	–

Information in this table derived from TRRL reports is reproduced with the permission of the Transport and Road Research Laboratory.

Appendix 4
Design flows of two-way urban roads

	2 lane carriageway Peak hourly flow vehicles per hour, both directions of flow*					Undivided carriageway Peak hourly flow vehicles per hour, one direction of flow				Dual carriageway Peak hourly flow vehicles per hour, one direction of flow		
						4 lane			6 lane	Dual 2 lane		Dual 3 lane
	6.1 m	6.75 m	7.3 m	9 m	10 m	12.3 m	13.5 m	14.6 m	18 m	Dual 6.75 m	Dual 7.3 m	Dual 11 m
Urban motorway					3000						3,600	5,700
All-purpose road, no frontage access, no standing vehicles, negligible cross traffic			2000			2,550	2,800	3,050		2,950†	3,200†	4,800†
All-purpose road, frontage development, side roads, pedestrian crossings, bus stops, waiting restrictions throughout day, loading restrictions at peak hours	1,100	1,400	1,700	2,200	2,500	1,700	1,900	2,100	2,700			

* 60 : 40 directional split can be assumed.

† Includes division by line of refuges as well as central reservation; effective carriageway width excluding refuge width is used.

Note: The recommended flows allow for a proportion of heavy vehicles equal to 15 per cent. No allowance will need to be made for lower proportions of heavy vehicles; the peak hourly flows at the year under consideration should be reduced when the expected proportion exceeds 15 per cent.

Source: 'Design flows for urban roads', Technical Memorandum H9/76, Department of the Environment. Reproduced with permission of the Controller of Her Majesty's Stationery Office.

Appendix 5 New Towns: financing of transport requirements

(Extract from Joint Circular from the Department of the Environment (Circular 53/76) and Welsh Office (Circular 73/76) reproduced with the permission of the Controller of Her Majesty's Stationery Office.)

SCOPE

4. Subject to the arrangements set out in the paragraphs which follow, county councils will retain in new towns, and include in their TPP[1] submissions, all the responsibilities for transport matters (including car parks) which they exercise outside new towns. But in accordance with TPP policies, and after consultation with the relevant county council, any development corporation may put proposals for the provision of car parking facilities, bus stations or subsidies for new town experimental bus services to the Department and these will be considered on their merits.

ROADS

5. Development corporations will, however, finance in the first instance the construction of roads (including busways) required by the development of a new town; this will cover both principal and non-principal roads, the distinction between them having ceased to be relevant for the purpose of financing following the abolition of principal road grant. Trunk roads, for which the Secretary of State will retain responsibility, and local distributor and access roads, which will continue to be the developer's responsibility, are not included in these arrangements.

6. Roads not falling into any of the categories described in paragraph 5 will remain entirely a county council responsibility. But where a road planned by a county council to meet non-new town requirements needs to be constructed either earlier than it would otherwise have been or to a higher standard than otherwise planned, by reason of the development of the new town, suitable proportions of the costs of advancement and/or of the higher standards may be accepted as falling within the new

arrangements.

7. The counties' statutory or other responsibilities for roads as highway authorities, or in any other regard, are in no way affected and there will be no change in the requirements for planning or other clearances, nor in the observance of construction standards at present normally applied.

8. Design and contractual responsibilities will depend, as before, on the precise nature of individual agreements between each development corporation and county council. The Department will expect future agreements to recognise the staffing commitments of both the development corporation and the county council brought about by previous arrangements governing their responsibilities.

FINANCING OF ROADS

9. Development corporations will finance new town roads by 60 year fixed interest Exchequer loans, repayable on an annuity basis, as authorised by the Secretary of State; no grant will be payable. County councils will be expected to make contributions to development corporations towards the cost of all roads that the latter finance under these arrangements, according to new cost-sharing agreements to be negotiated between the two parties and approved by the Department.

COST-SHARING GUIDELINES

10. The Department expects the following guidelines to be followed in the negotiation of cost-sharing agreements. Annual county councils contributions should be based on a percentage of the annual loan charges incurred by development corporations as a result of their financing road construction, and related land acquisition and design costs. For each year during the life of a project, defined as 30 years from the date when a road contract is started on site, the contribution would rise by annual increments of 1/30th according to the formula:

$$\frac{Y}{30} \times \frac{(100-T)}{100} \times A$$

(Where Y is the number of years since a road contract started on site, all fractions of a year being rounded up; T is the rate of TSG[2] in the year that a contract started on site, and A is the annuity sum incurred by the development corporation and attributable to the total cost of design, land acquisition and construction). Thus in the 30th year, the county council contribution would rise to meet the whole of the annuity payments, abated by the rate of TSG. The amount paid in the 30th year would continue to be paid in each of the remaining 30 years of the loan period. (In the event of the winding up of the development corporation, as would be expected within this term, the county council's liability would be to the body taking over the financial responsibility for repayment of the Exchequer loans in respect of the relevant costs.)

11. Alternatively, a county council might prefer to pay either a once-and-for-all capital contribution or capital contributions phased over the period of the new town road programme. There will be no objection to either such arrangement provided that the net present value of the chosen method, calculated by using a discount rate identical to the rate at which a development corporation is borrowing its funds, is no less than the net present value of the annuity contributions worked out on the above formula. If a county council chooses to adopt either of these arrangements, the Department would add the required amount to the block Key Sector Loan Sanction to be notified in December in respect of the following financial year.

12. It is recognised that the rate of TSG may vary during the years in which road contracts will be starting; to minimise uncertainty in this respect, the Department will re-examine, in consultation with the Associations, the workings of the above formula if the rate of TSG falls below that of RSG or if substantial changes occur to the framework of relevant Government grants.

13. County councils' contributions to development corporations will not be eligible for TSG. In consequence, these contributions should be identified separately in TPP submissions. Expenditure on schemes where contracts were let or, in a very small number of cases, were expected to be let, before 1 April 1975, will however be eligible for TSG. County expenditure on these schemes should therefore continue to be shown in TSG Finance Forms as eligible expenditure.

Notes

1 TPP – Transport Policies and Programme.
2 TSG – Transport Support Grant.

Bibliography

Architects Journal, 27 September, 1967.

Balchin, Jack, *First New Town*, Stevenage Development Corporation, 1980.

Barlow, A. M., *The Barlow Report*, HMSO, London, 1940.

Basildon Development Corporation, *Basildon New Town Master Plan Technical Report*, 1951.

Basildon Development Corporation, *Basildon Public Transport and the Road System*, date unknown.

Bellini, James, *Rule Britannia, A Progress Report for Domesday 1986*, Jonathan Cape Ltd, London, 1981.

Beresford, M., *New Towns of the Middle Ages*, Lutterworth Press, London, 1967.

Bracknell Development Corporation, *Bracknell: The Making of our New Town*, 1981.

British Road Federation, *Basic Road Statistics*, Published annually, British Road Federation.

Brown, Chris and Mackenzie, Jeremy, 'A Bus System Revitalised', *The Planner*, March, 1980

Buchanan, Colin, *Mixed Blessing: The Motor in Britain*, Leonard Hill Ltd, London, 1958.

Buchanan, Colin, 'Fifth Letter to a Politician', *Journal of the Institution of Highway Engineers*, 1981.

Buchanan, Colin et al., *Traffic in Towns*, Reports of the Steering

Group and Working Group appointed by the Minister of Transport, HMSO, London, 1963.

Buckinghamshire Department of Architecture and Planning, *The Case for the Monorail,* Buckinghamshire County Council, 1965.

Commission for the New Towns, *Crawley Town Centre Traffic Study,* Alastair Dick and Associates, 1976.

Cullen, Gordon, 'Prairie Planning in the New Towns', *Architectural Review,* 1953.

Cumbernauld Development Corporation, *Preliminary Planning Proposals and Addenda Reports,* Cumbernauld Development Corporation, 1959.

Cumbernauld Development Corporation, *Cumbernauld Traffic,* Report, 1967.

Department of Economic Affairs, *A Strategy for the South East,* HMSO, London, 1967.

Department of the Environment, 'Design flows for urban roads', *Technical Memorandum H9/76,* Department of the Environment, London, 1976.

Department of the Environment, 'New Towns: financing of transport requirements', *DOE Circular 53/76,* Department of the Environment, London, 1976.

Department of the Environment, *Residential Roads and Footpaths,* Design Bulletin 32. HMSO, London, 1977.

Esher, Lionel, *A Broken Wave: The Rebuilding of England. 1940-1980.* Allen Lane, London, 1981.

Gibberd, Frederick, *Town Design,* The Architectural Press, London, 1953.

Gibberd, Frederick, et. al., *Harlow: The Story of a New Town,* Publications for Companies, 1980.

Hillman, Mayer and Whalley, Anne, *Walking IS Transport,* Policy Studies Institute, London, 1979.

Holley, Stephen, *Washington: Quicker by Quango: The History of Washington New Town, 1964-1983,* Publications for Companies, 1983.

Hoskins, W. G., *English Landscapes,* BBC Publications, London, 1973. Permission to reproduce the quoted material was granted free of charge.

Howard, Ebenezer, *Garden Cities of Tomorrow,* (first published as *Tomorrow, a Peaceful Plan to Real Reform,* London, Swan, Sonnerschein 1898), reissued (1902) and reprinted with a preface by Sir Frederic Osborn and introductory essay by Lewis Mumford, Faber and Faber, London, 1945.

Jeffreys, William Rees, *The King's Highway,* Batchworth Press Ltd., London, 1949.

Jenkins, E., 'Highway Hierarchy – or Please Don't Bring your Car into the Living Room', *Journal of the Institution of Highway Engineers,* November 1975.

Livingston Development Corporation, *Livingston Plan,* Livingston Development Corporation, 1979.

McIntosh, A. J. W., *Report upon Anticipated Traffic Conditions and Volumes within the New Town,* Crawley Development Corporation, 1951.

Milton Keynes Development Corporation, *The Plan for Milton Keynes: Volumes 1 and 2, Technical Supplement 'Transportation' No. 7,* Milton Keynes Development Corporation, 1969.

Ministry of Housing and Local Government, *The South East Study 1961-1981,* HMSO, London, 1964.

Ministry of Housing and Local Government, *Notes on new street bylaws,* HMSO, London, 1964.

Ministry of Housing and Local Government, *People and Planning,* Report of the Committee on Public Participation in Planning, HMSO, London, 1969.

Ministry of Transport, *Design and Layout of Roads in Built-up Areas,* HMSO, London, 1946.

Ministry of Transport, *Traffic Signs Manual,* HMSO, London, 1965.

Ministry of Transport, *Roads in Urban Areas,* HMSO, London, 1966.

Ministry of Transport, *Traffic and Transport Plans,* Roads Circular No. 1/68, HMSO, London, 1968.

Ministry of Transport, *Transport Policy: A Consultation Document,* HMSO, London, 1976.

Ministry of Transport, *Lorries, People and the Environment* Cmnd 8439, HMSO, London, 1981.

Mooyman, N. J., *Relationship between urban structure, transport and mobility.* (n.d).

New Towns Technical Officers' Committee, *A Review of Public Transport in New Towns,* 1974.

Osborn, Frederic J. and Whittick, Arnold, *New Towns: Their Origins, Achievements and Progress,* Leonard Hill, London, 1977.

Peterborough Development Corporation, *Greater Peterborough Master Plan,* Peterborough Development Corporation, date unknown.

Peterborough Development Corporation, *Report on Cycleways,* Peterborough Development Corporation.

Potter, Stephen, *Transport and New Towns,* The Open University, Milton Keynes, 1976.

Potter, Stephen, *The Role of Segregation Planning and the Pedestrian/ Vehicle Conflict in Britain's New Towns.* The Open University, Milton Keynes, 1978.

Potter, Stephen, *Transport Planning in the Garden Cities,* The Open University, Milton Keynes, 1981.

Prince, E. J., 'Irvine new town', paper presented to Scottish branch of the Institution of Municipal Engineers, 1970.

Redditch Development Corporation, *Redditch New Town Planning Proposals,* Redditch Development Corporation, 1967.

Redditch Development Corporation, *Development Brief for Industry,* Redditch Development Corporation, 1979.

Runcorn Development Corporation, *Runcorn New Town Master Plan,* Runcorn Development Corporation, 1967.

Schaffer, Frank, *The New Town Story,* MacGibbon and Kee, London, 1970.

Skelmersdale Development Corporation, *Skelmersdale New Town Planning Proposals,* Skelmersdale Development Corporation, 1964.

Stein, Clarence S., *Toward New Towns for America,* Liverpool University Press, Liverpool, 1950.

Telford Development Corporation, *Telford Development Proposals,* Volume 1, 'Telford: central area: estimated car parking requirements', Telford Development Corporation, 1969.

Thomas, A. W., 'New towns in Britain – some notes on organisation and administration,' *Journal of the Institution of Municipal Engineers,* Vol. 92, July, 1965.

Transport and Road Research Laboratory, *Distribution of Accidents in Urban Areas of Great Britain,* Report 159 UC, 1975.

Transport and Road Research Laboratory, *Some Preliminary Results of the Harlow Dial-a-Bus Experiment,* Supplementary Report 214 UC, 1976a.

Transport and Road Research Laboratory, *Runcorn Busway Study,* Report 697, 1976b.

Transport and Road Research Laboratory, *Peterborough Experimental Cycle Route,* Report 975, 1981.

Tripp, H. Alker, *Town Planning and Road Traffic,* Edward Arnold, London, 1942.

Warrington Development Corporation, *Warrington New Town Outline Plan,* Warrington Development Corporation, 1972.

Washington Development Corporation, *Washington New Town Master Plan,* Washington Development Corporation, 1966.

Walsh, T., 'The role of the municipal engineer in industrial development and activity' presented at the Public Works Congress, November 1982. Published in *Municipal Engineer,* Vol. 110, no. 4, April 1983.

Wilson, A. Hugh, *Skelmersdale New Town Planning Proposals Report on Basic Plans.*

Index